PENG

PENGUIN

GENERAL EDITOR: CHRISTOPHER RICKS

SENECA IN ENGLISH

LUCIUS ANNAEUS SENECA, statesman, philosopher, advocate and man of letters, was born at Cordoba in Spain around 4 BC. He rose to prominence in Rome, pursuing a career in the courts and political life, for which he had been trained, while also acquiring celebrity as an author of tragedies and essays. Falling foul of successive emperors (Caligula in AD 39 and Claudius in AD 41), he spent eight years in exile, allegedly for an affair with Caligula's sister. Recalled in AD 49, he was made praetor and was appointed tutor to the boy who was to become, in AD 54, the emperor Nero. On Nero's succession, Seneca acted for some eight years as an unofficial chief minister. The early part of this reign was remembered as a period of sound government, for which the main credit seems due to Seneca. His control over Nero declined as enemies turned the emperor against him with representations that his popularity made him a danger, or with accusations of immorality or excessive wealth. Retiring from public life he devoted his last three years to philosophy and writing, particularly the *Letters to Lucilius*. In AD 65, following the discovery of a plot against the emperor, in which he was thought to be implicated, he and many others were compelled by Nero to commit suicide. His fame as an essayist and dramatist lasted until two or three centuries ago, when he passed into literary oblivion, from which the twentieth century has seen a considerable recovery.

DON SHARE was educated at Brown University, Simmons College and Boston University. His poems, essays and translations have been published widely in the United States. He received the PEN/New England Discovery Award for his translations of the poetry of Miguel Hernández, collected in the volume *I Have Lots of Heart*. Mr Share is Poetry Consultant for *Partisan Review* and a founding editor of *Salamander*.

THE POETS IN TRANSLATION SERIES

Published or forthcoming:

BAUDELAIRE IN ENGLISH
Edited by CAROL CLARK *and* ROBERT SYKES

THE BIBLE IN ENGLISH
Edited with an introduction by GERALD HAMMOND

DANTE IN ENGLISH
Edited by ERIC GRIFFITHS *and* MATTHEW REYNOLDS

HOMER IN ENGLISH
Edited with an introduction by GEORGE STEINER
with the assistance of AMINADAV DYKMAN

HORACE IN ENGLISH
Edited by D. S. CARNE-ROSS *and* KENNETH HAYNES
with an introduction by D. S. CARNE-ROSS

MARTIAL IN ENGLISH
Edited with an introduction by J. P. SULLIVAN *and* A. J. BOYLE

OVID IN ENGLISH
Edited with an introduction by CHRISTOPHER MARTIN

PETRARCH IN ENGLISH
Edited with an introduction by THOMAS P. ROCHE

THE PSALMS IN ENGLISH
Edited with an introduction by DONALD DAVIE

RILKE IN ENGLISH
Edited with an introduction by MICHAEL HOFMANN

VIRGIL IN ENGLISH
Edited with an introduction by K. W. GRANSDEN

SENECA IN ENGLISH

Edited by DON SHARE

PENGUIN CLASSICS

PENGUIN BOOKS

Published by the Penguin Group
Penguin Books Ltd, 27 Wrights Lane, London W8 5TZ, England
Penguin Books USA Inc., 375 Hudson Street, New York, New York 10014, USA
Penguin Books Australia Ltd, Ringwood, Victoria, Australia
Penguin Books Canada Ltd, 10 Alcorn Avenue, Toronto, Ontario, Canada M4V 3B2
Penguin Books (NZ) Ltd, 182–190 Wairau Road, Auckland 10, New Zealand

Penguin Books Ltd, Registered Offices: Harmondsworth, Middlesex, England

First published 1998
10 9 8 7 6 5 4 3 2 1

Set in 10/12.5 pt Monotype Bembo
Typeset by Rowland Phototypesetting Ltd, Bury St Edmunds, Suffolk
Printed in England by Clays Ltd, St Ives plc

For Jacquelyn Pope
Non est ad astra mollis e terris via.

CONTENTS

TRANSLATIONS AND IMITATIONS

RENAISSANCE SENECA

INTERIM SENECA

MODERN SENECA

ACKNOWLEDGEMENTS

I thank the following people for help and support of various kinds: Christopher Ricks, Jacquelyn Pope, Elizabeth Holmes, and, of the library staff at the Massachusetts Bay Community College, Catherine Lee, Rosemarie Golden, Cathy Ashton, and Pat Duggan.

For permission to reprint copyright material in translation in this book the editor and publishers gratefully acknowledge the following: Frederick Ahl: excerpts, *Troades; Hippolytus/Phaedra*, from *Three Tragedies: Trojan Women, Medea, and Phaedra*, translated and with Introductions by Frederick Ahl, copyright © 1986 by Cornell University, used by permission of the translator and the publisher, Cornell University Press; A. J. Boyle: excerpts, *Hippolytus/Phaedra*, from *Seneca's Phaedra* (Francis Cairns (Publications) Ltd, 1987), by permission of the publisher; Kelly Cherry: excerpt, *Octavia*, from *Seneca: The Tragedies*, edited by David R. Slavitt (Johns Hopkins University Press, 1992−5), reprinted by permission of the publisher; Caryl Churchill: chorus, *Thyestes*, from *Thyestes* by Seneca: translation copyright © Caryl Churchill 1995, published by Nick Hern Books, 14 Larden Road, London W3 7ST, used by permission of the publisher; Jane Elder: chorus, *Thyestes*, from *Thyestes* (midNag/Carcanet Press, 1982), by permission of Mid Northumberland Arts Group; T.S. Eliot: 'Marina', *Sweeney Agonistes*, from *Collected Poems 1909−1962*, copyright 1936 by Harcourt Brace and Company, copyright © 1964, 1963 by T. S. Eliot, reprinted by permission of Faber and Faber Ltd and Harcourt Brace and Company; Dana Gioia: excerpt, Thebäis, from *Seneca: The Tragedies*, edited by David R. Slavitt (Johns Hopkins University Press, 1992−5), reprinted by permission of the publisher; Rachel Hadas: excerpt, *Oedipus*, from *Seneca: The Tragedies*, edited by David R. Slavitt (Johns Hopkins

University Press, 1992–5), reprinted by permission of the publisher; Asa M. Hughes: chorus, *Thyestes*, from *Latin Poetry in Verse Translation*, edited by L. R. Lind (Houghton Mifflin, 1957); Ted Hughes: excerpt, *Oedipus*, from *Seneca's Oedipus* (Faber and Faber, 1968), reprinted by permission of the publisher; Robert Lowell: excerpt, *Racine's Phaedra: A Verse Translation* by Robert Lowell, translation copyright © 1960 by Robert Lowell and copyright renewed © 1988 by Harriet Lowell, Sheridan Lowell, and Caroline Lowell, reprinted by permission of Farrar, Straus and Giroux Inc and Faber and Faber Ltd; F. L. Lucas: excerpts, *Oedipus*; *Hippolytus/Phaedra*, from *Seneca and Elizabethan Tragedy* (Cambridge University Press, 1922), used by permission of the publisher; Douglass Parker: chorus, *Thyestes*, from *The Tenth Muse: Classical Drama in Translation*, edited by Charles Doria (Ohio University Press, 1980), reprinted by permission of Ohio University Press/Swallow Press, Athens; Stephen Sandy: excerpt, *Hercules Oetaeus*, from *Seneca: The Tragedies*, edited by David R. Slavitt (Johns Hopkins University Press, 1992–5), reprinted by permission of the publisher; J. P. Sullivan: excerpt, *Hercules Oetaeus*, from *Roman Poets of the Early Empire*, edited by A. J. Boyle and J. P. Sullivan (Penguin Classics, 1991). Selection, introductions, notes and glossary copyright © A. J. Boyle and J. P. Sullivan, 1991.

Every effort has been made to obtain permission from all copyright holders whose material is included in this book; but in some cases this has not proved possible. The publishers therefore wish to thank those translators who are included without acknowledgement. Penguin apologizes for any errors or omissions in the above list and would be grateful to be notified of any corrections that should be incorporated in the next edition of this volume.

GENERAL INTRODUCTION

1 Seneca's life and works

Lucius Annaeus Seneca was born in 4 BC or earlier in Cordoba, now southern Spain, into a family of great wealth and intellectual accomplishment. His father was Lucius Annaeus Seneca the Elder, otherwise known as Seneca the Rhetorician, who helped shape Roman education with his treatises. Rhetoric was essential in the preparation for public and intellectual life; as Dana Gioia puts it, 'A famous rhetorician like Seneca the Elder, therefore, commanded the sort of intellectual and social authority in Rome that today we might associate with a millionaire president of an Ivy League university who had also won the Nobel Prize in economics.'[1] Montaigne, Ben Jonson, and Pascal could quote from these treatises with the expectation that their audiences would recognize the citations. Seneca the Elder produced remarkable offspring. The oldest son, Annaeus Novatus, would become Roman governor of southern Greece, and is mentioned as Junius Gallio in the Acts of the Apostles (18:12–16) as an annoyed participant in the Jewish case against the blaspheming Saint Paul: he refused to punish Paul, and let the Greek crowd assault Paul's accusers. Annaeus Mela, the youngest son, was a businessman who eventually helped handle Nero's affairs; Mela's own son, Marcus Annaeus Lucanus, would be known as the last great epic poet of Rome, Lucan, who would haunt literature so deeply that he appeared in Dante's Purgatory alongside Homer, Horace, and Ovid. Despite all their talent and prosperity, all of Seneca the Elder's children, and also Lucan, were to die by suicide following the abortive conspiracy of Piso against Nero. As for the middle son, Lucius Annaeus, he had, by the time of his downfall, become a wealthy politician, and a dramatist and philosopher whose work would influence the course of literature for generations to come.

Although he was sickly as a boy, suffering from a tubercular condition

– so much so that he contemplated suicide, but refrained for his father's sake – Seneca became famous early on as a politician and public speaker, becoming a magistrate, and then a junior advocate. When he became known well enough to inspire Caligula's jealousy, he withdrew from public life. But following Caligula's assassination, Seneca became politically active again. It was a time of corruption and greed, in which assassination, suicide, and exile, and not the institutions of the old Republic, characterized the ensuing power struggles. At the beginning of Claudius's reign, Seneca was accused by the new empress, Messalina, of adultery with Caligula's sister, Julia Livilla, and was sent to Corsica for eight hard years, losing his liberty, and contact with his wife and son. Devastated, he wrote philosophical essays full of Stoic maxims later quoted by generations of schoolboys studying Latin. Messalina was executed in AD 48. A year later, following Agrippina's machinations on behalf of her son, Nero, Seneca was recalled to Rome to serve as a private tutor for the teenager, as well as praetor in the bureaucracy of the government. When Agrippina finally succeeded in poisoning Claudius, Seneca became part of a group of men who ruled Rome on young Nero's behalf. He used his political power and oratory skill – he was perhaps the first speechwriter in history – to keep the empire steady and Nero entertained. He even wrote Nero's hypocritical elegy for the murdered Claudius, and a nasty satire on the late emperor's deification (the *Apocolocyntosis*, or *Pumpkinification*), works which do not happily serve Seneca's reputation. Seneca's mentorship of Nero, guided by pragmatism and moral compromise, suggests a gulf between his writing and his own actual conduct. Inevitably, Nero came into his own. After botching an effort to kill his mother in AD 59 which involved a boat and lead weights, Nero got advice from Seneca while he figured out how to finish the job. A contemporary detractor, Sullius, claims that Seneca took over the estates of childless citizens to augment his wealth; whether true or not, he probably received gifts from Nero, and certainly had property exceeding the emperor's in size, including prized vineyards and houses. When Nero poisoned his close military adviser, S. Afranius Burrus, Seneca tried for a second time to leave public life – he even tried to give most of his estate to Nero along with his resignation; Nero refused. Seneca left Rome altogether, and history records Nero's subsequent rampages. In AD 65, a conspiracy grew to assassinate Nero, but the plot was exposed at the last minute by a servant. Badly shaken, Nero attempted to wipe out anybody he thought might have been involved. Among these was Seneca, his former mentor and adviser. Upon the arrival of Nero's men at his home, Seneca attempted to use his eloquence one last time by rebutting Nero's accusations in a letter; Nero's response was to order his soldiers to force Seneca to kill himself without leaving a will. Tacitus claims in his *Annales* that Seneca told his comrades, '*quod unum iam et tamen pulcherriumu habeat, imaginem uitae suae*' – 'Since I am forbidden to show you gratitude for your service, I give you the only possession I have left, my best possession: my life, and the way I lived it.' He then exclaimed, 'After murdering his own mother and brother, he completes the job by killing his teacher and tutor.' Seneca slit his wrists, yet, an austere man, he was too thin to bleed much. Next, he drank hemlock, and it, too, failed to kill him. At last he was put into warm water, and then suffocated in a steam bath. When, three years later, Nero was ordered by the Senate to be executed, he could not bring himself to take his own life, and even suggested to his servants that they kill themselves to give him courage – they demurred. Instead, Nero convinced his secretary to help him cut his own throat before soldiers arrived to arrest him. He bled to death as his servants looked on, and was heard to complain, 'How ugly and vulgar my life has become!'

Seneca's writing falls into two categories: prose works and the tragedies. Aside from the satire on Claudius and a scientific work, the former include philosophical texts, notably ten dialogues, the treatises *De Beneficiis* ('On Benefits'), *De Clementia* ('On Clemency', addressed to Nero), and the *Epistulae Morales ad Lucilium* ('Moral Epistles'). As A.J. Boyle writes, this work is characterized by Stoic notions of 'virtue, endurance, self-sufficiency, true friendship; the condemnation of evil, emotions and the false values of wealth and power; the praise of reason, wisdom, poverty; contempt for the fear of death'.[2] Seven tragedies are ascribed to Seneca: *Hercules Furens*, *Troades*, *Medea*, *Phaedra* (also called *Hippolytus*), *Oedipus*, *Agamemnon*, and *Thyestes*. Another tragedy, *Phoenissae* (also called *Thebäis*), apparently incomplete since it lacks choral odes, is also accepted as Senecan. Two other plays traditionally attributed to Seneca are no longer accepted as his: a play much longer than the others, *Hercules Oetaeus*, and a historical drama, *Octavia*, in which Seneca himself appears as a character. No dates of composition are known, though *Hercules Furens* was likely to have been composed no later than AD 54, at which time it seems to have been parodied. The first clear reference to any of Seneca's plays is in Quintilian, a generation after Seneca's death. The plays might have been composed during the period of exile to Corsica, which would date them between AD 41 and AD 49, though they certainly could have been written over a longer period of time. The tragedies are never mentioned in the prose works, though both stem from the same Stoic convictions.

'Seneca *tragicus*', Boyle writes, 'has received a variable press.'[3] The first printed edition of Seneca's tragedies appears from the press of Andreas Gallicus at Ferrara in 1474, and European versions of Senecan drama appear as early as 1315 in Padua and continue unabated through the seventeenth century in England, France, and Italy. Seneca's influence in the Renaissance has not always been kindly regarded. Thomas Nashe, in his preface to Greene's *Menaphon* (1589), gibed about 'vain-glorious tragedians' in his day who fed on 'crummes that fall from the translator's trencher', and sneered,

English Seneca read by candlelight yieldes manie good sentences – 'Bloud is a begger' and so forth; and if you intreate him faire in a frostie morning, he will afford you whole Hamlets, I should say handfulls, of tragical speeches.

In the 'Induction' to *A Warning for Faire Women*, dating from 1599, there is the following description of contemporary tragedy:

> How some damn'd tyrant to obtain a crown
> Stabs, hangs, impoisons, smothers, cutteth throats:
> And then a Chorus, too, comes howling in
> And tells us of the worryings of a cat:
> Then, too, a filthy whining ghost,
> Lapt in some foul sheet, or a leather pilch,
> Comes screaming in like a pig half-stick'd,
> And cries, Vindicta! – Revenge, Revenge!
> With that a little rosin flasheth forth,

Like smoke out of a tobacco pipe, or a boy's squib.
Then comes in two or three [more] like to drovers,
With tailors' bodkins, stabbing one another . . .

That the play is not altogether free of the faults it criticized, indicates just how deeply conventional the unpleasantly sanguinary had become by this time.

Dryden, despite borrowing from him, arraigned Seneca for 'false Eloquence' and moroseness in his commentary on Plutarch; in what might be both a compliment and complaint, Dryden remarks, in his *Of Dramatick Poesie* of 1668: 'One would think *unlock a door* was a thing as vulgar as could be spoken; yet Seneca could make it sound high and lofty in his Latin: *reserate clusos regii postes laris.'* Despite the admiration of some of his first translators – Alexander Neville thought that 'the grosenes of our owne Countrey language' could 'by no means aspire to the high lofty Latinists stile' – the enduring view was that, as the Earl of Shaftesbury put it, Seneca was the corrupter of Roman eloquence. Ezra Pound, observing the decline of the 'Lingua Romana' into a 'welter of rhetoric', complained that Seneca was symptomatic of a people in the process of 'losing grip of its empire and on itself'.[4] Carlyle, writing of Diderot's interest in defending 'poor Seneca, on occasion of some new Version of his Works, having come before the public and being roughly dealt with', colourfully anticipates this view:

notable Seneca, so wistfully desirous to stand well with Truth, and yet not ill with Nero, is and remains only our perhaps niceliest-proportioned Half-and-half, the plausiblest Plausible on record; no great man, no true man, no man at all; yet how much lovelier than such, – as the mild-spoken, tolerating, charity-sermoning, immaculate Bishop Dogbolt to some rude, self-helping, sharp-tongued Apostle Paul! Under which view, indeed, Seneca (though surely erroneously, for the origin of the thing was different) has been called in this generation, 'the father of all such as wear shovel-hats'.[5]

Even sympathetic scholarly commentators such as F. L. Lucas and John W. Cunliffe – themselves influential in keeping alive interest in Seneca's drama – were unable to resist the notion of Seneca as a plagiarists' quarry and little more: Cunliffe, in 1893, declared that 'the importance of Seneca's influence on the drama is at an end', and, moreover, that Seneca 'misled English dramatists into violence and exaggeration',[6] and Lucas concluded, in 1922, that 'his work is little remembered, still less regarded now'.[7] Saintsbury called Seneca's work 'classics that are no classics – that is to say, that enter into no school or university curriculum, and that are read, if they are read at all, for love, and not for duty or for money or for fame'.[8] By 1956, Herbert J. Miller, in *The Spirit of Tragedy*, could dispense with Seneca in a few pages in a chapter about Greek tragedy subtitled, 'Epilogue: The Decline to Seneca'. In this culmination of the age-old complaints against Seneca, he is reduced to an unconscious caricature of Greek tragedy – derivative, decadent, rhetorical (but not dramatic), indifferent to form, lurid, yet devoid of 'a tragic sense of life'.

In spite of this dire summation, Seneca was responsible for many innovations, among them

the five-act structure to frame the dramatic action with a beginning, middle, and end . . . He introduced a cast of helpful secondary characters to keep the narrative moving: the messenger to report important (and usually violent) off-stage events, the female confidante to elicit private thoughts from the heroine, the loyal friend or servant to listen to and advise the hero, as well as a decidedly un-Athenian version of a chorus that moralizes on events but never participates in them. Seneca also introduced the catalysing figure of the ghost who returns from death to provoke revenge.[9]

There is no end to controversy – a recent scholar calls these things 'a few generic features', and finds that not everything gathered 'under the rubric of Senecan necessarily traces back to Seneca even at some distant point'.[10]

Much less disputable is Seneca's 'other contribution', as Gioia calls it: the use of 'magnificent language'. His dramatic orations 'with their sonorous allusions, musical syntax, and dizzy rhetorical turns' not only 'encouraged hurricanes of theatrical bombast, they also demonstrated how mixing the techniques of poetry and oratory could create dramatic verse of powerful eloquence'.[11] Moreover, since the concision of Latin provided a perfect medium for epigram, Seneca's tragedies are filled with ingenious and quotable verse one-liners (*sententiae*) which 'announce turning points in soliloquies, and add edge to important conversations' (ibid.); a master of the Greek technique of stichomythia, he was able to incorporate these into dialogues consisting almost entirely of duelling exchanges of aphorisms which seem especially to have impressed Shakespeare.

Seneca provided a model not only for English Elizabethan drama, but also for French tragic theatre from La Péruse's adaptation of *Medea* in 1533, to Garnier, Corneille, and Racine, later on 'leaving his traces', Saintsbury wrote, 'even on Victor Hugo'. Artaud, in our own century, adapted Seneca's *Thyestes*, though Artaud's play is now lost, and called him 'the greatest tragic author in history'.

I weep upon reading his inspired drama, and in it behind the word I sense syllables crepitating in the most ghastly manner with the transparent boiling up of the forces of chaos . . . One cannot find anywhere a better *written* example of what is meant by cruelty in the theater than in all the Tragedies of Seneca, and especially in *Thyestes*.[12]

T. S. Eliot, for his part, introduced a 1927 edition of Newton's *Seneca: His Tenne Tragedies* with an essay soon given wider circulation as 'Seneca in Elizabethan Translation' in *Selected Essays* (1932), where it was accompanied by one of Eliot's most influential essays, 'Shakespeare and the Stoicism of Seneca'; Seneca would figure again in Eliot's Norton lectures at Harvard (1932–3), published as *The Use of Poetry*. Typically, Eliot's interest in Seneca helped rekindle interest among other poets and translators: poets from Robert Lowell and Ted Hughes to Stephen Sandy have translated or adapted Seneca right up to the moment this volume was prepared. Moreover, Gioia points out that since Seneca spent his adult life 'in a totalitarian state' it is illuminating to compare him to 'the poets of the modern totalitarian state' – Mandelstam, Akhmatova, Tsvetayeva, Benn, Radnóti, and even Solzhenitsyn.[13] As Boyle admonishes, those who think the themes of Seneca's tragedies merely rhetorical commonplaces 'have never stared into the face of a Caligula'.[14]

11 *Seneca in the English tradition*

The influence of Seneca in England was first felt in the schools and universities in the early sixteenth century in imitations composed in Latin. By the 1550s, Senecan tragedies were acted at Cambridge and Oxford. The first English translations began to appear in 1559, and in 1561, at the Christmas Revels of the Inner Temple at Westminster, the first English play in Senecan form – indeed, the first English drama in blank verse – *Gorboduc*, written by Oxford graduates Norton and Sackville, was performed. In 1579 at Cambridge, a Senecan tragedy about Richard III written by Legge in Latin appeared, and it, in turn, influenced an English play called *The True Tragedie of Richard III* upon which Shakespeare would later draw. Lucas notes, 'The universities did their part for tragedy in introducing into England that Senecan influence which spread by way of the Inns of Court to the popular theatres, and in educating many of the popular playwrights, like Marlowe, Greene, Nash and Peele.'[15] Although the popular stage was beneath the notice of the learned dons – Oxford even paid companies of players to stay away – as Frederick Boas points out, the patrons of acting companies must have been affected by the theatricals of their undergraduate days. Glynne Wickham comments:

It is difficult to attribute any precise measure of responsibility for the actual development of English drama to the Inns of Court [which might be described as a kind of university devoted to the studies of Law, located in London]; but situated as they were between the Court and the public playhouses, and responsible as they were for presenting comedies, histories, tragedies and masques which attracted the attention of both the Queen and Shakespeare, they undoubtedly assisted in bringing about that fusion of academic and popular traditions of play construction which gave Elizabethan and Jacobean drama its unique character and vitality.[16]

Henry VIII's break with Rome and the ensuing struggle between Reformers and Catholics resulted in periods of stage censorship during which enthusiasm for Latin studies could be dangerous. Nevertheless, interest in the precedents of classical drama ensured that translations and free adaptations of Seneca continued. When, in 1581 – coincident with the suppression of amateur performance of religious play cycles, and the establishment of the Revels Office as the instrument of government control of theatre – Thomas Newton collected and edited translations of each of Seneca's plays in the *Tenne Tragedies*, Seneca became the first classical poet whose complete dramatic work appeared in English.

While most English plays until about 1560 of which records have survived are rooted in religious themes, by the 1590s, revenge plays, and plays about English and foreign history, indicate a shift of interest to the secular. Consequently, a new wave of Senecan influence can be seen among the Elizabethans, notably in Kyd's *Spanish Tragedy*, and plays by, among others, Samuel Daniel, Fulke Greville, Marston, Chapman, Tourneur, Webster, and Beaumont and Fletcher.

Shakespeare is a special, and complex, case: the Thyestian pie consumed in *Titus Andronicus*; *Richard III*'s ghosts and tyrants; what Lucas identifies as 'the general resemblance of the atmosphere of murder, of the supernatural, and revenge' in *Macbeth*; the fatalism in *King Lear* – these indicate that Shakespeare had absorbed something of Seneca. Of the tragic attitude in Shakespeare, as evidenced by Macbeth's consenting to his destiny in the famous speech beginning 'Tomorrow, and tomorrow and tomorrow . . .' (Act V, Scene v) Santayana remarks:

Mr. Eliot says that this [Stoic] philosophy is derived from Seneca; and it is certain that in Seneca's tragedies, if not in his treatises, there is a pomp of diction, a violence of pose, and a suicidal despair not unlike the tone of this passage. But would Seneca ever have said that life signifies nothing? It signified for him the universal reign of law, of reason, of the will of God. Fate was inhuman, it was cruel, it excited and crushed every finite wish; yet there was something in man that shared that disdain for humanity, and triumphed in that ruthless march of order and necessity. Something superior, not inferior, Seneca would have said; something that not only raised the mind into sympathy with the truth of nature and the decrees of heaven, but that taught the blackest tragedy to sing in verse. The passions in foreseeing their defeat become prophets, in remembering it became poets; and they created the noblest beauties by defying and transcending death.[17]

While Seneca's philosophy re-echoes in the works of the Elizabethans, which employed (in Lucas's words) 'the same dogmas of tyranny' as Seneca, they were not, to use Santayana's formulation, merely unrolling 'the high maxims'. They put scepticism, cynicism, and resignation to dramatic ends – but in writing themselves, and writing of their own times, they had Seneca behind them. Eliot writes: 'No author exercised a wider or deeper influence upon the Elizabethan mind or upon the Elizabethan form of tragedy than did Seneca',[18] and elsewhere explains: 'No doubt *The Jew of Malta* or *Titus Andronicus* would have made the living Seneca shudder with genuine aesthetic horror; but his influence helped to recommend work with which he had little in common.'[19] Eliot suggests, moreover, that Senecan Stoicism is an important ingredient in Elizabethan drama because of its appeal in a period so characterized by dissolution and chaos; it is sobering to realize how many of Seneca's translators and imitators of this period had first-hand experience of shifting fortune, as the headnotes in this volume testify.

Senecan influence in English waned after the Elizabethans, although writers as diverse as Marvell and Rochester translated excerpts from the tragedies in the seventeenth century. For reasons which will be explored later in this volume, Seneca was significantly less appealing to poets, dramatists, and classicists of the nineteenth century. Our own century, however, has seen at least a dozen translations and adaptations of full tragedies by Seneca: his time has come again. William Levitan explains:

We have been watching, I think, the growing realization of a match between Seneca and the century. The plays have emerged from the last hundred years' experience of violence with a grim authority that could not have been predicted from the oscillation of taste alone or from the simple fact that academic bibliographies everywhere loathe a vacuum. At the end of the century, we can note something subtler, the deep rapport between Seneca (and all Latin literature, for that matter) and what are shaping up as some of the central concerns of contemporary literary discussion – rhetoric, theatricality, and power; extremity and the contingent authority of canons and norms; and the recasting of history in radical, even apocalyptic, terms.

The freakishness of Senecan drama, once the cause of its censure, has become the source of its greatest power ... At root, Senecan theatricality is the

imposition of will on time, and it collaborates with its own heroic monsters –
Atreus, Medea, the mad Hercules – to stage the impossible requirements of
their desires: to stop time if necessary, turn it back on itself if necessary, and
make the world watch. We do watch, and we are stunned.[20]

But not stunned into silence; and because Seneca's Stoicism, imagery,
and figures of speech have had for generations of writers in English
what Eliot calls 'some personal saturation value' which, at its best,
combusted spontaneously into originality, then the presence of the
Roman whom Jasper Heywood called 'the flowre of all writers' can
still be felt and acknowledged.

Notes

1. David R. Slavitt, ed., *Seneca: The Tragedies* (Baltimore, Johns Hopkins
University Press, 1995), vol. II, p. xix.

2. A. J. Boyle, *Seneca's Phaedra* (Leeds, Francis Cairns, 1987), p. 5.

3. ibid., p. 1.

4. Ezra Pound, *ABC of Reading* (New York, New Directions, 1934), p. 34.

5. Thomas Carlyle, *Critical and Miscellaneous Essays* (London, Chapman and
Hall, 1899), vol. III, p. 226.

6. John W. Cunliffe, *The Influence of Seneca on Elizabethan Tragedy* (London,
Macmillan, 1893), pp. 124–5.

7. F. L. Lucas, *Seneca and Elizabethan Tragedy* (Cambridge, Cambridge University
Press, 1922), p. 132.

8. Quoted in notes to Samuel Daniel, *Complete Works*, ed. Alexander B. Grosart
(New York, Russell and Russell, 1885), vol. III, pp. vii–xi.

9. Slavitt, ed., *Seneca: The Tragedies*, vol. II, pp. xiii ff.

10. Gordon Braden, *Renaissance Tragedy and the Senecan Tradition: Anger's Privilege*
(New Haven, Yale University Press, 1985), pp. 175, 178.

11. Dana Gioia in Slavitt, ed., *Seneca: The Tragedies*, vol. II, pp. xiii–xiv.

12. Quoted in Eric Sellin, *The Dramatic Concepts of Antonin Artaud* (Chicago,
University of Chicago Press, 1968), p. 32.

13. Dana Gioia in Slavitt, ed., *Seneca: The Tragedies*, vol. II, p. xxvii.

14. Boyle, *Seneca's Phaedra*, p. 5.

15. Lucas, *Seneca and Elizabethan Tragedy*, p. 100.

16. *English Drama to 1710*, ed. Christopher Ricks (London, Penguin, 1987),
p. 36.

17. George Santayana, *Essays in Literary Criticism*, ed. Irving Singer (New York, Scribner's, 1956), p. 267.

18. T. S. Eliot, *Selected Essays* (London, Faber and Faber, 1932; San Diego, Harcourt Brace Jovanovich, 1951), p. 65.

19. *Seneca: His Tenne Tragedies*, ed. Thomas Newton (New York, Knopf, 1927), p. xxiii.

20. William Levitan, 'What to Do With Seneca', *Bryn Mawr Classical Review*, vol. 3, no. 5 (1992).

FURTHER READING

A. J. Boyle, *Tragic Seneca: An Essay on the Theatrical Tradition*, London, Routledge, 1997.

Gordon Braden, *Renaissance Tragedy and the Senecan Tradition: Anger's Privilege*, New Haven, Yale University Press, 1985.

John W. Cunliffe, *The Influence of Seneca on Elizabethan Tragedy*, Hamden, Conn., Archon Books, 1893.

T. S. Eliot, *Selected Essays*, San Diego, Harcourt Brace Jovanovich, 1951.

F. L. Lucas, *Seneca and Elizabethan Tragedy*, Cambridge, Cambridge University Press; New York, Haskell House, 1922.

R. S. Miola, *Shakespeare and Classical Tragedy: The Influence of Seneca*, Oxford, Oxford University Press, 1972.

Seneca, His Tenne Tragedies, ed. Thomas Newton, Bloomington, Indiana University Press, 1927.

Seneca: The Tragedies, ed. David R. Slavitt, Baltimore, Johns Hopkins University Press, 1992–5.

ARGUMENTS OF
SENECA'S PLAYS

Oedipus

Laius, king of Thebes, was told by an oracle that he would be killed by his own son's hands. When a son was born to him, he gave the infant to a shepherd, to expose on Mount Cithaeron. Instead, the shepherd gave the baby to a wandering herdsman who served Polybus, king of Corinth. Years later, Oedipus, said to be the son of Polybus, fled Corinth to escape the fate prophesied to him by an oracle: that he would kill his father. While making his way north, he met and killed an old man who argued with him about the right of way on the narrow road. When he arrived in Thebes, Oedipus read the riddle of the Sphinx, destroying the monster Juno had sent to harass that country. For this service, Oedipus was made the husband of Jocasta, the widowed queen of Laius, and assumed the throne. Many years have passed, and Oedipus and Jocasta have had several children. A pestilence afflicts the state, and Oedipus has sent Creon to consult the oracle, to learn the cause and find out how the scourge can be relieved. As he awaits his messenger's return, he grieves for the plight of his kingdom.

Thebäis

Self-blinded and self-exiled, Oedipus has wandered for three years, attended by his daughter Antigone. She alone, despite his fated sins, has remained attached to him. His sons have agreed to reign in alternate years, but Eteocles refuses to give up the throne even though his year's reign is over. Polyneices, his brother, is marching against the gates of Thebes with seven armies to claim his right to the throne. In this version, Jocasta did not kill herself but is still living on in grief and shame, striving to reconcile her sons.

Medea

Though the play is confined in time to the final day of catastrophe at Corinth, the background is the whole story of the Argonauts: how Jason and his heroic comrades undertook their quest for the golden fleece, and the three deadly labours imposed upon Jason before the fleece could be won – the yoking of the fiery bulls, the contest with the giants that sprang from the sown serpent's teeth, and overcoming the sleepless dragon that guarded the fleece. Medea, smitten by love for Jason, defied her father, Aeëtes, and used her magic to help Jason in these labours and accompanied him in his flight. To delay the king's pursuit she slew her brother and scattered his mangled remains in the path as they fled. She promised to rejuvenate Jason's father with her charms, but tricked his daughters into slaying him. For this act, Medea and her husband were exiled from Thessalia and lived in Corinth. For ten years she lived there happily, her past almost forgotten, without using her magic. But now Jason has been gradually won away from his wife and is about to wed Creüsa, the daughter of Creon. Wedding festivities have begun as the play opens and reveals Medea invoking all the powers of heaven and hell in punishment of her unfaithful husband.

Hercules Furens

Juno in her jealous wrath has imposed twelve mighty and destructive tasks on Hercules, her hated stepson. These he has triumphantly accomplished. Abandoning her plan of crushing him by such toils, she will turn his hand against himself in order to destroy him. When Hercules returns from hell she causes him to go mad, precipitating the tragedy which forms the action of the play.

Hippolytus / Phaedra

Theseus married Antiope, and they had a child, Hippolytus, who grew up to love the chaste, austere and beautiful, shunning the haunts of men and scorning the love of women. Meanwhile, Theseus had slain Antiope and married Phaedra. Now the king has not been seen for four years – he has descended into Tartarus and no one believes he will return. Deserted, the hapless Phaedra has conceived a hopeless passion for Hippolytus. Venus has sent this madness on her, just as her own mother was cursed with a mad and fatal malady.

Hercules Oetaeus

The long, heroic life of Hercules has neared its end. He has completed his twelve great tasks. Now, having overcome the world and the underworld, Hercules aspires to heaven. He sacrifices to Jove and prays to be received into heaven.

Thyestes

Pelops had banished his sons for the murder of their half-brother, Crysippus, levying a curse that they would kill each other. When Pelops died, Atreus returned home and took possession of his father's throne. Thyestes also claimed the throne and sought to gain it by seducing Aërope, his brother's wife, and stealing the magical, golden-fleeced ram from Atreus' flock, said to give the right to rule. For this act he was banished by the king. But Atreus has been planning a complete revenge on his brother and has recalled him from banishment in pretended friendship, offering him a place beside him on the throne, in order to have Thyestes entirely in his power.

Troades

The long siege of Troy is over: she has been overthrown, her defenders are dead or exiled. The victorious Greeks have gathered the spoils of Troy on the shore, including the Trojan women, whom they have raped. The women wait to be assigned to Grecian lords and taken away. But now the ghost of Achilles has risen from the tomb, and demanded that Polyxena be sacrificed to him before the Greeks are allowed to sail away. Calchas orders that Astyanax be slain, for only then can Greece be safe from any future Trojan war. So the Trojan captives, who have endured so much, must endure further tragedy.

Agamemnon

The blood feud between Atreus and Thyestes did not end with the terrible vengeance Atreus wreaked upon his brother. Thyestes lived to have a son by his own daughter – Aegisthus, who was to slay Atreus and bring ruin and death on Agamemnon. The Trojan war is over, and the arrival of the victorious king has been announced. Clytemnestra, enraged at Agamemnon because he sacrificed her daughter Iphigenia at Aulis, and jealous because he is bringing Cassandra home as her rival, estranged by her separation from Agamemnon but also by her guilt at her union with Aegisthus, is plotting to slay Agamemnon on his return, thereby gaining revenge and safety from his wrath.

Octavia

Octavia is the only extant Roman historical drama; though traditionally attributed to Seneca, its authorship is uncertain. The action takes place at Rome over the course of two days in AD 62. Nero, quarrelling with his wife, Octavia, condemns her to exile and death as he plans to marry his mistress, Poppaea. Seneca, having been recalled from exile by Nero, and now one of his principal advisers, counsels moderation, but to no avail. The ghost of Agrippina, Nero's mother, appears, and threatens the new marriage with calamity. The chorus sympathizes with the unfortunate Octavia.

RENAISSANCE SENECA

HENRY HOWARD, EARL OF SURREY (?1517–1547)

Poet, translator, soldier, and Tudor courtier, beheaded for high treason in 1547 after political missteps during the illness of Henry VIII. With Sir Thomas Wyatt, brought Petrarch and the Italian sonnet into English, and was thereby instrumental in the development of the English or Shakespearean sonnet. Surrey's translation of Books II and IV of Virgil's *Aeneid* inaugurated the formation of English blank verse. His innovative work, including this version of Seneca's *Hippolytus/Phaedra*, 761–74, was published in Tottel's *Miscellany* in 1557.

The frailtie and hurtfulnes of beautie.

Brittle beautie, that nature made so fraile,
Wherof the gift is small, and short the season,
Flowring to day, to morowe apt to faile,
Tickell treasure abhorred of reason,
5   Daungerous to dele with, vaine, of none auaile,
Costly in keping, past not worthe two peason,
Slipper in sliding as is an eles taile,
Harde to attaine, once gotten not geason,
Iewel of ieopardie that perill dothe assaile,
10   False and vntrue, enticed oft to treason,
Enmy to youth: that moste may I bewaile.
Ah bitter swete infecting as the poyson:
Thou farest as frute that with the frost is taken,
To day redy ripe, to morowe all to shaken.

6 *peason* peas   **8** *geason* rare

SIR THOMAS WYATT (?1503–1542)

Diplomat and courtier with a rocky diplomatic career – he was imprisoned in the Tower of London in 1536 on suspicion of being one of Anne Boleyn's lovers, and accused in 1541 of misconduct as ambassador to Charles V. His poems were not printed in his lifetime, but, like Surrey, he helped bring the sonnet into English, giving it a rhyming last couplet; he also experimented with forms new to English such as the *rondeau* and *terza rima*. This version of *Thyestes*, 391–403, was published in Tottel's *Miscellany* in 1557. H. A. Mason argues that the poem is 'no ordinary translation'; measuring it alongside Cowley's version of the same passage, he remarks, 'We have only to contrast the comparative security of gentlemen in Restoration England with the perilous situation of Wyatt to understand how he came to turn Seneca's moral commonplaces into a haunting poem' (*Humanism and Poetry in the Early Tudor Period*, London, Routledge and Kegan Paul, 1959, pp. 180–85).

Of the meane and sure estate.

Stond who so list vpon the slipper whele,
Of hye astate and let me here reioyce.
And vse my life in quietnesse eche dele,
Vnknowen in court that hath the wanton toyes.

5   In hidden place my time shall slowly passe
And when my yeres be past withouten noyce
Let me dye olde after the common trace
For gripes of death doth he to hardly passe
That knowen is to all: but to him selfe alas,
10   He dyeth vnknowen, dased with dreadfull face.

1 *slipper* slippery

ANONYMOUS

This anonymous rendering of a part of the first chorus of *Hippolytus/Phaedra* was also published in Tottel's *Miscellany* in 1557.

The power of loue ouer gods them selues.

For loue Appollo (his Godhead set aside)
    Was seruant to the kyng of Thessaley,
Whose daughter was so pleasant in his eye,
That bothe his harpe and sawtrey he defide.
5 And bagpipe solace of the rurall bride,
Did puffe and blowe and on the holtes hy,
His cattell kept with that rude melody,
And oft eke him that doth the heauens gyde.
Hath loue transformed to shapes for him to base
10 Transmuted thus sometime a swan is he,
Leda taccoye, and eft Europe to please,
A milde white bull, vnwrinckled front and face,
Suffreth her play tyll on his backe lepeth she,
Whom in great care he ferieth through the seas.

4 *sawtrey* psaltery   **6** *holtes* hills   **11** *taccoye* to entice

THOMAS SACKVILLE,
1st EARL OF DORSET (1536–1608)
and THOMAS NORTON (1532–1584)

Sackville and Norton collaborated to produce what some regard as the first English tragedy in blank verse, *Gorboduc*, in 1561. Sackville was a statesman as well as a poet and playwright, and delivered the death sentence to Mary, Queen of Scots; Norton was a lawyer and translator, and was Cranmer's son-in-law. *Gorboduc*, a close imitation of Seneca, which was set in ancient Britain, abandoned the tradition of the English morality play. The following excerpt is an unmistakable example of Senecan thought and speechifying.

> Knowe ye that lust of kingdomes hath no lawe;
> The Goddes do beare and well allowe in kinges
> The thinges they abhorre in rascall routes.
> When kinges on sclender quarrels ron to warres,
> And than in cruell and vnkindely wise,
> Cōmaunde theftes, rapes, murder of innocentes,
> To spoile of townes & reignes of mightie realmes,
> Thinke you such princes do suppresse them selues
> Subiect to lawes of kinde and feare of Gods,
> Yet none offence, but decked with glorious name
> Of noble conquestes in the handes of kinges,
> Murders and violent theftes in priuate men
> Are heynous crymes and full of foule reproche.

RICHARD EDWARDS (?1523–1566)

Though popular among his contemporaries, little is known about
Richard Edwards. One of the 'philosophers' of Christ Church, Oxford,
who were elected 'theologians', he seems to have left Oxford around
1551 just after his election. The Senecan *Damon and Pithias* was probably
performed before Elizabeth at Whitehall around Christmas 1564, but
was entered in the Stationers' Register in 1567, and the earliest known
edition published in 1571. The following passage, which imitates part
of the *Octavia*, is an example of Senecan 'stichomythia', in which almost
every line is a moral maxim.

DIONISIUS: Let Fame talke what she lyst, so I may lyve in
    safetie.
EUBULUS: The onely meane to that, is to use mercie.
DIONISIUS: A milde Prince the people despiseth.
EUBULUS: A cruell kynge the people hateth.
DIONISIUS: Let them hate me, so they feare mee.
EUBULUS: That is not the way to lyve in safetie.
DIONISIUS: My sword and power shall purchase my quietnesse.
EUBULUS: That is sooner procured by mercy and gentilnesse.
DIONISIUS: Dionisius ought to be feared.
EUBULUS: Better for him to be welbeloved.
DIONISIUS: Fortune maketh all thinges subject to my power.
EUBULUS: Beleve her not, she is a light Goddesse, she can
    laugh and lowre.
DIONISIUS: A kinges prayse standeth in the revenging of his
    enemie.
EUBULUS: A greater prayse to winne him by clemencie.
DIONISIUS: To suffer the wicked live, it is no mercie.
EUBULUS: To kill the innocent, it is great crueltie.
DIONISIUS: Is Damon innocent, which so craftely
    underminded Carisophus,
    To understand what he could of kinge Dionisius?
    Which survewed the Haven and eche Bulwarcke in the Citie,

Where battrie might be layde, what way best to approche?
   shall I

Suffer such a one to live, that worketh me such dispite?

No, he shall die, then I am safe, a dead dogge can not bite.

EUBULUS: But yet, O mightie King, my dutie bindeth me,

   To geve such counsell as with your honour may best agree,

   The strongest pillers of Princely dignitie,

   I finde this: justice with mercy, and prudent liberalitie.

   The one judgeth all thinges by upright equitie,

   The other rewardeth the worthy, flying eche extremitie:

   As to spare those, which offend maliciously,

   It may be called no justice, but extreame injurie:

   So upon suspicion, of each thinge not well proved,

   To put to death presently, whom envious flattery accused,

   It seemeth of tiranny, and upon what fickle ground al tirants
      doo stand,

   Athenes and Lacedemon can teache you yf it be rightly
      scande:

   And not only these Citezens, but who curiously seekes,

   The whole Histories of all the world, not only of Romaines
      and Greekes,

   Shall well perceyve of all Tirantes the ruinous fall,

   Their state uncertaine, beloved of none, but hated of all:

   Of mercifull Princes to set oute the passyng felycitie

   I neede not: ynough of that, even these dayes do testifie:

   They live devoid of feare, their sleapes are sound, they
      dreed no enemie,

   They are feared and loved, and why? they rule with Justice
      and mercie.

   Extendyng Justice to such, as wickedly from Justice have
      swarved,

   Mercie unto those, where opinion, simplenesse have mercie
      deserved:

   Of lybertie nought I say, but onely this thynge,

   Lybertie upholdeth the state of a kynge . . .

TANCRED AND GISMUND

Tancred and Gismund was a tragedy by Robert Wilmot, Christopher Hatton, Henry Noel, and others, derived from a story by Boccaccio. It was acted by the Gentlemen of the Inner Temple before Elizabeth in 1568 in a rhyming version with the title *Gismond of Salerne*; the version published in 1591 changed the title and is in blank verse. Senecan in style and structure – Lucas (*Seneca and Elizabethan Tragedy*, p. 101) called it a 'combination of the Romantic Italian Renaissance love story with the classic form of Seneca' – the following excerpt, from the rhymed version, is typical in its elaboration of a horrible crime, and resembles *Thyestes*, 743–51.

CHORUS: O dáned deed.
RENU: What deem you this to be
   Al the sayd newes that I haue to vnfould?
   Is here (think you) end of the crueltie
   That I haue seen?
CHORUS: Could any heauier woe
   Be wrought to him, then to destroy him so?
RENU: What, think you this outrage did end so well?
   The horror of the fact, the greatest griefe,
   The massaker, the terror is to tell.
CHORUS: Alack what could be more? they threw percase
   The dead body to be deuourd and torne
   Of the wild beasts.
RENU: Would God it had been cast a sauage praie
   To beasts and birds.

GEORGE GASCOIGNE (?1525–1577)

Poet, playwright, translator, who brought many foreign literary forms
into English for the first time. *Jocasta*, published in 1573, was the first
Greek tragedy performed on the English stage. It featured dumb shows
or charades before each act, a feature of early English tragedies. The
passage given here is a Senecan chorus.

> O fierce and furious *Mars*, whose harmefull harte,
> Rejoyceth most to shed the giltlesse blood,
> Whose headie wil doth all the world subvert,
> And doth envie the pleasant mery moode,
> Of our estate that erst in quiet stoode.
> Why doest thou thus our harmelesse towne annoye,
> Which mightie *Bacchus* governed in joye?
>   Father of warre and death, that dost remove
> With wrathfull wrecke from wofull mothers breast,
> The trustie pledges of their tender love,
> So graunt the Gods, that for our finall rest,
> Dame Venus pleasant lookes may please thee best,
> Wherby when thou shalt all amazed stand,
> The sword may fall out of thy trembling hand.
>   And thou maist prove some other way full well
> The bloudie prowesse of thy mightie speare,
> Wherwith thou raisest from the depth of hell,
> The wrathfull sprites of all the furies there,
> Who when the[y] w[a]ke, doe wander every where,
> And never rest to range about the coastes,
> Tenriche that pit with spoile of damned ghostes.
>   And when thou hast our fieldes forsaken thus,
> Let cruell discorde beare thee companie,
> Engirt with snakes and serpents venemous,
> Even she that can with red virmilion dye
> The gladsome greene that florisht pleasantly,
> And make the greedie ground a drinking cup,

To sup the bloud of murdered bodyes up.
    Yet thou returne O joye and pleasant peace,
From whence thou didst against our wil depart,
Ne let thy worthie minde from travell cease,
To chase disdaine out of the poysned harte,
That raised warre to all our paynes and smarte,
Even from the brest of *Oedipus* his sonne,
Whose swelling pride hath all this jarre begonne.
    And thou great God, that doest all things decree,
And sitst on highe above the starrie skies,
Thou chiefest cause of causes all that bee,
Regard not his offence but heare our cries,
And spedily redresse our miseries,
For what ca[n] we poore wofull wretches doe
But crave thy aide, and onely cleave therto?

SENECA: HIS TENNE TRAGEDIES

In 1581, Thomas Newton collected what he called the *Tenne Tragedies* of Seneca, which consisted of existing translations done separately over a period of some eight years. The individual translators knew, or knew of, Gascoigne, and Sackville and Norton; at the same time, they would have been familiar with Latin versions and imitations of Seneca produced at the universities and Inns of Court.

    C. S. Lewis, describing what he called 'Drab Age Verse' (*English Literature in the Sixteenth Century*, Oxford, Oxford University Press, 1954, p. 256), called this work 'execrable: the metre is a torment to the ear, the language at once artless and unnatural', and complained that 'all the sharp detonations of the original' disappear in the 'yokel garrulity' of the translators' style (pp. 254, 256). But in 'Seneca in Elizabethan Translation' (1927), T. S. Eliot claimed that 'if we look at the dates we cannot overlook the probability that these translations helped to direct the course of events ... It is not only as an embryonic form of Elizabethan tragedy that these translations have documentary interest. They represent the transformation of the older form of versification into the new – consequently the transformation of language and sensibility as well' (*Selected Essays*, San Diego, Harcourt Brace Jovanovich, 1951, p. 84).

JASPER HEYWOOD (1535–1597)

His father was the epigrammist, John Heywood, his mother was related to Sir Thomas More, and John Donne was his nephew. He entered Oxford at the age of 12. Exiled as a Roman Catholic after being imprisoned for a year in the Tower of London, he taught philosophy and theology abroad, and died in Naples. Heywood, who became a Jesuit shortly after completing his *Thyestes*, varied Seneca's abrupt ending of that tragedy by adding a scene in which Thyestes, who has been fed his murdered children by his brother, pronounces himself a criminal, and begs punishment. Heywood also created a prologue for *Thyestes* in which he asks the Fury of Seneca's first scene for inspiration. In his *Troas*, Heywood makes a place for the spirit of Achilles – 'the first vengeful ghost of Tudor revenge tragedy', as John Kerrigan notes (*Revenge Tragedy: Aeschylus to Armageddon*, London, Oxford University Press, 1996, pp. 112–13) – to call for retribution against the Greeks. Heywood's alterations are clearly more Christian than Stoic in nature.

Of the last six lines of the chorus in Act V of Heywood's translation of *Hercules Furens*, Eliot wrote that 'nothing can be said of such a translation except that it is perfect'. C. S. Lewis (see p. 11 above) said that Eliot had picked

with exquisite taste, the only lines which deserve praise: and even those no man could construe unless he had seen the Latin first. In my sad progress [through Newton's collection] I have sometimes thought that I could find others to set beside them: but it was only the same sort of illusion which might make a man, by long residence in Lincolnshire, come to take a mound for a mountain.   (*English Literature in the Sixteenth Century*, p. 256)

In this first excerpt from *Hercules Furens* (published 1560), the world of nature is glad with life, while in the cities men repeat their rounds of greedy questing for power and wealth: all are speeding to the underworld. Even Hercules has gone down to Pluto's realm, without yet returning.

> CHORUS: The fading starres now shyne but seelde in sighte
> In stipye skye, night overcome with day
> Plucks in her fyres, while spronge agayne is light.
> The day starre drawes the cleresome beames theire waye,
> The yoye signe of haughtye poale agayne,
> With seven starres markt, the Beares of Arcadye,
> Do call the light with overturned wayne.
> With marble horse now drawne, hys waye to hye
> Doth Titan toppe of Oetha over spred
> The bushes bright that nowe with berryes bee
> Of Thebes strewde, by daye do blushe full redde.
> And to returne doth Phœbus syster flee.
> Now labor harde beginnes, and everye kynde
> Of cares it styrres, the Shepehearde doth unfolde:
> His flockes unpende, do grase their foode to fynde,
> And nippes the grasse with hoary frost full colde.
> At will doth play in open medow faire
> The Calfe whose brow did damme yet never teare,
> The empty Kyne their udders doe repayre.
> And lyght with course uncertayne here and there,
> In grasse full soft the wanton kidde hee flynges.
> In toppe of boughe doth sitte with chaunting songe,
> And to the Sunne newe rose to spreade her wynges,
> Bestirres herselfe her mourneful nestes amonge
> The Nightingall: and doth with byrdes aboute
> Confuse resound with murmure mixed ryse
> To witnes day, his sayles to wynde set out
> The shypman doth committe in doubt of lyfe,

10

20

7 *wayne* cart

Whyle gale of wynde the slacke sayles filles full strayte

30   He leaning over hollow rocke doth lye,

And either his begiled hookes doth bayte,

Or els beholdes and feeles the pray from hye with paised
        hand

The trembling fish he feeles with line extent.

This hope to them to whom of hurtles lyfe,

Is quiet rest, and with his owne content,

And lytle, house, such hope in fieldes is ryfe

The troblous hopes with rolling whirlewynd great

And dredful feares their wayes in cityes keepe.

He proude repayre to prince in regall seate,

40   And hard court gates without the rest of sleepe

Esteemes, and endless happynes to hold

Doth gather goods, for treasure gaping more,

And is ful pore amid his heaped gold.

The peoples favour him (astonied sore)

And commons more unconstant then the sea,

With blast of vayne renoume liftes up full proude.

He selling at the brawling barre his plea,

Full wicked, sets his yres and scoulding loud

And woordes to sale, a fewe hath knowne of all

50   The careles rest, who mindfull how doth flitte

Swift age away, the tyme that never shall

Returne agayne do holde: while fates permitte,

At quiet live: the lyfe full quickly glydes

With hastned course, and with the winged day

The wheele is turnde of yere that hedlong slides,

The sisters hard perfourme their taskes alway,

Nor may agayne untwist the threede once sponne

Yet mankind loe unsure what way to take

To meete the greedy destenyes do thronne

60   And willingly wee seke the Stigian lake.

To much Alcides thou with stomacke stoute

32 *paised* appeasing

The sory sprites of hell dost hast to see.
With course prefixt the fates are brought aboute
To none once warnd to come may respite bee
To none to passe their once appointed day,
The tombe all people calde by death doth hyde
Let glory him by many landes awaye
Display, and fame throughout all cityes wyde
Full babling praise, and even with skye to stande
70   Avaunce and starres: let him in chariot bright
Ful haughty goe: let me my native land
In safe and secrete house keepe close from sight
To restful men hoare age by course doth fall,
And low in place, yet safe and sure doth lye,
The poore and base estate of cottage small:
The prowder pompe of minde doth fall from hye
But sad here comes with losed lockes of heare
Loe Megara with litle company,
And slowe by age drawes Hercles father neare.

In the next excerpt, Hercules speaks, exultant from slaying Lycus, when
suddenly the madness planned for him by Juno takes hold.

but what meanes this? myd day
The darkenes have incloas'd aboute lo Phœbus goeth his way
With face obscure without a clowde who dryves the day to
flight,
And turnes to east? from whence doth now his dusky hed the
night
Unknowne bring forth? whence fil the poale so many rownde
about
Of daytyme starres? lo here behold my laboure first ful stout
Not in the lowest parte of heaven the Lyon shyneth bryght,
And fervently doth rage with yre, and byttes prepares to fyght.
Even now loe he some star wil take, with mouth full wyde to
see

He threatning standes, and fires out blowes and mane up
    rustleth he
Shaking with necke the harvest sad of shape, what ever thinge,
And what soever winter colde in frosen tyme doth bring,
He with one rage wil overpasse, of spring tyme bull he will
Both seeke and breake the neckes at once.

                              *

Goe hurtles soules, whom mischiefe hath opprest
Even in fyrst porch of lyfe but lately had,
And fathers fury goe unhappy kind
O litle children, by the way ful sad
    Of journey knowen.
    Goe see the angry kynges.

In this excerpt from *Troas* (published 1559), the chorus describes the
comfort of company to those in grief. However, the Trojan women
are about to be scattered in exile and will suffer alone, after a last sad
glimpse of Troy.

CHORUS: A Comfort is to mans calamity
        A dolefull flocke of felowes in distres.
        And sweete to him that mournes in miserie
        To here them wayle whom sorowes like oppres
        In deepest care his griefe him bites the les,
        That his estate bewayles not all alone,
        But seeth with him the teares of many one.

        For still it is the chiefe delight in woe,
        And joy of them that sonke in sorrowes are,
        To see like fates by fall to many moe,
        That may take part of all their wofull fare,
        And not alone to be opprest with care.
        There is no wight of woe that doth complayne,
        When all the rest do like mischaunce sustayne.

In all this world if happy man were none,
None (though he were) would thinke himselfe awretch,
Let once the ritch with heapes of Gold be gone,
Whose hundred head his pastours overretch,
Then would the poore mans hart begin to stretch.
There is no wretch whose life him doth displease,
But in respect of those that live at ease.

Sweete is to him that standes in deepe distresse,
To see no man in joyful plight to bee,
Whose onely vessel wind and wave oppresse,
Ful sore his chaunce bewayles and weepeth hee,
That with his owne none others wracke doth see
When he alone makes shipwracke one the sand,
And naked falles to long desyred land.

A thousande sayle who seeth to drench in Seas,
With better will the storme hath overpast
His heavy hap doth him the lesse displease
When broaken boardes abroade be many cast,
And shipwrackt shippes to shore they flit ful fast,
With doubled waves when stopped is the floud,
With heaps of them that there have lost theyr good.

Ful sore did Pirrhus Helens losse complayne,
What time the leader of his flocke of shepe,
Uppon his backe alone he bare them twayne,
And wet his Golden lockes amid the deepe,
In piteous playnt (alas) he gan to weepe.
The death of her it did him deepe displease,
That shipwracke made amid the drenching seas.

And piteous was the playnt and heavy moode
Of woful Pyrrha and eke Deucalion
That nought beheld aboute them but the floud,
When they of all mankynd were left alone

Amid the seas ful sore they made their mone
To see themselves thus left alive in woe
When neyther land they saw, nor fellowes moe.

Anone these playnts and Troyans teares shall quaile,
And here and there the ship them tosse by seas:
When trompets sound shal warne to hoyse up sayle,
And through the waves with wind to seeke their waies
Then shall these captives goe to ende their dayes
In land unknowne: when once with hasty ore
The drenching deepe they take and shunne the shore.

What state of mynd shal then in wretches bee?
When shore shall sinke from sight and seas aryse?
When Idey hill to lurke aloofe they see?
Then poynt with hand from farre wher Troia lies,
Shall child and mother: talking in this wyse:
Loe yonder Troy, where smoke it fumeth hie,
By this the Troyans shal their countrey spie.

In this excerpt from *Thyestes* (published 1560), Tantalus is raised from
Hell by Megaera to instil mortal hatred between his nephews Thyestes
and Atreus, who alternate in ruling Mycenae. In the next excerpt, a
messenger recounts the slaying of Thyestes's children.

TANTALUS, MEGÆRA

What furye fell enforceth mee to fle, th' unhappy seat,
That gape and gaspe with greedye jawe, the fleeyng food to
    eate
What God to Tantalus the bowres wher breathing bodyes dwel
Doth shew agayne? is ought found worse, then burning
    thyrst of hel
In lakes alow? or yet worse plague then hunger is there one,
In vayne that ever gapes for foode? shal Sisyphus his stone,

That slipper restles rollyng payse uppon my backe be borne,
Or shall my lymmes with swifter swinge of whirling whele
    be torne?
Or shal my paynes be Tytius panges th' encreasyng liver
    still,
10   Whose growing guttes the gnawing gripes and fylthy foules
    do fyll?
That styl by nyght repayres the panch that was devourd by
    day,
And wondrous wombe unwasted lieth a new prepared
    pray
What ill am I appoynted for? O cruell judge of sprites,
Who so thou be that tormentes new among the fowles
    delytes
Stil to dispose, ad what thou canst to all my deadly woe,
That keeper even of dungeon darke would sore abhorre to
    knowe.
Or hel it selfe it quake to se: for dread wherof likewyse
I tremble wold, that plague seke out: lo now there doth
    aryse
My broode that shal in mischiefe farre the grandsyers gilt
    out goe,
20   And gyltles make: that first shall dare unventred ills to do.
What ever place remayneth yet of all this wicked land,
I wil fill up: and never once while Pelops house doth
    stand
Shall Minos idle be.
MEGÆRA: Go forth thou detestable sprite
And vexe the Goddes of wicked house with rage of furyes
    might.
Let them contend with all offence, by turnes and one by
    one
Let swordes be drawne: and meane of ire procure there may
    be none,

11 *panch* paunch

Nor shame: let fury blynd enflame theyr myndes and
    wrathful will,
Let yet the parentes rage endure and longer lasting yll
Through childrens children spreade: nor yet let any leysure
    be
The former fawte to hate, but still more mischiefe newe to
    see,
Nor one in one: but ere the gylt with vengeance be acquit,
Encrease the cryme: from brethren proud let rule of
    kingdom flyt
To runnagates: and swarving state of all unstable thinges,
Let it by doubtfull dome be toste, betwene thuncertaine
    kyngs.
Let mighty fall to misery, and myser clime to might,
Let chaunce turne thempyre upsydowne both geve and take
    the right.
The banyshed for gylt, when god restore theyr country
    shall.
Let them to mischiefe fall a fresh as hatefull then to all,
As to themselves: let Ire thinke nought unlawfull to be
    doon,
Let brother dread the brothers wrath, and father feare the
    soon,
And eke the soon his parents powre: let babes be murdered
    yll,
But worse begot? her spouse betrapt to treasons trayne to kyll,
Let hatefull wyfe awayte, and let them beare through seas
    their warre,
Let bloodshed lye the lands about and every field a farre:
And over conqueryng captaynes greate, of countreys far to see,
Let lust tryumphe: in wicked house let whoredome counted
    be
The light'st offens: let trust that in the breasts of brethren
    breedes,
And truth be gone: let not from sight of your so heynous
    deedes

The heavens be hyd, about the poale when shyne the starres
on hye,
50 And flames with woonted beames of light doe decke the
paynted skye.
Let darkest night bee made, and let the day the heavens
forsake.
Dysturbe the godds of wicked house, hate, slaughter,
murder make.
Fyll up the house of Tantalus with mischieves and debates,
Adorned be the pillers hygh with bay, and let the gates
Be garnysht greene: and worthy there for thy returne to
sight,
Be kyndled fyre: let mischyefe done in Thracia once, theyr
lyght
More manyfolde, wherefore doth yet the uncles hand
delaye?
Doth yet Thyestes not bewayle his childrens fatall day?
Shall he not finde them where with heat of fyres that under
glowe
60 The cawderne boyles? their limmes eche one a peeces let
them go
Disperste: let fathers fires, with blood of chyldren fyled bee:
Let deynties such be drest: it is no mischiefe newe to thee,
To banquet so: behold this day we have to thee releast,
And hunger starved wombe of thyne we send to such a
feast.
With fowlest foode thy famyne fyll, let bloud in wyne be
drownd,
And dronke in sight of thee: loe now such dishes have I
found,
As thou wouldst shonne, stay whither doste thou hedlong
way now take?
TANTALUS: To pooles and floods of hell agayne and styll
declining lake,
And flight of tree ful frayght with fruite that from the lippes
doth flee,

70   To dungeon darke of hateful hell let leeful be for me
      To goe: or if to light be thought the paynes that there I
          have,
      Remove me from those lakes agayne: in midst of worser
          wave
      Of Phlegethon, to stand in seas of fyre beset to bee.
      Who so beneath thy poynted paynes by destenyes decree
      Dost stil endure who soo thou bee that underliest alow
      The hollow denne, or ruyne who that feares and overthrow
      Of fallyng hyl, or cruel cryes that sound in caves of hell
      Of greedy roaryng Lyons throats or flocke of furyes fell
      Who quakes to know or who the brandes of fyre in dyrest
          payne
80   Halfe burnt throwes of harke to the voyce of Tantalus:
          agayne
      That hastes to hel, and, whom the truth hath taught beleeve
          wel mee
      Love wel your paynes, they are but small when shall my hap
          so bee
      To flee the light?
MEGÆRA: Disturbe thou fyrst thys house with dire
          discord
      Debates and battels bring with thee, and of th' unhappy
          sworde
      Ill love to kinges: the cruel brest stryke through and hateful
          hart,
      With tumult mad.
TANTALUS: To suffer paynes it seemeth wel my part,
      Not woes to worke: I am sent forth lyke vapoure dyre to
          ryse,
      That breakes the ground or poyson like the plague in
          wondrouse wyse

70 *leeful* lawful

That slaughter makes, shall I to such detested crymes, applye

90   My nephewes hartes? o parentes great of Gods above the
　　　skie

And myne (though sham'de I be to graunt) although with
　　　greater pain

My tongue be vext, yet this to speake I may no whit
　　　refrayne

Nor hold my peace: I warne you this least sacred hand with
　　　bloud

Of slaughter dyre, or fransie fell of frantike fury wood

The aulters slayne, I wil resist: And garde such gylt away.

With strypes why dost thou me affryght? why threatst thou
　　　me to fraye

Those crallyng snakes? or famine fyxt in empty wombe,
　　　wherfore

Dost thou revyve? now fries within with thyrst enkindled
　　　sore

My harte: and in the bowels burnt the boyling flames do
　　　glow.

100   MEGÆRA: I follow thee: through all this house now rage and
　　　fury throwe

Let them be driven so, and so let eyther thirst to see

Each others blood ful wel hath felt the comming in of thee

This house, and all with wicked touch of the begune to
　　　quake.

Enough it is, repayre agayne to dens and loathsome lake,

Of floud well knowen, the sadder soyle with heavy fote of
　　　thyne

Agreeved is, seest thou from springes how waters do
　　　declyne

And inward sinke? or how the bankes lye voyd by drughty
　　　heate?

And hoatter blast of fyery wynde the fewer cloudes doth
　　　beate?

The treese be spoyld, and naked stand to sight in withred
        woddes,

110   The barayne bowes whose fruites are fled: the land betwene
        the floods

With surge of seas on eyther syde that wonted to resound,

And nearer foordes to seperat sometyme with lesser ground,

Now broader spred, it heareth how aloofe the waters ryse.

Now Lerna turnes agaynst the streame Phoronides likewyse

His poores be stopt, with custom'd course Alphéus dryves
        not still,

His hollie waves, the trembling tops of high Cithæron hill,

They stand not sure: from height adowne they shake their
        sylver snowe,

And noble fieldes of Argos feare, theyr former drought to
        know.

Yea Tytan doubtes himselfe to rolle the worlde his wonted
        way,

120   And drive by force to former course the backward drawing
        daye.

*

MESSINGER: As hungry Tygre wonts that doth in gengey
        woods remayne

With doubtfull pace to range and roame betweene the
        bullocks twayne,

Of eyther pray full covetous and yet uncertayne where

She fyrst may byte, and roaring throate now turnes the tone
        to teare

And then to th' other strayght returnes, and doubtfull
        famyne holdes:

So Atreus dyre, betwene the babes doth stand and them
        beholdes

On whom he poynctes to slake his yre: first slaughter where
        to make,

Hee doubts: or whom he shoulde agayne for second offring
        take,

Yet skills it nought, but yet he doubtes and such a cruelty
It him delights to order well.
CHORUS: Whom take he fyrst to dy?
MEGÆRA: First place, least in him thinke yee might no piete to
        remayne
To graundsier dedicated is, fyrst Tantalus is slayne.
CHORUS: With what a minde and count'nesice, could the boy
        his death sustayne?
MEGÆRA: All careles of him selfe he stoode, nor once he
        would in vayne
His prayers leese. But Atreus fierce the sword in him at last
In deepe and deadly wound doth hide to hilts, and gryping
        fast
His throate in hand, he thrust him through. The sword then
        drawne away
When long the body had uphelde it selfe in doubtfull stay,
Which way to fall, at length upon the unckle downe it
        falles.
And then to th' aulters cruelly Philisthenes he tralles,
And on his brother throwes: and strayght his necke of
        cutteth hee.
The Carcase headlong falles to ground: a piteous thing to see,
The mourning head with murmure yet uncertayne doth
        complayne.
CHORUS: What after double death doth he and slaughter then
        of twayne?
Spares he the Child? or gilt on gilt agayne yet heapeth he?
MESSINGER: As long maynd Lyon feerce amid the wood of
        Armenie,
The drove pursues and conquest makes of slaughter many
        one,
Though now defyled be his jawes with bloud and hunger
        gone
Yet slaketh not his yreful rage with bloud of Bulles so great,
But slouthful now with weary tooth the lesser Calves doth
        threate

None other wyse doth Atreus rage, and swelles with anger
    straynd,
And holding now the sword in hand, with double slaughter
    staynd,
Regarding not where fell his rage, with cursed hand unmild
He strake it through his body quite, at bosome of the Child
The blade goeth in, and at the backe agayne out went the
    same,
He falles and quenching with his bloud the aulters sacred
    flame,
Of eyther wound at length he dieth.

CHORUS: O heynous hateful act.

MESSINGER: Abhorre ye this? ye heare not yet the end of all
    the fact,
There followes more.

CHORUS: A fiercer thing, or worse then this to
    see
Could Nature beare?

MEGÆRA: Why thinke ye this of gylt the end to
    be?
It is but part.

CHORUS: What could he more? to cruel beastes he cast
Perhappes their bodyes to be torne, and kept from fyres at
    last.

MEGÆRA: Would God he had: that never tombe the dead
    might over hyde,
Nor flames dissolve, though them for food to foules in
    pastures wyde
He had out throwen, or them for pray to cruell beastes
    would flinge.
That which the worst was wont to be, were here a wished
    thing,
That them their father saw untombd: but oh more cursed
    crime
Uncredible, the which denye will men of after tyme:

From bosomes yet alive out drawne the trembling bowels
    shake,
The vaynes yet breath, the feareful hart doth yet both pant
    and quake:
But he the stringes doth turne in hand, and destenies
    beholde,
And of the guttes the sygnes each one doth vewe not fully
    cold.
When him the sacrifyce had pleasd, his diligence he puttes
To dresse his brothers banquet now: and streight a sonder
    cuttes
The bodyes into quarters all, and by the stoompes anone
The shoulders wyde, and brawnes of armes he strikes of
    everychone.
He layes abroad their naked lims, and cuts away the bones:
The onely heads he kepes and handes to him committed
    once.
Some of the guttes are broacht, and in the fyres that burne
    full sloe
They drop, the boyling licour fome doth tomble to and froe
In moorning cawderne: from the flesh that overstandes aloft
The fyre doth flye, and skatter out and into chimney ofte
Up heapt agayne, and there constraynd by force to tary yet
Unwilling burnes: the liver makes great noyse upon the spit,
Nor easely wot I, if the flesh, or flames they be that cry,
But crye they do: the fyre like pitch it fumeth by and by:
Nor yet the smoke it selfe so sad, like flithy miste in sight
Ascendeth up as wont it is, nor takes his way upright,
But even the Gods and house it doth with fylthy fume
    defile.
O pacient Phœbus though from hence thou backeward flee
    the whyle,
And in the midst of heaven above dost drowne the broken
    day,
Thou fleest to late: the father eats his children, well away,

And limmes to which he once gave life, with cursed jaw
    doth teare.
He shynes with oyntment shed ful sweete all round about
    his heare,
Replete with wyne: and oftentymes so cursed kynd of food
His mouth hath held, that would not downe, but yet this
    one thing good
In all thy yls (Thyestes) is that them thou dost not knoe,
And yet shal that not long endure, though Titan backward
    goe
And chariots turne agaynst himselfe, to meete the wayes he
    went,
And heavy night so heynous deede to kepe from sight be
    sent,
And out of tyme from East aryse, so foule a fact to hyde,
Yet shall the whole at length be seene: thy ylles shall all be
    spide.

JOHN STUDLEY (?1545–?1590)

Studley published his translations of Seneca while an undergraduate at
Cambridge, which he entered in 1563. He ran into trouble as a Fellow
of Trinity College in 1573, when he was forced to resign because of
his Puritan convictions. He may have become a lawyer subsequently,
and was perhaps killed at the siege of Breda. In this excerpt from
Hippolytus/Phaedra, Phaedra, in exile and living in wedlock with her
father's enemy, feels deserted, and admits to an unlawful love for her
stepson, Hippolytus, despite her nurse's warnings. The second excerpt,
from the chorus, describes the power of love.

PHAEDRA: I know the truth ye teach
    O Nurce, but fury forceth mee at worser thinges to reach:

My mynd even wittingly to vyce falles forward prone and
  bent
To holesome counsell backe agayne in vayne it doth
  relente:
As when the Norman tugges and toyles to bring the
  fraighted Barke
Agaynst the striving streame, in vayne he loseth al his carke
And downe the shallow streame perforce the Shyp doth
  hedlong yeeld,
Where reason preaseth forth, there fighting fury winnes the
  field,
And beares the swinging sway, and cranke Cupidoes
  puissant might
10 Tryumpheth over all my breast this flighty winged wight
And puissant potestate throughout the world doth beare the
  stroke,
And with unquenched flames doth force Joves kindled
  breast to smoake,
The Battelbeaten Mars hath felt these bitter burning
  brandes,
And eke the God hath tasted these whose fervent fierye
  handes,
The thumping thunder bouncing boltes three forked wyse
  doth frame,
And he that ever busied is about the furious flame,
In smoltring Fornace raging hoat on dusky top so hie
Of foggye Aetna mount: and with such slender heat doth
  frie,
And Phœbe himselfe that weldes his dart upon his twanging
  string,
20 With aymed shaft directlie driven the wimpled Ladde doth
  sting.

6 *carke* load **11** *potestate* mighty power

With powre he scoures along the Earth and Marble Skye
    amayne.
Lust favoring folly filthily did falsely forge and fayne
Love for a God: and that he might hys freedome more
    attayne.
Ascribes the name of fayned God to shittel bedlame rage.
Erycina about the world doth send her roving page,
Who glyding through the Azure skies with slender joynted
    arme
His perlous weapons weildes at will, and working grievous
    harme,
Of bones and stature beyng least great might he doth display
Upon the Gods, compelling them to crouch and him obey.
Some Brainsicke head did attribute these thinges unto
    himselfe,
And Venus Godhead with the bow of Cupid little else.
Who cockred is, tryumphing much in fauning fortunes lap,
And flotes in welth, or seekes and sues for thinges that
    seldome hap,
Lust (mighty fortunes mischeous mate) assaulteth straight his
    breast,
His tooth contempneth wonted fare and victuals homly
    drest.
Nor hansome houses pleaseth him, why doth this plague
    refuse
The simple sort, and to annoy doth stately bowers chuse?
How haps it matrimony pure to byde in Cottage base?
And honest love in middle sort of men doth purchase place?
And thinges that be of meane estate themselves restraine ful
    wel,
But they that wallow in their luste whose stately stomackes
    swell,
Puft up and bolstred bigge with trust of Kingly scepter
    proude
Do greater matters enterprise then may be well alowde.

Hee that is able much to do, of powre wil also bee
To do these thinges he cannot doe.
[NURCE:]   Now Lady dost thou see
   What thinges do thee beseeme thus staid on stately throne
      on hie?
   Mistrust the scepter of thy spouse returning by and by.
PHAEDRA: In me I beare a violent and mighty payse of love,
   And no mans comming home againe to terrour may me
      move.
50   He never stepped backe agayne, the welkin skie to touch,
   That swallowed once and sunke in gulfe and glummy cave
      did couch
   Shut up in shimering shade for ay.
NURCE: Yet do not thou suppose,
   Though dreadful Ditis lock with barres, and bolt his
      dongeon close:
   And though the hideous hellicke hounde do watch the
      griesly gates,
   Not Theseus alone shal have his passage stopt by fates.
PHAEDRA: Perhaps he pardon wil the cryme of loves procuring
   heate.

*

CHORUS: This peevish Elfe the Countreys all doth keepe,
   Whose quarrels sting the Marble faced rout
   Of water Nimphes, that with the Waters deepe
   The brand that burnes in breast cannot quench out,
   The flying fowle doth feele the foystring flames.
   What cruell Skirmish doe the Heyffers make?
   Prickt up by lust that nice Dame Venus frames
   In furious sorte for all the Cattels sake?
   If fearefull Hearts their Hindes doe once mistrust,
   In love disloyall then gladly dare they fight,
   And bellowings out, they bray to witnesse just
   Their angry moode, conceyv'de in irefull spright

The paynted coast of India then doth hate
The spotty Hyded Tygar, then the Bore
Doth whet his Tuskes to combat for his mate,
And fomes at mouth: the ramping Lyons rore
And shake their Manes, when Cupids corsies move:
Wyth grunts and grones the howling frythes doe murn:
The Dolphin of the raging Sea doth love:
The Elephants by Cupids blaze doe burn:
Dame nature all doth challeng as her owne,
And nothing is that can escape her lawes:
The rage of wrath is quencht and overthrowne,
When as it pleaseth Love to bid them pawes:
Blacke hate that rusting frets in cankred breast,
And all olde grudge is dasht by burning love.
What shall I make discourse more of the rest
Stout Stepdames doth this gripe to mercy move.

This excerpt is from a debate between Hippolytus and the nurse about his austerity and disdain for women. He rhapsodizes on his life in the woods, calling it a Golden Age, before the fall of innocence which he attributes to womankind. In the subsequent excerpt, a messenger describes to Theseus the death of Hippolytus, which was ordered in response to the spurned Phaedra's false accusations. Of this passage, Geoffrey Hill writes, 'In the Elizabethan "hinterland", where spectacular "closet" horror can at any time become the routine hideousness of public spectacle, how can one say where metaphor ends and reality begins?' (*The Lords of Limit*, London, A. Deutsch, 1984, p. 34).

HIPPOLYTUS: No life is more devoyd of sinne, and free from
        grievous thralles,
    And keeping fashions old, then that which leaving Townish
        walles,
    Doth take delight in pleasant Woods, he is not set on fyre,
    Enraged sore with burning Byle of covetous desyre.

Who hath addict himselfe among the mountaynes wilde to
    live,
Not prickt with pratling peoples bruite, no credit doth he
    geve.
To th' Vulgar sort disloyall still, unto the better part
Nor cankred rancour pale doth gnaw his blacke and fretting
    hart.
Nor fickle favour forceth he, he bound doth not obay
The payse of Scepter proude: but weildes the massy scepter
    sway
At ebbing honours gapes he not, nor moyles for fleeting
    mucke,
Removed farre from hovering hope and dread of backward
    lucke,
Not bitter gnawing Envy rancke teares him with tooth
    unkind,
Not quaynted with the mischiefe that in Cittyes and in
    mynd
Of people presseth thicke: nor quakes at every blast that flies
With guilty conscience to himselfe, nor frames himselfe to
    lies.
Nor covets rich with thousand pillers close his head to
    shroude,
Nor guildes his beames with glisteryng gold for fancy fond
    and proude,
Nor gushing streames of bloud upon his innocent Alters
    flow.
Nor Bullockes bright their hundred heads as whyte as flakie
    Snow,
Do yeeld to Axe, whyle scattered is on thaulter sacred
    grayne,
But al the quiet countrey round at wil he doth obtayne.
And harmles walketh too and froe amid the open ayre,
And onely for the brutish Beast contrives a trapping snare.

Another whyle uppon the swift Alpheus banckes he walkes

Now up and downe the breary Brakes of bushy woods he
    stalkes

Where lukewarme Lernas christall floud with water cleare
    doth shine,

And chaunging course his Channell out another way doth
    twyne:

And heare the piteous plaining Birds with chirping charmes
    do chide,

And Braunches trembling shake whereon soft windye puffes
    do glyde.

And spreading Beches old do stand, to fast and shake my
    shankes:

To stampe and daunce it doth me good on running Rivers
    bankes:

Or els upon a withred clod to steale a nap of sleepe,

Whereas the fountayne flowes amayne with gushing waters
    deepe.

Or els among the baulmy flowres out braying savours
    sweete,

Wheras with pleasant humming noise the bubbling brooke
    doth fleete.

The Apples beaten of the tree do ravening hunger staunch,

An Strawberyes gathered of the bush soone fill with hungry
    paunch.

He shoons assaultes, that doth himselfe from regall royall
    hold.

Estates do quaffe theyr dreadful drinke in Bolles of massye
    Golde:

How trimme it is water to lap in palme of naked hand:

The sooner drowsye Morpheus byndes thy Browes with
    sleepy bande:

The carelesse corpes doth rest at ease upon the hardest
    Couch:

The Cabin base hauntes not by Nookes, to prig and filch a
    pouch:

In house of many corners blynd his head he doth not hyde,
He loves to come abroade and in the light to be espyde:
The Heavens beare witnesse of his life, they lived in this
    wise.
I thinke, that scattred did of Gods in alder time arise.
No doting covetous blinde desire of Golde in them was
    found:
No stones nor stakes set up in field did stint the parted
    ground:
The sayling Ship with brazen Stem cut not the waltring
    wave,
But every man doth know his coast and how much he
    should have.
No hugy Rampires raysed were, nor Ditches delved deepe,
Nor countermured Castle strong the walled Townes to
    keepe.
The Souldier was not busied his blunted Tooles to whet,
Nor rapping Pellets, Cannon shot the barred Gates downe
    bet,
Nor soyle with yoaked Oxe was strainde to beare the
    cutting share,
The field even fertill of it selfe did feede the World with
    fare,
The plentifull aboundant Woods great wealth by nature
    gave:
A house of nature eake they had a dimme and darksome
    Cave:
The covetous minde to scrape up wealth, and despret
    furious ire,
And greedy Lust (that eggeth on the minde all set on fire.)
First brake the bands, and eger thirst of bearing sway stept
    in,
To be the strongers ravening pray the weaker did begin,

And might went for oppressed right: the naked Fist found
  out
To scratch and cuffe, to box and bum, with dealing blowes
    about.
The knarrie Logs, and snaggie shive were framed weapons
    strong,
The gatten Tree ungrayned was with Pikes of Yron long.
No nor the rusty Fawchon then did hang along the side,
Nor Helmet crest upon the head stood percking up for
    pride,
Pale spightfull griefe invented Tooles, and warlick Mars his
    braine
Contriv'de new sleights, a thousand kinde of deathes he did
    ordaine:
By meanes hereof eche Land is fild with clottred gore
    yshed,
With streames of bloud the Seas are dyde to hue of sanguine
    red,
Then Mischiefe wanting measure gan through every house
    to passe,
No kinde of vitious villany that practise wanted was.
By Brother, Brother reft of Breath, and eake the Fathers
    Life
By hand of Childe, eake murthred was the husband of his
    Wyfe,
And Mother lewde on mischiefe set destroyde their bodies
    seede.
I overpasse the Stepdame with her guilt and haynous deede.
And no where pitty planted is, as in the brutish beast:
But womankinde in mischiefe is ringleader of the reast,
The instrument of wickednesse enkindling first desire,
Whose vile uncesteous whoredome set so many Townes on
    fire.

So many Nations fall to warre, eake Kingdomes
    overthrowne,
And raysed from the ground, to crushe so many people
    downe.
Let other passe: by Jasons Wyfe Medea may wee finde
By her alone, that Women are a plaguy crabbed kinde.

*

NUNTIUS: Hippolytus (ay woe is me) is slayne by doleful death.
THESEUS: Now Father do I know my Sonne bereaved of his
    breath,
For why the Leacher life is lost: shew in what sort he dide.
NUNTIUS: In all poast hast as fugitive to shunne the Towne he
    hyde
Once having caught his cutting course apace he scuddes
    away,
His prauncing Palfrayes straite he doth with Collers close
    araye
With curbed bittes their snaffled heads at wil he brydles in,
Then talking much unto himselfe to curse he doth beginne
His native soyle: alas deare Father, Father stil he cryes:
And angry lasheth with his whip, whyle loose his Bridle lies:
Then sodenly a hugy swolve gan swel amid the deepe,
And starteth up into the starres no pipling wind doth
    sweepe
Along the Seas in Heaven so lith no noyse at all there was:
The Seas ful calme even as their kindly Tyde doth drive
    them, passe.
Nor yet no boysterous Southerne wynd the Sycill sand
    turmoyles.
Nor yet with fomie ramping surge the raging gulph up
    boyles,
Heavde up by Westerne puffes: when as the rockes with
    flappyng flash
Do shake and drownd Lucates clive the hoary fome doth
    dash.

The tombling waves togeather tost on hils are heaped hie,
The swelling swolve with Monster much to land alofe doth
    flye,
Nor only shaken ships in Seas do suffer wracke hereby:
The land in hazard lyes of stormes a waltring wave is rold
In tottering wise a wallowing gulph with winding compas
    fold,
Drives downe I know not what withall: a flat uprisyng new
An head above the water brim doth rayse the Starres to
    vew.
In foggie cloud eclipsed is Apollos dusky gleede,
And Scyros Rocks whom Trumpe of Fame advaunst by
    dreary deede
Corynthus take whom double Sea on eyther side assayle:
While greatly we agriefd, these thinges do languishing
    bewayle,
The belking Seas yell out the grunting Rockes with all do
    rore:
The stabby Clive doth reke, from whence the water ebde
    before,
It frothes, and keping course by course it spewes the waters
    out,
As doth Physeter fish (that flittes the Ocean Coast about)
And gulping doth from yawning throat his flouds of water
    spoute.
The shaken surge did tottre strayte and brake it selfe in
    twayne:
With wracke (more violent then wee did feare) it rusht
    amayne
Agaynst the shore, beyond the bankes it breakes into the
    land:
And hideous Monster followes: these for feare did quaking
    stand.

THESEUS: What shape that uncouth Monster had and body vast
    declare.

NUNTIUS: A boasting Bull, his marble necke advaunced hye
    that bare,

Upraysd his lofty bristled Mayn on curled forhead greene

With shaggy eares prickt up his divers speckled hornes were
    seene.

(Whom Bacchus earst possessed had, who tames the Cattell
    wyld,

And eake the God that borne in flouds was bred a water
    Chyld)

Now puffing he perbraketh flames, and now as leaming
    light

With sparckling beams his goggle eyes do glare and glister
    bright.

His greasy larded necke (a marke for to be noted well)

With tough and knobby turnels hie out bumping big do
    swell.

His snorting Nostrilles wyde do grunt and yawning gulphes
    they sosse,

His breast and throtebag greenishly are dawbd with clammy
    mosse,

His side along begrymed is with Lactuse red of hue,

On snarling knots his wrinckled rumpe toward his face he
    drue,

His scaly haunch, and lagging tayle most ugly dragges hee
    up,

As Pristis in the deepe of Seas the swallowed Keele doth
    sup.

Or else perbraketh out agayne the undigested pup.

The earth did quake, the Cattel feard about the field do
    rampe,

The hunter starke with chilling feare beginnes to stare and
    stampe,

The heirdman had no mynd his scattrynge Heyfers to
    pursue,
The Deere amazed brake the pale and bad the Laundes
    adue.
But onely yet Hippolytus, devoyde of faynting feare
His neyng horses with the raynes of Bridles hard doth
    beare,
With wonted woordes he cheareth up his nymble Nagges
    afraide:
A steepe hie way at Argos lies with stony clives decaide,
That nodding overhangs the Sea which underfleetes that
    wayes:
That ugly Royle heere heates him selfe, and raging wrath
    doth rayse,
And kindling courage hoate, him force with burning breast
    assayes,
And chaufing efe himselfe before gan fret with angry hart.
Lo then into a scouring course on sodayne doth hee start,
With whirling pace he girding forth doth scarcely touch the
    ground,
Lighting a front the trimbling Cart with glaring Eyes hee
    glowmd.
Then also doth thy threatning Son with lowring browes
    upstart,
Nor chaungeth Countenaunce, but speakes with stout
    couragious hart.
This foolish feare doth not appaule my bold and hardned
    brest,
It comes to mee by kinde, that Bulls by mee should bee
    opprest.
His Steedes defying strait the Raynes plonge forward with
    the Cart,
As rage did prick them, sore afright beside the way they
    start.

This bias way among the Rocks they raunge, and wander
    wyde,
But as the Pylot (least the Barke should totter to one syde)
Doth beare it even in wrastling waves: so while his horses
    skip,
He ruleth them, now raines them hard, and now with
    winding whip
Free lashes on their buttocks layes: his Foe doth him
    pursue,
Now step by step, now meeting full agaynst his face hee
    flue.
Provoking terror every where. No further fly they might:
The horned beast with butting Browes gan run upon them
    right.
The trampling Gennets straught of wits doe straight way
    breake their ray,
The struggle striving hard to slip the Collar if they may.
And prauncing on their hinder Feete, the burden hurle on
    ground:
Thy Son flat falling on his Face, his body fast was bound,
Entangled in the winding ropes, the more he strives to
    loose
The slipping knots, he faster sticks within the sliding noose.
The Horses doe perceyve the broyle: and with the Waggon
    light
While none there is to rule the Raynes, with skittish feare
    afright
At randon out they ramping runne, (even as the Welkin hye
The Cart that mist his woonted waight, disdayning in the
    Skye
The dreery day that falsely was commit unto the Sun,
From off the fiery Marble Poale that downe askew doth
    run,

Flang Phaeton topsie torvey tost) his bloud begores the
    ground:
And dingd agaynst the rugged Rocks his head doth oft
    rebound:
The brambles rent his haled hayre: the edged flinty stones,
The beauty batter of his Face, and breake his crashing
    bones:
At Mouth his blaring tongue hangs out with squeased eyne
    out dasht,
His Jawes and Skull doe crack, abrode his spurting Braynes
    are pasht,
His cursed beauty thus defoylde with many wounds is spent:
The jotting Wheeles do grinde his guts, and drenched lims
    they rent.
At length a Stake with Trunchion burnt his ripped Paunch
    hath caught,
From rived Grine to th' Navell stead within his wombe it
    raught:
The Cart upon his Maister pawsde agaynst the ground
    ycrusht,
The Fellies stuck within the wounds, and out at length they
    rusht:
So both delay and Maisters limbs are broke by stresse of
    Wheeles:
His dragling guts then trayle about the wincing horses
    heeles.
They thumping with their horny Hooves agaynst his Belly
    kick,
From bursten Paunch on heapes his blouddy bowells jumble
    thick:
The scraiting Bryers on the Brakes with needle poynted
    pricks
His gory Carkas all to race with spelles of thorny sticks

And of his flesh ech ragged shrub a gub doth snatch and
rent,
His men (a mourning troupe God knowes) with brackish
teares besprent
Doe stray about the fielde, whereas Hippolytus was tore:
A piteous signe is to bee seene by tracing long of gore:
His howling Dogges their Maisters limmes with licking
follow still:
The earnest toyle of woful Wights can not the coats up
fill,
By gathering up the gobbets sparst and broken lumps of
flesh.
Is this the flaunting bravery that comes of beauty fresh?
Who in his Fathers Empyre earst did raigne as pryncely
Peare
The Heyre apparant to the Crowne, and shone in honour
cleare,
Lyke to the glorious Stars of Heaven, his Limmes in pieces
small
Are gathred to his fatall Grave, and swept to funerall.
THESEUS: O Nature that prevaylste too much, (alas) how dost
thou binde
Whyth bonds of bloud the Parents breast? how love we
thee by kinde?
Maugre our Teeth whom guilty eeke we would have reft of
breath?
And yet lamenting with my teares I doe bewayle thy death.
NUNTIUS: None can lament with honesty that which he wisht
destroyde.
THESEUS: The hugiest heape of woes by this I thinke to be
enjoyde,
When flickering Fortunes cursed wheele doe cause us cry
alas,
To rue the wrack of things which earst wee wished brought
to passe.

NUNTIUS: If stil thou keepe thy grudge, why is thy Face with
     teares besprent?
THESEUS: Because I slue him, not because I lost him, I repent.

*

THESEUS: The shreadings of this deare beloved carkasse bring
     to mee,
  His mangled members hether bring on heapes that tombled
     be:
  This is Hyppolytus, I do acknowledge myne offence,
  For I it is, that have deprived thee of life and sense.
  Least that but once, or onely I should be a guilty Wight,
  I Sire attempting mischiefe have besought my Fathers
     might.
  Lo I enjoy my fathers gift, O solitarinesse,
  A grievous plague when feeble yeares have brought us to
     distresse.
  Embrace these lims, and that which yet doth of thy sonne
     remayne.
  O woeful wight in baleful breast preserve and entertayne.
  These scattred scraps of body torne O Syre in order set,
  The straying gobbetts bring agayne, here was his right hand
     set:
  His left hand here instructed well to rule the raynes must
     be.
  His left syde rybbs (ful wel I know to be bewayld of mee
  With bitter teares) as yet alas are lost and wanting still,
  O trembling handes behold this woful busines to fulfil,
  And withered Cheekes forbid your streams of flowing tears
     to runne
  Whyle that the father do accompt the members of his
     Sonne.
  And eke patch up his body rent, that hath his fashion lost,
  Disfigured foule with gorye woundes, and all about betost:
  I doubt, if this of thee be peece, and peece it is of thee:
  Here, lay it here, in th' empty place, here let it layed be,

Although perhap it lye not right: (aye me) is this thy face?
Whose beauty twinckled as a starre, and eake did purchase
    grace,
In sight of Foe procurd to ruth. Is this thy beauty lost?
O cruell will of Gods, O rage in sinne prevayling most.
Doth thus the Syre that great good turne perfourme unto
    his sonne?
Lo let thy fathers last farewel within thyne eares to runne,
My child whom oft I bid farewell: the whilst the fire shall
    burne
These bones, set ope his buriall bower, and let us fall to
    mourne
With loude lamenting Mopsus wise for both the coarses
    sake:
With Princely Pompe his funerall fire see that ye ready
    make,
And seeke ye up the broken parts in field dispersed round,
Stop hir up hurlde into a Pit, let heavy clodds of ground
        Lie hard upon his cursed hed.

In this excerpt from *Medea*, Medea chants her incantations, calling upon
the gods of the ghostly underworld before she sends her sons to Jason's
bride with a deadly robe.

O flittring Flockes of grisly ghostes that sit in silent seat
O ougsome Bugges, O Gobblins grym of Hell I you intreat:
O lowryng Chaos dungeon blynde, and dreadfull darkned
    pit,
Where Ditis muffled up in Clowdes of blackest shades doth
    sit,
O wretched wofull wawling soules your ayde I doe
    implore,
That linked lye with gingling Chaynes on wayling Limbo
    shore,

O mossy Den where death doth couche his gastly carrayne
    Face:
Relesse your pangues, O spryghts, and to this wedding hye
    apace.
Cause yee the snaggy wheele to pawse that rentes the
    Carkas bound,
Permit Ixions racked Lymmes to rest upon the ground:
Let hungry bytten Tantalus wyth gawnt and pyned panche
Soupe up Pirenes gulped streame his swelling thyrst to
    staunche.
Let burning Creon byde the brunt and gyrdes of greater
    payne,
Let payse of slyppery slyding stone type over backe agayne
His moylyng Father Sisyphus, amonges the craggy Rockes.
Yee daughters dyre of Danaus whom perced Pychers
    mockes
So oft with labour lost in vayne this day doth long for you
That in your lyfe with bloudy blade at once your husband
    slewe.
And thou whose aares I honored have, O torch and lampe
    of night,
Approche O Lady myne with most deformed vysage dight:
O threefolde shapen Dame that knitst more threatning
    browes then one,
According to the countrey guise with dagling locks undone
And naked foote, the secrete grove about I halowed have,
From dusky dry unmoysty cloudes the showers of rayne I
    crave.
Through me the chinked gaping ground the soked seas hath
    drunk,
And mayner streame of th' ocian floud beneath the earth is
    sunk,
That swelteth out through hollow gulph with stronger
    gushing rage.
Then were his suddy wambling waves whose power it doth
    asswage

The heavens with wrong disturbed course and out of order
    quight,
The darkned sonne, and glimmering stars at once hath
    shewed theyr light,
And drenched Charles his stragling wayne hath ducte in
    dasshing wave,
The framed course of roaming time racte out of frame I
    have.
So my enchauntments have it wrought, that when the
    flaming sunne
In sommer bakes the parched soyle then hath the twigges
    begunne,
With sprowting blossom fresh to blome, and hasty winter
    corne
Hath out of harvest seene the fruite to barnes on suddein
    borne.
Into a shallowe foorde his sture distreame hath Phasis wast,
And Isters channell being in so many braunches cast,
Abated hath his wrackfull waves, on every silent shore
He lyeth calme: The tumbled flouds with thundring noyse
    did rore,
When couched close the windes were not moving pippling
    soft,
With working wave the praluncing seas have swolne and
    leapt aloft,
Whereas the wood in alder time with thicke and braunched
    bowe
Did spread his shade on gladsome soyle no shade remayneth
    now.
I rolling up the magicke verse at noone time Phœbus stay,
Amyd the darkned Sky, when fled was light of drowsy day.
Eke at my charme the watry flockes of Heyæds went to
    glade.
Time is it Phœba to respect the service to thee made:

To thee with cruell bloudy hands these garlands greene
 were twynde
Which with his folding circles nyne the serpent rough did
 bynde.
Have here Tiphoias fleshe, that doth in Ætnas Fornace
 grone,
That shoke with battery violent king Joves assaulted trone.
This is the Centaures paysoned bloud which Nessus villayne
 vyle
Who made a rape of Dianire entending her to fyle,
Bequethed her when newly wounde he gasping lay for
 breath,
While Hercles shaft stack in his Ribs, whose launce did
 worke his death:
Beholde the Funerall cinders heere which up the poyson
 dryed
Of Hercules who in his fyre on Oeta mountayne dyed:
Loe heere the fatall brand, which late the fatall sisters three
Conspyred at Meleagers byrth, such should his destny bee,
To save alyve his brethyng corpes, while that might whole
 remayne,
Which saufe his mother Althe kept, till he his uncles
 twayne,
(That from Atlanta would have had the head of conquered
 Bore,)
Had reft of lyfe whose spightfull death Althea tooke so sore,
That both she shewed her ferventnesse in systers godly love,
When to revenge her brothers death meere nature did her
 move,
But yet as mother most unkynde, of nature most unmylde,
To hasten the untymely grave of her beloved chylde,
Whyle Meleagers fatall brande she wasted in the flame,
Whose swelting guts and bowels moult consumed as the
 same,

These plumes the Harpyes ravening fowles for hast did leave
    behinde
In hidden hole whose cloase accesse no mortall wight can
    fynd.
When fast from Zethes chasing them with speedy flight
    they fled.
Put unto those the fethers which the Stymphal byrde did
    shed,
Whom duskyng Phœbus dymned lyght syr Hercules did
    stynge,
And galled with the shafte, that he in Hydraes hyde did
    flynge.
You Aares have yeelde a clattring noyse I knowe, I knowe
    of olde,
How unto mee my Oracles are wonted to bee toulde,
That when the trembling flowre doth shake then hath my
    Goddes great,
Vouchsafe to graunt mee my request as I did her intreate,
I see Dianas waggon swife, not that whereon shee glydes,
When all the night in darkned Sky with Face full ope shee
    rydes:
With countnaunce bright and blandishing but when with
    heavy cheare,
With dusky shimmering wanny globe, her lampe doth pale
    appeare.
Or when shee trots about the heavens wyth horseheade
    rayned strayte,
When Thessayle Witches with the threats of charming her
    doe bayte.
So with thy dumpish dulled blase, thy cloudy faynting lyght,
Sende out, amid the lowring sky, the heart of people
    smyght
Wyth agonies of suddeyne dread, in straung and fearfull
    wyse,
Compell the pretious brasen pannes with jarring noyse to
    ryse

Through Corinth countrey every where, to shielde thee
    from this harme,
Least headlong drawne thou be from heaven to earth by
    force of charme.
An holy solempne sacryfice to worship thee wee make,
Imbrewed with a bloudy turphe the kindled Torch doth
    take
Thy sacred burning night fyre at the dampishe mory grave.
Sore charged with thy troubled ghost my head I shaken
    have,
And ducking downe my Necke alowe with shryking lowde
    have shrig,
And groveling flat on floore in traunce have lyen in
    deadmans plight.
My ruffled Lockes about myne eares downe dagling have
    ben bownd,
Tuckt up about my temples twayne with gladsome garland
    crownde
A drery braunche is offred thee from filthy Stigis flood.
As is the guise of Bacchus priestes the Coribanthes wood,
With naked breast and dugges layde out Ile pricke with
    sacred blade
Myne arme, that for the bubling bloude an issue may bee
    made,
With trilling streames my purple bloude let drop on
    Th'aulter stones.
My tender Childrens crusshed fleshe, and broken broosed
    bones
Lerne how to brooke with hardned heart: in practise put
    the trade
To florishe fearce, and keepe a coyle, with naked glittring
    blade:
I sprinkled holy water have, the launce once being made,
If tyred thou complaynest that my cryes thee overlade,
Give pardon to my ernest suite, O Perseus sister deare,
Still Jason is the onely cause that urgeth mee to reare

With squeking voyce thy noysome beames, that sting like
    shot of bo
So season thou those sawced robes to worke Creusas woe,
Wherewith when shee shall pranke her selfe the poyson by
    and by
To rot her inward mary out, within her bones may fry,
The secret fyer bleares their eyes with glosse of yeallow
    golde,
The which Prometheus gave to mee that fyer fylcher bolde.
On whom for robbery that he did in heavens above
    commit,
With massy payse great Caucasus th'unweldy hill doth sit,
Where under with unwasted wombe he lyes, and payes his
    payne,
To feede the cramming foule with gubs of guts that growes
    agayne.
He taught mee with a prety sleyght of conning, how to
    hyde
The strength of fyer close kept in, that may not be espyde,
This lyvely tinder Mulciber hath forged for my sake,
That tempred is with brymstone quick at fyrst touch and
    take.
Eke of my Cosen Phaëton a wyldefyer flake I have
His flames the monstrous staghard rough Chimera to mee
    gave,
In head and breast a Lyon grim, and from the Rump
    behynde
He sweepes the flower with lagging Tayle of Serpent fearce
    by kynde
In Rybbes, and Loynes along his paunche yshaped lyke a
    Goate.
These Fumes that out the Bull perbrakte from fyry
    spewinge throat
I gotten have and brayde it with Medusas bitter gall
Commaunding it in secret sorte to duske and cover all:

Breath on these venoms Hecate, with deadly myght
    inspyre,
Preserve the touching poulder of my secret covert fyre,
O graunt that these my cloked craftes so may bewitch theyr
    Eyes,
That lykelyhoode of treason none they may heerein
    surmyse:
So worke that they in handling it may feele no kynde of
    heate:
Her stewing breast, her seathing vaynes, let fervent fyer
    freate
And force her rosted pyning lymmes to drop and melt
    away,
Let smoke her rotten broyling bones: enflame this bryde to
    day
To cast a lyght with greater gleede on fryseled blasing heare
Then is the shyning flame that doth the wedding torches
    beare.
My suite is harde, thryse Hecate a dreadfull barking gave
From dolefull cloude a sacred flash of flamy sparkes shee
    drave.
Eche poysons pryde fulfilled is: call forth my chyldren
    deare,
By whom unto the cursed Bryde these presentes you may
    beare:
Goe forth, goe forth my lytle Babes, your mothers cursed
    fruite,
Goe, goe, employ your paynes with brybe and earnest
    humble suite
To purchase grace, and eke to earne you favour in her sight.
That both a mother is to you, and rules with Ladies might.
Goe on, apply your charge apace, and hye you home
    agayne,
That with embracing you I may my last farewell attayne.

This excerpt from *Agamemnon* is Cassandra's vision of the king's murder.

> O shall a King be murthered, by a banisht wretches hande?
> Out, shall Th'adulterer destroy the husbande of the Wyfe?
> The dreadful destinies approcht, the foode that last in lyfe
> He tasted of before his death, theyr maysters bloud shall see,
> The gubs of bloude downe dropping on the wynde shall
>   powred bee.
> By traytrous tricke of trapping weede his death is brought
>   about,
> Which being put upon his heade his handes coulde not get
>   out,
> The stopped poake with mouth set ope his muffled head
>   doth hyde,
> The mankinde dame with trembling hand the swerd drew
>   from her side,
> Nor to the utmost of her might it in his flesh shee thrast,
> But in the gieving of the stroke shee stayed all agast,
> Hee as it were a bristled Bore entangled in the net
> Among the bryars in busshy woodes yet tryeth out to get.
> With strugling much the shrinking bands more streightly he
>   doth bind,
> He stryves in vayne, and would slip of the snare that doth
>   him blind.
> Which catcheth holde on every syde. But yet th' entangled
>   wreatch
> Doth grope about, his subtle foes with griping hand to
>   catch.
> But furious Tyndaris preparde the Pollaxe in her hande,
> And as the priest to sacrifice at Th'alter side doth stande,
> And vewes with eye the Bullockes necke, eare that with
>   Axe he smite,
> So to and fro shee heaves her hand to stryke and leavell
>   right.

He hath the stroke: dispatcht it is: not quite chopt of the
head,
It hangeth by a litle crop: heere from the Carkasse dead
The spouting bloude came gusshing out: and there the head
doth lye,
With wallowing, bobling, mumbling tongue: nor they do
by and bye
Forsake him so: the breathlesse coarse Ægist doth all to
coyle:
And mangled hath the gasshed corpes: whyle thus hee doth
him spoyle,
She putteth to her helping hand: by detestable deede
They both accorde unto the kynde, whereof they doe
proceede.

In this excerpt from *Hercules Oetaeus*, the nurse suggests to Deianira
that she use magic to punish Hercules for his infatuation with Iole.

NURSE: It is almost a common guise, that wedded wyves doe
haunte,
Theyr husbands hearts by magicke Arte, and witchcraft to
enchaunte.
In winter coulde I charmed have the woods, to make them
sprout,
And forst the thunder dint recoyle, that hath bin boulting
out.
With waltring surges I have shooke the seas amid the calme,
I smoothed have the wrastling waves, and layde downe
every walme.
The dry ground gaped hath like gulphs, and out new
springs have gusht,
The roring rocks have quaking sturd, and none thereat hath
pusht.
Hell gloummy gates I have brast oape, where grisly ghosts
all husht

Have stood and aunswering at my charme the goblins grim
    have scoulde.
The threefolde headded hounde of hell with barking
    throates hath houlde.
Thus both the seas, the lande, the heavens, and hell bowe at
    my becke.
Noone day to midnight, to and froe turnes at my charming
    checke.
At my enchauntment every thing declynes from natures
    lawe.
Our charme shall make his stomacke stoupe, and bring him
    more in awe.
DEIANIRA: What hearbes doe grow in Pontus sea? Or els on
    Pindus hill?
To trownce this machelesse champion, where shall I finde
    the ill?
The magicke vearse enchaunts the Moone from Starry skies
    to ground,
And fruictfull harvest is thereby in barren winter found.
The whisking flames of lightning leames oft sorcery doth
    stay,
And noonetyde topsy turvy tost doth dim the dusky day.
And leave the welkin to the starres, and yet not cause him
    stoupe.
NURSE: The Gods themselves by charme of love have forced
    bin to droupe.
DEIANIRA: Perhap hee shall be woon by one, and yeelde to her
    the spoyle.
So love shall be to Hercules the last and latest toyle.

THOMAS NUCE (d. 1617)

Nuce graduated from Cambridge, after which he published his translation of the *Octavia* in 1566, while a rector in Norfolk. Here, Seneca
appears as himself, debating in stichomythia with Nero.

NERO: A light thing tis for to be just, I see,
    For him whose heart is voyd of shrinking feare.
SENECA: A soveraigne salve for feare is for to beare
    Your selfe debonair to your subjectes all.
NERO: Our foes to slea, a cheftaynes vertue call.
SENECA: A worthier vertue tis in countries syre,
    His people to defend with sword and fyre.
NERO: It wel beseemes such aged wightes to teach
    Unbridled springolles yong, and not to preache
    Both to a man and prince of ryper yeares.
SENECA: Nay, rather frolicke youthful bloud appeares,
    To have more neede of counsell wyse and grave.
NERO: This age sufficient reason ought to have.
SENECA: That heavenly powers your doinges may allow.
NERO: A madnes 'twere to Gods for me to bow,
    When I my selfe can make such Gods to be:
    As Claudius now ycounted is we see.
SENECA: So much the more because so much you may.
NERO: Our power permittes us all without denay.
SENECA: Geve slender trust to Fortunes flattring face:
    She topsie turvy turnes her wheele apace.
NERO: A patch he is that knoweth not what he may.
SENECA: A Princes prayse I compted have alway,
    To do that same which with his honor stoode,
    Not that which franticke fancy counteth good.
NERO: If that I were a meacocke or a slouch,
    Each stubborne, clubbish daw would make mee couch.
SENECA: And whom they hate, with force they overquell.
NERO: Then dynt of sword the prince defendeth well.

SENECA: But fayth more sure defence doth seeme to mee.
NERO: Ful meete it is that Cæsar dreaded be.
SENECA: More meete of subjectes for to be belov'd.
NERO: From subjects myndes, feare must not be remov'd.
SENECA: What so by force of armes you do wringe out,
    A grievous worke it is to bring aboute.
NERO: Well hardly then our will let them obay.
SENECA: Will nothing then but that which wel you may.
NERO: We wil decree what we shall best suppose.
SENECA: What peoples voyce doth joyntly bynd or lose,
    Let that confirmed stand.
NERO: Swordes bloudy dynt
    Shall cause them else at me to take their hint.

THOMAS NEWTON (?1542–1607)

Newton translated the *Thebäis* to complete his edition of Seneca's tragedies collected in 1581. Little is known of him but that he studied at both Oxford and Cambridge, and became a rector in Essex in 1583. In this excerpt, Oedipus, in exile with his devoted daughter Antigone, yearns for death.

Why dost thou (Daughter) labour loose in usyng further
    speech?
To alter this my stony hart why dost thou mee beseech?
I tell thee playne, I fully meane this bloud of myne to spill,
That long with Death hath struggling kept: and thereupon I
    will
Descend to darke infernall Lake: for this same darknes blynd
Of both myne eyes is nothing such, as fact of myne should
    fynd.
It were my Blisse to bee in Hell in deepest dungeon fast:
Now that which should long since have bene, I wil perfourme
    at last.

I cannot be debard from Death: wilt thou deny me glave
10   Or Sword, or knife? wilt thou no toole for mischiefe let me
          have?
    Wilt thou both watch and ward each way, where daunger lies
          in wayte?
    Shall such a sinful Caytife wretch as I, be kept so straite?
    Wilt thou not suffer me with Coard to breake my hatefull
          Necke?
    Canst thou kepe mee from poysonous herbes? hast thou them
          al at beck?
    What shall it thee prevayle to take for mee such earnest care?
    Death ech where is: and wayes to death in thousand corners
          are.
    Herein hath God good order tane, that every selie Foe,
    May take away an others life: but Death hee cannot so.
    I seeke not anye toole to have: this desprate mynd of myne
20   Can use the service of my hand, my threede of lyfe t' untwine.
    Now hand, thy maister at a pinch assist to worke his feate,
    Helpe him with all thy power and strength, t' exployt his
          purpose great.
    I poynt thee not in this my Corps unto one place alone:
    Alas, each part of me with guilt is plaunch and overgrowne.
    In which soever part thou wilt, thy Massacre beginne,
    And seeke to bring me to my death which way thou mayst it
          winne.
    In pieces crush this body all, this hart that harbors sinne
    Pluck out, out all my entrailes pull, proceede, and never linne
    To gash and cut my wezand pype. My vaynes asonder scratch,
30   And make the Bloud come spowting out, or use that other
          match,
    Which heretofore thou used haste: digge where myne eyes
          earst stood:
    And let these woundes gush out apace much mattry filth and
          blood.

9 *glave* lance   12 *Caytife* captive

Hale out of mee this loathed soule that is so hard and stout:
And thou deare father Laius stand up and looke about:
Behold where ever that thou standst: I Umpyre doe the make,
And eyed Judge of all my plagues that justly heere I take.
My fact so lewde, so horrible, so loathsome to bee tolde
I never thought with any pryce or tormentes manifolde
Could have full expiation: ne thought I it inough
40   To die this death: or in one part to be beslashed through.
By piecemeale I am well content to suffer tormentes all
And even by piecemeale for to die: for plagues to plague mee
      call,
Exact the punishment that's due: I heere most ready stand
To satisfie with any death that law and righte hath scand.
My former smartes, when as mine eyes I raked out with pawes,
Were but as tastes of sacrifice, somewhat to helpe my cause.
Come therefore (Father) neare to mee, and thrust this hand of
      myne
More nearer into every wound. It swerv'de and did decline
For feare, when first it tooke th' assay mine eyes to ransacke
      out.
50   I beare it still in memory, my eyes then star'de about
And seemed to disswade the hand from doing of the charge
Whereto it was enjoyned tho, and had Commission large.
Thou shalt well thinke that Œdipus dissembleth not a whit
But what his word hath warranted, his deede hath firmely
      quit.
Thy stoutnes then was not so great when eyes thou pulledst
      out
As was thy manhoode, when thou threwst them from thee
      round about.
Now, by those Eyeholes thrust thy hand into the very braine:
That part where death attempted was, let death be sought
      againe.

ALEXANDER NEVILLE
(1544–1614)

Neville entered Cambridge at the age of 12. He translated *Oedipus* in 1560, and it was published in 1563. He stayed loyal to the English Church, and may have been a member of Parliament. He was buried in Canterbury Cathedral. In this excerpt, Creon describes Tiresias's rites to determine the cause of the plague. The spirits of the dead testify, including Laius, who declares that Oedipus is the cause, since he murdered his own father and married his own mother.

CREON: Than in the Sheepe, and Oxen blacke, by backwarde
    course are drown.
And odoures sweete, and Frankencence, on flaming fyres
    are thrown.
The beasts on burning Altars cast, do quake with schorched
    lims:
And bloudy streames with fyre mixt, about the Aultars
    swims.
Than on the darke infernall Gods, and him that rules them
    all:
With deadly shriking voyce aloude, the Prophet gins to call.
And rouls the Magick verse in mouth, and hidden Artes
    doth prove:
Which eyther power have to appease or els the Gods to
    move.
Than bloudy streaming Lycours black, with broyling heate
    doe boyle:
And all the Beasts consume and burn. The Prophet than to
    toyle
Begins. And mixed wyne and Mylke upon the Aultars
    throwes.
And all the Dongeon darke, and wyde with streaming bloud
    it flowes.

Than out with thundring voyce agayne the Prophet calles
and cryes,

And straight as much with mumbling mouth he champs in
secret wyse.

The trees do turne. The Rivers stand. The ground with
roring shakes.

And all the world as seemes to mee, with fearefull trembling
quakes.

I am heard, I am heard, than out aloude the Priest began to
cry:

Whan all the dampned soules by heapes abrode outrushing
fly.

Then woods with rumbling noyse, doe oft resounding
make.

And Heaven, and Earth together goe. And bowes and trees
do crake.

And Thunders roore. And Lightnings flash. And waves aloft
doe fly.

And ground retyres: and Dogs doe bawl: and Beastes are
heard to cry.

And whyther long of Acheron, that lothsom Flud that
flowes

All stinking streames: or of the earth, that out her Bowels
throwes,

Free place to Sprights to geve: or of that fierce infernall
Hound,

That at such times doth bustling make with chayns, and
ratling sound.

The Earth al wide it open gapes. And I did see on ground,

The Gods with colour pale and wan, that those dark
kingdoms keepe.

And very night I saw in deede, and thousand shapes to
creepe,

From out those filthy stinking Lakes, and lothsom pits of
Hell.

Where all the evils under Son, in darksom shades doe dwell.

So quaking all for feare I stoode with minde right sore
    apalde,
Whilst on those Gods with trembling mouth the Priest full
    often calde.
Who all at once, out of theyr dens did skip with griesly
    Face.
And Monsters grim, and stinging Snakes seemd wander in
    that place.
And all the fowlest Feendes of Hell, and Furies all were
    theare.
And all transformed Ghosts and sprights, that ever Hell did
    beare.
With Cares, and all Diseases vyle, that mortall mynds doe
    crush,
All those, and more I sawe out of those Dongeons deepe to
    rush.
And Age I sawe, with riveled Face, and Neede, and Feare,
    and Death,
And Fyre, and flames, and thousand ills out from those Pits
    to breath.
Then I was gon: and quight amazd The wenche in worser
    case.
And yet of olde, acquaynted with her Fathers Artes she was.
The Priest himselfe unmooved stoode, and boldly cited
    owt:
Whole Armies of king Ditis men, who clustring in a Rowt:
All flittring thin like Cloudes, disperst abrode in Ayre doe
    fly.
And bearing sundry shapes and formes doe scud about in
    Sky,
A thousand woods I thinke have not so many leaves on
    trees.
Ten thousand medowes fresh have not so many flowers for
    bees.

Ten hundred thousand rivers not so many Foule can show:
Nor all the drops and streams, and gulphes that in the Seas
   do flow,
If that they might be wayed, can sure so great a number
   make
As could those shapes and formes that flew from out of
   Limbo lake:
Both Tantalus and Zetus too, and pale Amphions Ghost:
And Agave, and after her ten thousand Sprightes do post.

THE TRAGEDY OF LOCRINE

The Tragedy of Locrine, which Eliot called 'popular and atrocious',
was included among the additional pieces added to the third folio of
Shakespeare's works in 1664. Its authorship is uncertain, but it was
written around 1585 and published in 1595, and resembles the work
of Robert Greene (?1558–1592), a pamphleteer and playwright, and
George Peele (see p. 81).

Madam, where resolution leads the way,
And courage followes with imboldened pace,
Fortune can neuer vse her tyrannie,
For valiantnesse is like vnto a rocke
That standeth in the waues of Ocean,
Which though the billowes beat on euery side,
And *Borras* fell with his tempestuous stormes,
Bloweth vpon it with a hideous clamour,
Yet it remaineth still vnmooueable.

THOMAS HUGHES (d. 1623)

Hughes was largely responsible for *The Misfortunes of Arthur*, a pastiche of Senecan borrowings published in 1587. Lucas called it 'the most slavishly Senecan of all English plays'. The play was presented before Elizabeth in 1588 in a production which may have been instigated by Francis Bacon. It was the last play by gentlemen from one of the Inns of Court to be performed for the queen; and the eighty-ninth drama printed in England.

From *Thyestes*:

Omit no plague, and none will be inough.   (I.ii. 46, cf. 256)

Who strives to stand in pompe of Princely port,
On guiddy top and culme of slippery Court,
Findes oft a heavy Fate, whiles too much knowne
To all, he falles unknown unto himselfe.
                    (III Chorus 35–8; cf. 391–2, 401–3)

GILDAS: What greater sinnes could hap, then what be past?
    What mischiefes could be meant, more then were wrought?
NUNCIUS: And thinke you these to be an end to sinnes?
    No. Crime proceedes: those made but one degree.
                    (IV.ii. 15–16, cf. 745–7)

The safest passage is from bad to worse.   (I.iv. 77, cf. 115)

He is a foole, that puts a meane in crimes.   (I.iv. 79. cf. 150)

Extremest cures must not be used first.   (I.iv. 82, cf. 153)

In desperate times, the headlong way is best.   (I.iv. 83, cf. 154)

From *Phaedra*:

T'is safest then to dare when most you feare.

(III.i. 145, cf. 722)

Small griefes can speake: the great astonisht stand.

(IV.ii. 14, cf. 607)

From *Troades*:

A hopelesse feare forbids a happy Fate.   (III.iv. 6, cf. 425)

Declare: we joy to handle all our harmes. (IV.i. 8, cf. 1066–7)

From *Hercules Oetaeus*:

Unlawfull love doth like, when lawfull lothes. (I.ii. 70, cf. 357)

From *Medea*:

My selfe am left, ther's left both seas and lands,
And sword, and fire, and chaines, and choice of harmes.

(I.iii. 20–21, cf. 166–7)

From *Octavia*:

The more you may, the more you ought to feare.

(II.ii. 19, cf. 450)

From *Oedipus*:

Small manhood were to turne by back to Chance.

(II.iii. 107, cf. 86)

Death onely frees the guiltlesse from anoies. (III.i. 124, cf. 934)

SIR EDWARD DYER (1543–1607)

A poet, courtier, diplomat, and alchemist who knew Sir Philip Sidney and Fulke Greville, his own poems were preserved in commonplace books, and were written in a plain, but melancholy style. Like much Elizabethan verse, his was set to music; 'My Mind to Me a Kingdom Is', printed in 1588, was his most famous lyric, set to music by William Byrd. The sentiment is from *Thyestes*, II. 380: *Mens regnum bona possidet* – 'A good mind possesses a kingdom.'

My Mind to Me a Kingdom Is

1
My mynde to me a kyngdome is,
Suche perfect ioy therin I fynde,
That it excells all other blisse
That worlde afords or growes by kynde:
    Though muche I wante which most would haue,
    Yet still my mynde forbides to craue.

2
No princely pompe, no wealthy store,
No force to wine the victorye,
No wilye witt to salue a sore,
No shape to feade a louinge eye;

To none of these I yealde as thrall:
For why? my minde dothe serue for all.

3
I see how plenty suffers ofte,
And hasty clymers sone do fall:
I see that those whiche are alofte
Myshapp dothe threaten moste of all:
   They get with toylle, they keepe with feare;
   Such cares my mynde coulde neuer beare.

4
Contente I liue, this is my staye:
I seeke no more than maye suffyse,
I presse to beare no haughtie swaye;
Look, what I lack my mynde suppliese:
   Lo, thus I tryumphe lyke a kynge,
   Content with that my mynde doth bringe.

5
Some haue to muche, yet still do craue,
I little haue, and seeke no more:
They are but poore, though muche they haue,
And I am ryche with lytle store:
   They poore, I ryche; they begg, I geve:
   They lacke, I leaue; they pyne, I lyue.

6
I laugh not at an others loss,
I grudge not at an others gaine:
No worldly waues my mynde can toss,
My state at one dothe still remayne:
   I feare no foe, I fawne no freende,
   I lothe not lyfe, nor dread no ende.

7
Some waye theyre pleasure by theyre luste,
Their wisdom by theyre rage of will:
Theire treasure is theire only truste,
A cloked crafte theyre store of skyll:
    But all the pleasure that I fynde
    Is to mayntayne a quiet mynde.

8
My wealthe is healthe and perfecte ease,
My conscience cleere my chiefe defense:
I neither seeke by brybes to please,
Nor by deserte to breede offence:
    Thus do I lyue, thus will I dye;
    Would all did so, as well as I.

THOMAS KYD (1558–1594)

The Spanish Tragedy, acted around 1588 and printed in 1599, is a notable adaptation of Seneca. Lucas calls it a literary curiosity: 'From the first act to the last nothing whatever happens.' The excerpt below is an adaptation of *Agamemnon*, 57–73.

    Infortunate condition of Kings,
Seated amidst so many helpeles doubts.
First we are plast vpon extreamest height,
And oft supplanted with exceeding hate;
But euer subiect to the wheele of chance;
And at our highest neuer ioy we so,
As we both doubt and dread our ouerthrow.
So striueth not the waues with sundry winds,
As Fortune toyleth in the affaires of Kings,
That would be feard, yet feare to be beloued,
Sith feare or loue to Kings is flatterie . . .

QUEEN ELIZABETH I (1533–1603)

Scarcely a poet, yet her writings are part of English literature: she wrote
prose, original verse, and translations. A free paraphrase or rough draft
(the first thirty-one lines have no parallel in the Latin), this chorus from
Hercules Oetaeus cannot be dated, and possibly is not hers – it does not
exist in the queen's own hand. Horace Walpole transcribed it in 1806,
and identified it as her work. The passage concerns the disloyalty of
subjects to their leaders and the treachery of public office.

> What harming hurl of fortune's arm thou dreadest,
> Let fraught of faith the burden of care relieve,
> And take thou such, to fear approved by proof,
> The unpicked locks of certain trust to hold;
> For geason is the faith, and rarely kept is trust,
> Where puffed sails from best forewinds be fallen.
> The weight of scepter's sway if choice must bear,
> Albeit the vulgar crew fill full thy gates,
> And hundred thresholds with their feet be smoothed:
> Though with thy gleaves and axes thou be armed,
> And root full great do glory give thy name,
> Amid the view of all these sundry sorts
> One faultless faith her room even scant may claim.
> The golden ledge full wrathful spites besets,
> And where the gates their posts draw forth by breadth
> More easy way to guiles and passed safe.
> Heed then the clocks of warned harms with good,
> And let the hidden blade not wrong thee work,
> For when most show by gazers' eyes is spied,
> And presence great thy honor most advance,
> This gift retain as fellow to thy room:
> Disdain may frown, but envy thrust thee through.
> No ofter doth the east the night's care release
> And makes the shady dark with light abash
> Than kings be made in an instant short, and marred;

So icy is their joy and hopeless woe.
The love of kingdom's rule observed with care,
But for himself a king but few regard.
The court's luster a stale guest made for me,
Delighted with the shine no woe forethought.
And this man seeks the nearest room to prince,
To glittering view amid the streets he comes;
While broiled is with cark the miser's breast
In search of gainful grasp his name to spread.
In compass of the hoarded heaps to find
One bit to slake desire's wave he seeks.
Not all the coast where Istrus' trade doth haunt,
With gems bedecked through hue of diverse kind,
Nor Lydia fair with sweetest streams suffice
To quench nor answer all such thirst by half;
Nor yet the soil that bides Zephirus' slave,
Abashed at golden shining Tagus' beams,
Nor Hebrus' service may content at full,
Rich though Hydaspes' hedge his fields throw out,
Though Ganges' course his confines all do graze
With filled force to water all his lands.
To greedy grating wights enough not all
That nature well doth please his lack not so.
This man doth homage unto kingly force,
And harbor Rome adores where last he haunts,
Not meaning that this plowshare should advance
Like crooked hind his master's gain with clots
By murdering the ground; no ease of toil
Though thousand leas his husbandmen turn up.
Well pleased rests his hearth with goods even such
As pleasure may by gift another need.
A badder sort the prince's court regard
With foiled foot that stumble gives at all
And each to lose with no avail to one.
That might may equal harm they power achieve
Whose living's thread drawn out is of such length

Whom hap nor takes ere nature calls away.
The horned newed moon them blessed calls
Whose wane them misers judges when day doth fall.
A man full rarely happy is and old.
More surer sleeps thee downy turfs procure:
All Tyre, where purple woven is and made,
Not so sound slumber doth his owner yield.
The gilded roofs the quiet rest bereave,
And waking nights the purple draws from ease.
O that the breasts of rich men naked were,
The smoothed dreads of lofty lucks that hide;
The Brutian stream more milder course doth hold
When eastern wind him strikes with force's stroke.
In franched mind from care the silly soul possest,
A pot of beechen tree full sure he keeps
With steady hand that fears no snatch from hold.
No sudden fright affrays, no thief he dreads;
With ease y-got and single show he feeds
And recks not for the girded blades to thigh.
The golden cup of bloody mixture keeps.
The wife that is y-tied to man of mean estate
No carking hath in order pain to set,
Nor shining gift of reddy sea she wears
Her ears free from the pluck of gemmy weight;
No stone of Eoas' waves her cumber makes.
Soft wool ingrained with Sidon's purple fair
Drinks not the red for use that her befalls;
No Maeon needle filleth she with skeins
By parted hues that give the shade with art.
The silky land that lies to sunny east
Needs not the fruit from eastern tree to pluck;
Every herb the colors' die may mix
That distaff fills with yarn that skill not spun.
She nursed not the doubts of wedlock bed;
Of lewd suspect of weary works she shuns.
The wrathful lamp Erinis lighteth up

The feastful day adorns by pestering rout.
The poor man deemeth not his happy state
Till wealthy folk by fall it show.
Who so, therefore, the middle way eschews
The wry and crooked balk's most sure to tread.
While Phaeton boy one day of father got
To rule the reins and eke his wain to guide
In leaving wonted walk and worned ways
Which by slide, while the uncouth skies he shares
Such place as heat of Phoebus' flame knew nòt.
His ruin was the world his fellow plain.
Daedalus yet more larger scope and broader took,
Who never yet a sea by name did grace.
Though Icarus sought the true and living birds
By guile to pass and win the tryer's right,
His father's feathered wings despised with scorn,
To Phoebus near with swifty gait he hies,
And christened by this slip the sea was sure.
Evil bought the great where ill exceeds the good.
Let one full happy be and highly flee.
God shield that mighty me the vulgar call.
The lee of shore my silly boat shall loathe,
Let no full wind to depth my bark bequeath.
From safest creeks doth fortune glide and shun,
With search in middest sea for tallest ship
And takes its dearest prey the nearer to cloud.

UNKNOWN

The True Tragedie of Richard III (?1591, published 1594) derives from a play written by Legge in Latin, and is of interest because Shakespeare used it for his own play (see p. 83); both feature Senecan presentiment of evil, ghosts, and a tyrant.

> The hell of life that hangs upon the Crowne,
> The daily cares, the nightly dreames,
> The wretched crewes, the treason of the foe,
> And horror of my bloodie practise past,
> Strikes such a terror to my wounded conscience,
> That sleepe I, wake I, or whatsoever I do,
> Meethinkes their ghoasts comes gaping for revenge,
> Whom I have slaine in reaching for a Crowne.
> Clarence complaines, and crieth for revenge.
> My Nephues bloods, Revenge, revenge, doth crie.
> The headlesse Peeres comes preasing for revenge.
> And every one cries, let the tyrant die.
> The Sunne by day shines hotely for revenge.
> The Moone by night eclipseth for revenge.
> The stars are turnd to Comets for revenge.
> The Planets chaunge their courses for revenge.
> The birds sing not, but sorrow for revenge.
> The silly lambes sits bleating for revenge.
> The screeking Raven sits croking for revenge.
> Whole heads of beasts comes bellowing for revenge.
> And all, yea all the world I thinke,
> Cries for revenge, and nothing but revenge.
> But to conclude, I have deserved revenge.
> In company I dare not trust my friend,
> Being alone, I dread the secret foe:
> I doubt my foode, least poyson lurke therein.
> My bed is uncoth, rest refraines my head.
> Then such a life I count far worse to be,

Then thousand deaths unto a damned death:
How, wast death I said? who dare attempt my death?
Nay who dare so much as once to thinke my death?
Though enemies there be that would my body kill,
Yet shall they leave a never dying minde.
But you villaines, rebels, traitors as you are,
How came the foe in, preasing so neare?
Where, where, slept the garrison that should a beat them back?
Where was our friends to intercept the foe?
All gone, quite fled, his loyaltie quite laid a bed?
Then vengeance, mischiefe, horror, with mischance,
Wilde-fire, with whirlewinds, light upon your heads,
That thus betray'd your Prince by your untruth.

MARY SIDNEY, COUNTESS OF PEMBROKE (1561–1621)

Sister to Sir Philip Sidney, and Sir Robert Sidney, a less well-known poet who was father to Lady Mary Wroth. She learned French, Italian, Latin, Greek, and Hebrew with her brothers, and married Henry Herbert, Earl of Pembroke, when she was 15 (he was 50). After this marriage, she retained the Sidney coat of arms, and set up her home as an academy for artists and writers. With Philip, she translated Psalms, also contributing editorial work to his *Arcadia*. Among her own works are various original writings, and translations – including *The Tragedy of Antonie*, a play meant for private performance based on Robert Garnier's *Marc Antoine* (1592). Mary Sidney converted Garnier's alexandrines to English blank verse, retaining his neo-Senecan stoicism. The passages given below are very close to Seneca's *Agamemnon*, 664 ff.; 589–92; 598–600; and *Hercules Oetaeus*, 184–208.

CHORUS: Lament we our mishaps,
  Drowne we with teares our woe:
  For lamentable haps
  Lamented easie growe:
  And much lesse torment bring
  Than when they first did spring.
We want that wofull song,
  Wherwith wood-musiques Queene
  Doth ease her woes, among
  Fresh springtimes bushes greene,
  On pleasant branch alone
  Renewing ancient mone.
We want that monefull sound,
  That pratling *Progne* makes
  On fields of *Thracian* ground,
  Or streames of *Thracian* lakes:
  To empt her brest of paine
  For *Itys* by her slaine.
Though *Halcyons* do still,
  Bewailing *Ceyx* lot,
  The Seas with plainings fill
  Which his dead limmes have got,
  Not ever other grave
  Then tombe of waves to have.
And though the bird in death
  That most *Meander* loves
  So sweetly sighes his breath
  When death his fury proves,
  As almost softs his heart,
  And almost blunts his dart.
Yet all the plaints of those,
  Nor all their tearfull larmes,
  Cannot content our woes,
  Nor serve to waile the harmes,
  In soule which we, poore we,
  To feele enforced be.

Nor they of *Phœbus* bredd
    In teares can do so well,
    They for their brother shedd,
    Who into *Padus* fell,
    Rash guide of chariot cleere
    Surveiour of the yeare.
Nor she whom heav'nly powers
    To weping rocke did turne,
    Whose teares distill in showers,
    And shew she yet doth mourne,
    Wherewith his toppe to Skies
    Mount *Sipylus* doth rise.
Nor weping drops which flowe
    From Barke of wounded tree,
    That *Mirrhas* shame doth showe
    With ours compar'd may be,
    To quench her loving fire
    Who durst embrace her sire.
Nor all the howlings made
    On *Cybels* sacred hill
    By Eunukes of her trade,
    Who *Atys*, *Atys* still
    With doubled cries resound,
    Which *Eccho* makes rebound.
Our plaints no limits stay,
    Nor more than do our woes:
    Both infinitely straie
    And neither measure knowes.
    In measure let them plaine:
    Who measur'd griefes sustaine.

*

CHORUS: Alas, with what tormenting fire
    Us martireth this blind desire
        To stay our life from flieing!
    How ceasleslie our minds doth rack,

How heavie lies upon our back
　　This dastard feare of dieing!
　Death rather healthfull succour gives,
　Death rather all mishaps relieves
　　That life upon us throweth:
And ever to us doth unclose
The dore whereby from curelesse woes
　　Our weary soule out goeth.
What Goddesse else more milde then she
To burie all our paine can be,
　　What remedie more pleasing?
Our pained hearts when dolor stings,
And nothing rest, or respite brings,
　　What help have we more easing?
Hope which to us doth comfort give,
And doth our fainting hearts revive,
　　Hath not such force in anguish:
For promising a vaine reliefe
She oft us failes in midst of griefe,
　　And helples lets us languish.
But Death who call on her at neede
Doth never with vaine semblant feed,
　　But when them sorrow paineth,
So riddes their soules of all distresse
Whose heavie weight did them oppresse,
　　That not one griefe remaineth.
Who feareles and with courage bolde
Can *Acherons* black face behold,
　　Which muddie water beareth:
And crossing over in the way
Is not amaz'd at Perruque gray
　　Olde rusty *Charon* weareth?
Who voide of dread can looke upon
The dreadfull shades that roame alone,
　　On bankes where sound no voices:
Whome with her fire-brands and her Snakes

No whit afraide *Alecto* makes,
   Nor triple-barking noises:
Who freely can himselfe dispose
Of that last hower which all must close,
   And leave this life at pleasure:
This noble freedome more esteemes,
And in his heart more precious deemes,
   Then crowne and kinglie treasure.
The waves which *Boreas* blasts turmoile
And cause with foaming furie boile,
   Make not his heart to tremble:
Nor brutish broile, when with strong head
A rebell people madly ledde
   Against their Lords assemble:
Nor fearefull face of Tirant wood,
Who breaths but threats, and drinks but bloud,
   No, nor the hand which thunder,
The hand of *Jove* which thunder beares,
And ribbs of rocks in sunder teares,
   Teares mountains sides in sunder:
Nor bloudy *Marses* butchering bands,
Whose lightnings desert laie the lands
   Whome dustie cloudes do cover:
From of whose armour sun-beames flie,
And under them make quaking lie
   The plaines wheron they hover:
Nor yet the cruell murth'ring blade
Warme in the moistie bowels made
   Of people pell-mell dieing
In some great Cittie put to sack,
By savage Tirant brought to wrack,
   At his colde mercie lieing.
How abject him, how base thinke I,
Who wanting courage can not dye
   When need him thereto calleth?
From whome the dagger drawne to kill

The cureles griefes that vexe him still
   For feare and faintnes falleth?
   O *Antonie* with thy deare mate
Both in misfortunes fortunate!
   Whose thoughts to death aspiring
Shall you protect from victors rage,
Who on each side doth you encage,
   To triumph much desiring.
That *Cæsar* may you not offend
Nought else but death can you defend,
   Which his weake force derideth.
And all in this round earth containd,
Pow'rles on them whome once enchaind
   Avernus prison hideth:
Where great *Psammetiques* ghost doth rest,
Not with infernall paine possest,
   But in sweete fields detained:
And olde *Amasis* soule likewise,
And all our famous *Ptolomies*
   That whilome on us raigned.

SIR ROBERT SIDNEY (1563–1626)

Robert was the younger brother of Sir Philip Sidney. His poetry was not printed while he was alive, and remained unpublished until 1984. Ian Ousby points out that Sidney's work 'is chiefly remarkable as the largest body of original verse to have descended to us from the Eliza- bethan period in a text entirely set down by the poet himself' (*Literature in English*, Cambridge, Cambridge University Press, 1996, p. 360). Sidney was lord of the manor to whom Jonson's *To Penshurst* is addressed.

The first poem is a straightforward rendering of *Thyestes*, lines 607– 16; the second poem is from a chorus in the same play, lines 398–403 – a passage which has also been translated by Wyatt and Heywood. Sidney's editor, Peter Croft, remarks that while Wyatt and Heywood used decasyllabics and, in order to maintain this metre, introduced phrases which have no equivalent to Seneca, Sidney, in both poems given here, took 'evident care to reproduce as closely as possible not only the sense but also the syllabic structure' of the original (*The Poems of Robert Sidney*, ed. P.J. Croft, Oxford, Clarendon Press, 1984, p. 327). Compare Marvell's version (p. 132 below) of the second passage, rendered in catalectic trochaics.

Translated out of Seneca

Yow vnto whome hee that rules sea and land
of lyfe and death grants the lawgiuing hand
puft vp and sullein hawty lookes forbeare
That wch from yow the meaner man doth feare
the same to yow, a greater lorde doth threate
All power is vnder heauyer power sett:
He whoe of coming day was lofty fownd
him the departing day saw on the grownd
let no man trust to much to seasons fayre
let none cast down of better tymes despayre.

In another place

So when wth out all noyse of mee
the dayes shall ouerpassed bee
a homely olde man I shall dy
On him a heauy death doth ly
whoe vnto all men to much known
vnto himself doth dy vnknown.

UNKNOWN

The Tragedy of Master Arden of Faversham (published 1592) was once thought to have been written by Shakespeare. It was based on an actual murder documented in Holinshed's *Chronicles* (1577). The play is full of sinister Senecan rhetoric, including the following, which can be compared with *Hippolytus/Phaedra*, 1135–40.

> Well fares the man how ere his cates do taste
> That tables not with foule suspition:
> And he but pines amongst his delicats,
> Whose troubled minde is stuft with discontent.
> My goulden time was when I had no gould,
> Though then I wanted, yet I slept secure,
> My dayly toyle, begat me nights repose:
> My nights repose made daylight fresh to me.
> But since I climbd the toppe bough of the tree,
> And sought to build my nest among the clouds.
> Each gentle stary gaile doth shake my bed:
> And makes me dread my downfall to the earth . . .

GEORGE PEELE (1558–1596)

An impoverished playwright and poet, and one of the 'University Wits' who were better educated than their contemporaries, Jonson and Shakespeare. *King Edward I* was published in 1593; the excerpt below imitates Seneca.

> EDWARD: Now trothles King what fruites haue brauing
>   boastes,
>   What end hath Treason but a soddaine fall?
>   Such as haue knowne thy life and bringing vp,

    Haue praised thee for thy learning and thy art,
    How comes it then that thou forgetst thy bookes,
    That schoold thee to forget ingratitude,
    Vnkinde, this hand hath nointed thee a king,
    This tongue pronounst the sentence of thy ruth,
    If thou in lue of mine vnfaigned loue,
    Hast leuied armes for to attempt my crowne,
    Now see thy fruites, thy gloryes are dispearst,
    And his, for like sith thou hast past thy bounds,
    Thy sturdie necke must stoope to beare this yoke.

BALIOLL: I tooke this lesson *Edward* from my booke,
    To keepe a iust equality of minde,
    Content with euery fortune as it comes,
    So canst thou threat no more then I expect.

EDWARD: So sir your moderation is enforst,
    Your goodly gloses cannot make it good.

BALIOLL: Then will I keepe in silence what I meane,
    Since *Edward* thinkes my meaning is not good.

EDMUND: Naie *Balioll* speake forth, if there yet remain,
    A little remnant of perswading Art.

BALIOLL: If cunning haue power to win the king,
    Let those imploy it that can flatter him.
    If honored deede may reconcile the King,
    It lies in me to giue and him to take.

EDWARD: Why what remaines for *Balioll* now to giue?

BALIOLL: Alegeance as becomes a roiall king.

EDWARD: What league of faith where league is broken once?

BALIOLL: The greater hope in them that once haue falne.

EDWARD: But foolishe are those Monarches that doe yeelde
    A conquered Realme vppon submissiue vowes.

BALIOLL: There take my crowne and so redeme my life.

EDWARD: I sir that was the choisest plea of both,
    For who so quels the pomp of haughtie windes.

And breakes their staffe, wheron they build their trust,
Is sure in wanting power they carrie not harme.
Balioll shall liue, but yet within such bounds,
That if his wings grow fllig, they may be clipt.

WILLIAM SHAKESPEARE
(1564–1616)

Richard III (performed 1594) is full of Senecan presentiment of evil, featuring ghosts and a tyrant – and also contains long passages of Senecan epigrammatic stichomythia, as here in I.ii and IV.iv.

ANNE: No beast so fierce, but knowes some touch of pitty.
RICHARD: But I know none, and therefore am no Beast.
ANNE: O wonderfull, when diuels tell the truth!
RICHARD: More wonderfull, when Angels are so angry.

*

RICHARD: Say she shall be a High and Mighty Queene.
QUEENE: To vaile the Title, as her Mother doth.
RICHARD: Say I will loue her euerlastingly.
QUEENE: But how long shall that title euer last?
RICHARD: Sweetly in force, vnto her faire liues end.
QUEENE: But how long fairely shall her sweet life last?
RICHARD: As long as Heauen and Nature lengthens it.
QUEENE: As long as Hell and *Richard* likes of it.
RICHARD: Say I her Soueraigne, am her Subiect low.
QUEENE: But she your Subiect, lothes such Soueraignty.
RICHARD: Be eloquent in my behalfe to her.
QUEENE: An honest tale speeds best, being plainly told.
RICHARD: Then plainly to her, tell my louing tale.
QUEENE: Plaine and not honest, is too harsh a style.
RICHARD: Your Reasons are too shallow, and to quicke.

QUEENE: O no, my Reasons are too deepe and dead,
  Too deepe and dead (poore Infants) in their graues,
  Harpe on it still shall I, till heart-strings breake.
RICHARD: Harpe not on that string Madam, that is past.
  Now by my George, my Garter, and my Crowne.
QUEENE: Prophan'd, dishonor'd, and the third vsurpt.
RICHARD: I sweare.
QUEENE: By nothing, for this is no Oath:
  Thy George prophan'd, hath lost his Lordly Honor;
  Thy Garter blemish'd, pawn'd his Knightly Vertue;
  Thy Crowne vsurp'd, disgrac'd his Kingly Glory:
  If something thou would'st sweare to be beleeu'd,
  Sweare then by something, that thou hast not wrong'd.
RICHARD: Then by my Selfe.
QUEENE: Thy Selfe, is selfe-misvs'd.
RICHARD: Now by the World.
QUEENE: 'Tis full of thy foule wrongs.
RICHARD: My Fathers death.
QUEENE: Thy life hath it dishonor'd.
RICHARD: Why then, by Heauen.
QUEENE: Heauens wrong is most of all:
  If thou didd'st feare to breake an Oath with him,
  The vnity the King my husband made,
  Thou had'st not broken, nor my Brothers died.

Bottom's promise to speak in 'Ercles vaine', in *A Midsummer Night's Dream* I.ii (performed 1596, published 1600), has been supposed by several commentators to be a parody of Studley's translation of *Hercules Oetaeus*.

QUINCE: You *Nicke Bottome* are set downe for *Pyramus*.
BOTTOME: What is *Pyramus*, a louer, or a tyrant?
QUINCE: A Louer that kills himselfe most gallantly for loue.
BOTTOME: That will aske some teares in the true performing of
    it: if I do it, let the audience looke to their eies: I will
    mooue stormes; I will condole in some measure. To

> the rest yet, my chiefe humour is for a tyrant. I could
> play *Ercles* rarely, or a part to teare a Cat in, to make all
> split the raging Rocks; and shiuering shocks shall break
> the locks of prison gates, and *Phibbus* carre shall shine
> from farre, and make and marre the foolish Fates. This
> was lofty. Now name the rest of the Players. This is
> *Ercles* vaine, a tyrants vaine: a louer is more condoling.

King John III.iv (published 1623) strongly resembles *Hercules Furens* (345–9).

> A Scepter snatch'd with an vnruly hand,
> Must be as boysterously maintain'd as gain'd.
> And he that stands vpon a slipp'ry place,
> Makes nice of no vilde hold to stay him vp:

Compare this adaptation of Seneca's *Hippolytus/Phaedra*, 615 ('*curae leues loquuntur ingentes stupent*') in *Macbeth* IV.iii 209–10 (performed *c.*1606) with Webster's, which appears on p. 108.

> Giue sorrow words; the griefe that do's not speake,
> Whispers the o're-fraught heart, and bids it breake.

ANONYMOUS

The following passage from *Edward III* (published 1596) – which Shakespeare may have had a hand in – adapts *Oedipus*, 987–92.

> To die is all as common as to liue
> The one in choice the other holds in chase,
> For from the instant we begin to liue,
> We do pursue and hunt the time to die,
> First bud we, then we blow, and after seed,

Then presently we fall, and as a shade
Followes the bodie, so we follow death,
If then we hunt for death, why do we feare it?
If we feare it, why do we follow it?
If we do feare, how can we shun it?
If we do feare, with feare we do but aide
The thing we feare, to seize on vs the sooner,
If wee feare not, then no resolued proffer,
Can ouerthrow the limit of our fate,
For whether ripe or rotten, drop we shall,
As we drawe the lotterie of our doome.

SAMUEL DANIEL (1562/3-1619)

Poet, playwright, translator, critic, and historian. While best remembered for his sonnet sequence *Delia*, his tragedies, *Cleopatra* (1594) and *Philotas* (1600-1604) – modelled on French versions of Seneca – were what Lucas called 'good minor drama'. Saintsbury felt that Daniel had an 'almost unsurpassed faculty of ethical verse'. Eliot (*Selected Essays*, p. 78) wrote of these two plays that 'They contain many lovely passages, they are readable all through, and they are well built'; but noted that while Daniel was a 'good poet' and there was something to be learned from him, he 'had no influence'.

    And God forbid, that euer souldiers words
Should be made liable vnto misdeeds;
When fainting in their march, tir'd in the fight,
Sicke in their tent, stopping their wounds that bleeds;
Or haut and iolly after conquest got,
They shall out of their heate vse words vnkinde;
Their deeds deserue, to haue them rather thought
The passion of the season, than their minde:
For souldiers ioy, or wrath, is measurelesse,

Rapt with an instant motion: and we blame,
We hate, we prayse, we pity in excesse,
According as our present passions frame.
Sometimes to passe the Ocean we would faine,
Sometimes to other worlds, and sometimes slacke
And idle, with our conquests, entertaine
A sullen humor of returning backe:
All which conceits one trumpets sound doth end,
And each man running to his ranke doth lose
What in our tents dislikt vs, and we spend
All that conceiuèd wrath vpon our foes.
And words, if they proceede of leuity,
Are to be scorn'd, of madnesse, pitied;
If out of malice or of iniury,
To be remiss'd or vnacknowledgèd:
For of themselues, they vanish by disdaine,
But if pursude, they will be thought not vaine.

THE TRAGICAL REIGN
OF SELIMUS

The Tragical Reign of Selimus, published in 1594, was ascribed to 'T.G.',
who may have been either Thomas Greene or Thomas Goffe, a writer
of 'Turkish' tragedies. T.S. Eliot felt that the play was 'obviously written
by some one who had not yet experienced the influence of Marlowe',
and felt that its declamatory blank verse was 'in its impulse, if not in its
achievement, Senecan'. The passage quoted adapts *Thyestes*, 204–18.

AGAMEMNON: O see my Lord, how fell ambition
    Deceiues your sences and bewitcyes you,
    Could you vnkind performe so foule a deed,
    As kill the man, that first gaue life to you?
    Do you not fear the peoples aduerse fame?

ACOMAT: It is the greatest glorie of a king
 When, though his subiects hate his wicked deeds
 Yet are they forst to beare them all with praise.
AGAMEMNON: Whom feare constraines to praise their princes
   deeds,
 That feare, eternall hatred in them feeds.
ACOMAT: He knowes not how to sway the kingly mace,
 That loues to be great in his peoples grace:
 The surest ground for kings to build vpon,
 Is to be fear'd and curst of euery one.
 What though the world of nations me hate?
 Hate is peculiar to a princes state.
AGAMEMNON: Where ther's no shame, no care of holy law,
 No faith, no iustice, no integritie,
 That state is full of mutabilitie.
ACOMAT: Bare faith, pure vertue, poore integritie,
 Are ornaments fit for a priuate man,
 Beseemes a prince for to do all he can.

JOHN MARSTON (1576–1634)

The playwright and poet who owed the most to Seneca of all the
Elizabethan dramatists, especially in his two-part *Antonio and Mellida*
(1599–1600), which contained nine quotations in Latin taken directly
from Seneca's plays, in addition to less direct borrowings. The passages
below adapt, respectively, *Thyestes*, 342 ff. and *Phoenissae*, 152 ff. (both
from *Antonio and Mellida*); *Thyestes*, 205–15 and *Medea*, 155–6 (both
from *Antonio's Revenge*).

 Why man, I never was a Prince till now.
 Tis not the bared pate, the bended knees,
 Guilt tipstaves, Tyrrian purple, chaires of state,
 Troopes of pide butterflies, that flutter still

In greatnesse summer, that confirme a prince:
Tis not the unsavory breath of multitudes,
Showting and clapping, with confused dinne;
That makes a Prince. No, *Lucio*, he's a king,
A true right king, that dares doe aught, save wrong,
Feares nothing mortall, but to be unjust,
Who is not blowne up with the flattering puffes
Of spungy Sycophants: Who stands unmov'd,
Despight the justling of opinion:
Who can enjoy himselfe, maugre the throng
That strive to presse his quiet out of him:
Who sits upon *Joves* footestoole, as I doe,
Adoring, not affecting, majestie:
Whose brow is wreathed with the silver crowne
Of cleare content: this, *Lucio*, is a king.
And of this empire, every man's possest,
That's worth his soule.

*

Each man take hence life, but no man death:
Hee's a good fellow, and keepes open house:
A thousand thousand waies lead to his gate,
To his wide-mouth'd porch: when niggard life
Hath but one little, little wicket through.
We wring our selves into this wretched world,
To pule, and weepe, exclaime, to curse and raile,
To fret, and ban the fates, to strike the earth
As I doe now. *Antonio*, curse thy birth,
And die.

*

PIERO: Tis just that subjectes acte commaunds of kings.
PANDULPHO: Commaund then just and honorable things.
PIERO: Even so my selfe then will traduce his guilt.
PANDULPHO: Beware, take heed least guiltlesse blood be spilt.

PIERO: Where onely honest deeds to kings are free,
   It is no empire, but a beggery.
PANDULPHO: Where more than noble deeds to kings are free,
   It is no empire, but a tyranny.
PIERO: Tush juicelesse graybeard, tis immunity,
   Proper to princes, that our state exactes,
   Our subjects not alone to beare, but praise our acts.
PANDULPHO: O, but that prince that worthfull praise aspires,
   From hearts, and not from lips, applause desires.
PIERO: Pish, true praise, the brow of common men doth ring,
   False, only girts the temple of a king.
   He that hath strength, and 's ignorant of power,
   He was not made to rule, but to be rul'd.
PANDULPHO: Tis praise to doe, not what we can, but should.

*

            That griefe is wanton sick,
   Whose stomacke can digest and brooke the dyet
   Of stale ill relisht counsell. Pigmie cares
   Can shelter under patience shield: but gyant griefes
   Will burst all covert.

SIR WILLIAM ALEXANDER, EARL OF STIRLING (c.1567–1640)

Poet and playwright, and courtier to James I and Charles I. Though he had been Secretary of State, as well as Earl of Stirling, he died in poverty. His four monarchical tragedies, written from 1603 to 1607, struck Lucas as 'extremely Senecan and consumedly dull' and he referred to Alexander as 'a seedy jackdaw masquerading in mouldy owl's feathers'. The passages below are from *Darius* and *The Alexandrian Tragedy*. Eliot called these 'poor stuff' (*Selected Essays*, p. 77) – 'I imagine

that they are more important in the history of the Union than in the
history of the Drama, since they represent the choice, by a Scotsman
of accidental eminence, to write verse in English instead of in Scots.'

> CHORUS: Time, through *Ioves* judgement just,
>   Huge alterations brings:
>   Those are but fooles who trust
>   In transitory things,
>   Whose tailes beare mortall stings,
>   Which in the end will wound;
>   And let none thinke it strange,
>   Though all things earthly change:
>   In this inferiour round
>   What is from ruine free?
>   The elements which be
>   At variance (as we see)
>   Each th' other doth confound:
>   The earth and ayre make warre,
>   The fire and water are
>   Still wrestling at debate,
>   All those through cold and heat,
>   Through drought and moisture jarre.
>   What wonder though men change and fade,
>   Who of those changing elements are made?
>
>   How dare vaine worldlings vaunt
>   Of fortunes goods not lasting,
>   Evils which our wits enchant:
>   Expos'd to losse and wasting!
>   Loe, we to death are hasting,
>   Whil'st we those things discusse:
>   All things from their beginning,
>   Still to an end are running,
>   Heaven hath ordain'd it thus;
>   We heare how it doth thunder,
>   We see th' earth burst asunder,

And yet we never ponder
What this imports to us:
Those fearefull signes doe prove,
That th' angry pow'rs above
Are mov'd to indignation
Against this wretched nation,
Which they no longer love:
    What are we but a puffe of breath
    Who live assur'd of nothing but of death?

Who was so happy yet
As never had some crosse?
Though on a throne he sit,
And is not us'd with losse,
Yet fortune once will tosse
Him, when that least he would;
If one had all at once,
Hydaspes precious stones,
And yellow *Tagus* gold;
The orientall treasure,
And every earthly pleasure,
Even in the greatest measure,
It should not make him bold:
For while he lives secure,
His state is most unsure;
When it doth least appeare,
Some heavy plague drawes neare,
Destruction to procure.
    Worlds glory is but like a flowre,
    Which both is bloom'd, and blasted in a houre.

In what we most repose,
We finde our comfort light,
The thing we soonest lose
That's precious in our sight;
For honour, riches, might,

Our lives in pawne we lay;
Yet all like flying shadowes,
Or flowers enamelling meadowes,
Doe vanish and decay.
Long time we toile to finde
Those idols of the minde,
Which had, we cannot binde
To bide with us one day:
Then why should we presume
On treasures that consume,
Difficult to obtaine,
Difficult to retaine,
A dream, a breath, a fume:
   Which vexe them most, that them possesse,
   Who starve with store, and famish with excesse.

*

'So change all things which subject are to sight:
'Disorder order breeds, and order it:
'Next light comes darknesse, and next darknesse light,
'This never-changing change transcends our wit.
'Thus health and sicknesse, poverty and state,
'Dishonour, honour, life and death, with doubt,
'Still inter-changing (what a true deceit!)
'All link'd together, slide by turnes about;
'To worldly states the heavens a height appoint,
'Where, when they once arrive, they must descend,
'And all perfections have a fatall point,
'At which excellency it selfe must end.
'But as all those who walke on th' earth, are cross'd
'With alterations, happ'ning oft, and strange,
'The greatest states with greatest stormes are toss'd,
'And (sought of many) must make many a change.'
Nor speake I this by speculation mov'd,
(As gathering credit out of ancient scroules)

'No, I have liv'd at court, and oft have prov'd
'Nothing below more vex'd, then great mens soules;
'The tyrant honours thralls, while as they mone,
'Their plaints to vulgar eares loath to impart,
'They all the weight of woes must beare alone,
'Where others of their griefe lend friends apart.
'Their verie rising o're us to the height,
'Which seemes their best is worst, for, being lords,
'They never know the truth that comes to light,
'When franke society speakes naked words.
'Whil'st sadnesse oft seemes majestic, time tels
'How deare they buy their pompe with losse of rest:
'Some but three furies faine in all the hels;
'There are three thousand in one great mans brest.'

GEORGE CHAPMAN (c.1560–1634)

Immortalized in Keats's famous sonnet, Chapman was a translator, playwright, and poet about whom little is known. His plays are filled with Senecan mannerisms and adaptations. The first three passages below are from *Bussy D'Ambois* (1604), Acts II, III, and V, respectively; the last of these adapts *Agamemnon*, 49–56. The next two excerpts are from *The Revenge of Bussy D'Ambois*, Acts V and IV (1610). The two passages following are from *The Conspiracy of Charles Duke of Byron* (1608); the first, from Act II, adapts *Hercules Oetaeus*, 454–71, while the second, from Act III, imitates the ironic dialogue between Oedipus and Creon in *Oedipus*, 511–29.

NUNTIUS: What *Atlas*, or *Olympus* lifts his head
        So farre past Couert, that with aire enough
        My words may be inform'd? And from his height
        I may be seene, and heard through all the world?
        A tale so worthie, and so fraught with wonder,
        Sticks in my iawes, and labours with euent.

*

MONSIEUR: Peace, peace, I pray thee peace.
BUSSY: Let him peace first that made the first warre.
MONSIEUR: Hee's the better man.
BUSSY: And therefore may doe worst?
MONSIEUR: He has more titles.
BUSSY: So *Hydra* had more heads.
MONSIEUR: Hee's greater knowne.
BUSSY: His greatnesse is the peoples, mine's mine owne.
MONSIEUR: Hee's noblie borne.
BUSSY: He is not, I am noble.
And noblesse in his blood hath no gradation,
But in his merit.

*

MONSIEUR: Not so the Sea raues on the Lybian sandes,
Tumbling her billowes in each others necke:
Not so the surges of the euxine Sea
(Neere to the frostie Pole, where free *Bootes*
From those darke-deepe waues turns his radiant Teame)
Swell being enrag'd, euen from their inmost drop,
As Fortune swings about the restlesse state
Of vertue, now throwne into all mens hate.

*

CLERMONT D'AMBOIS: A man to ioyne himselfe with
th'Vniuerse,
In his maine sway, and make (in all things fit)
One with that all, and goe on, round as it;
Not plucking from the whole his wretched part,
And into straites, or into nought reuert,
Wishing the compleate Vniuerse might be
Subiect to such a ragge of it as hee . . .

*

GUISE: In his most gentle, and vnwearied minde,
   Rightly to vertue fram'd; in very nature;
   In his most firme inexorable spirit,
   To be remou'd from any thing hee chuseth
   For worthinesse; or beare the lest perswasion
   To what is base, or fitteth not his obiect;
   In his contempt of riches and of greatnesse;
   In estimation of th'Idolatrous vulgar;
   His scorne of all things seruile and ignoble,
   Though they could gaine him neuer such aduancement;
   His liberall kinde of speaking what is truth,
   In spight of temporising; the great rising,
   And learning of his soule, so much the more
   Against ill fortune, as shee set her selfe
   Sharpe against him, or would present most hard,
   To shunne the malice of her deadliest charge;
   His detestation of his speciall friends,
   When he perceiu'd their tyrannous will to doe,
   Or their abiection basely to sustaine
   Any iniustice that they could reuenge;
   The flexibilitie of his most anger,
   Euen in the maine careere and fury of it,
   When any obiect of desertfull pittie
   Offers it selfe to him; his sweet disposure
   As much abhorring to behold, as doe
   Any vnnaturall and bloudy action;
   His iust contempt of Iesters, Parasites,
   Seruile obseruers, and polluted tongues:
   In short, this Senecall man is found in him,
   Hee may with heauens immortall powers compare,
   To whom the day and fortune equall are,
   Come faire or foule, what euer chance can fall,
   Fixt in himselfe, hee still is one to all.

*

If knowledge of the sure euents of things,
Euen from the rise of subiects into Kings:
And falles of Kings to subiects, hold a powre
Of strength to worke it; I can make it good;
And tell him this to; if in midest of winter
To make black Groues grow greene; to still the thunder;
And cast out able flashes from mine eies,
To beate the lightning back into the skies,
Proue powre to do it, I can make it good;
And tell him this too; if to lift the Sea
Vp to the Starres, when all the Windes are still;
And keepe it calme, when they are most enrag'd:
To make earths driest palms, sweate humorous springs
To make fixt rocks walke; and loose shadowes stand,
To make the dead speake: midnight see the Sunne,
Mid-daie turne mid-night; to dissolue all lawes
Of nature, and of order, argue powre
Able to worke all, I can make all good.
And all this tell the King.

*

LABROSSE: Forbeare to aske me, sonne,
   You bid me speake, what feare bids me conceale.
BYRON: You haue no cause to feare, and therefore speake.
LABROSSE: Youle rather wish you had beene ignorant,
   Then be instructed in a thing so ill.
BYRON: Ignorance is an idle salue for ill,
   And therefore do not vrge me to enforce,
   What I would freely know; for by the skill
   Showne in thy aged hayres, ile lay thy braine
   Here scattered at my feete, and seeke in that,
   What safely thou must vtter with thy tongue,
   If thou deny it.
LABROSSE: Will you not allow me
   To hold my peace? what lesse can I desire?
   If not, be pleasd with my constrained speech.

BYRON: Was euer man yet punisht for expressing
   What he was chargde? be free, and speake the worst.

CYRIL TOURNEUR (c.1575–1626)

The attribution of *The Revenger's Tragedy* (1607) to Tourneur has been questioned – it is sometimes suggested that Thomas Middleton (c.1580–1627) may be the author. The play is an example of what John Addington Symonds called the 'tragedy of blood', and is Senecan in its themes of lust, murder, and fatalism, using the devices of what Cunliffe called 'the ghastly relics of mortality'. Eliot wrote, 'What gives Tourneur his place as a great poet is this one play, in which a horror of life, singular in his own or any age, finds exactly the right words and the right rhythms' (*Selected Essays*, p. 169). The passage below adapts *Hippolytus/Phaedra*, 679–82.

   O thou almighty patience, tis my wonder,
   That such a fellow, impudent and wicked,
   Should not be clouen as he stood:
   Or with a secret winde burst open!
   Is there no thunder left, or ist kept vp
   In stock for heauier vengeance? [*Thunder*] there it goes!

BEN JONSON (1572–1637)

Jonson modelled his tragic style upon Seneca's. *Sejanus* (1603) and *Catiline* (1611) provide many parallels to *Thyestes* and *Oedipus*, as seen below. Jonson's 'Epode', a poem published in the collection *The Forrest* (1616), concludes with a paraphrase of *Hippolytus/Phaedra*, 162–4. The concluding excerpt, a parody of a Senecan speech, is from Jonson's play, *The Staple of News* (1625). Of this last, H.A. Mason comments,

'Even without the Latin before us, we can still see Latinisms sticking out' (*Humanism and Poetry in the Early Tudor Period*, London, Routledge and Kegan Paul, 1959, p. 270).

Sejanus

Men are deceiu'd, who thinke there can be thrall
Beneath a vertuous prince. Wish'd liberty
Ne're louelier lookes, then vnder such a crowne.
But, when his grace is meerely but lip-good,
And, that no longer, then he aires himselfe
Abroad in publique, there, to seeme to shun
The strokes, and stripes of flatterers, which within
Are lechery vnto him, and so feed
His brutish sense with their afflicting sound,
As (dead to vertue) he permits himselfe
Be carried like a pitcher, by the eares,
To euery act of vice: this is a case
Deserues our feare, and doth presage the nigh,
And close approach of bloud and tyranny.
Flattery is midwife vnto princes rage:
And nothing sooner, doth helpe foorth a tyranne,
Then that, and whisperers grace, who haue the time,
The place, the power, to make all men offenders.

*

SEIANUS: If this be not reuenge, when I haue done
    And made it perfect, let *Ægyptian* slaues,
    Parthians, and bare-foot *Hebrewes* brand my face,
    And print my body full of iniuries.
    Thou lost thy selfe, childe DRVSVS, when thou thought'st
    Thou could'st out-skip my vengeance: or out-stand
    The power I had to crush thee into ayre.
    Thy follyes now shall taste what kinde of man

They haue prouok'd, and this thy fathers house
Cracke in the flame of my incensed rage,
Whose fury shall admit no shame, or meane.
Adultery? it is the lightest ill,
I will commit. A race of wicked acts
Shall flow out of my anger, and o're-spread
The worlds wide face, which no posterity
Shall e're approoue, nor yet keepe silent: Things,
That for their cunning, close, and cruell marke,
Thy father would wish his; and shall (perhaps)
Carry the empty name, but we the prize.
On then, my soule, and start not in thy course;
Though heau'n drop sulphure, and hell belch out fire,
Laugh at the idle terrors: Tell proud IOVE,
Betweene his power, and thine, there is no oddes.
'Twas onely feare, first, in the world made gods.

TIBERIVS, SEIANVS.

Is yet SEIANVS come?
SEIANVS: He's here, dread CAESAR.
TIBERIVS: Let all depart that chamber, and the next:
    Sit downe, my comfort. When the master-prince
    Of all the world, SEIANVS, saith, he feares;
    Is it not fatall?
SEIANVS: Yes, to those are fear'd.
TIBERIVS: And not to him?
SEIANVS: Not, if he wisely turne
    That part of fate he holdeth, first on them.
TIBERIVS: That nature, bloud, and lawes of kinde forbid.
SEIANVS: Doe policie, and state forbid it?
TIBERIVS: No.
SEIANVS: The rest of poore respects, then, let goe by:
    State is inough to make th'act iust, them guilty.
TIBERIVS: Long hate pursues such acts.
SEIANVS: Whom hatred frights,
    Let him not dreame on sou'raignty.

TIBERIVS: Are rites
   Of faith, loue, piety, to be trod downe?
   Forgotten? and made vaine?
SEIANVS: All for a crowne.
   The prince, who shames a tyrannes name to beare,
   Shall neuer dare doe any thing, but feare;
   All the command of scepters quite doth perish
   If it beginne religious thoughts to cherish:
   Whole Empires fall, swaid by those nice respects.
   It is the licence of darke deeds protects
   Eu'n states most hated: when no lawes resist
   The sword, but that it acteth what it list.

*

Catiline

ACT I

SYLLA'S GHOST
Do'st thou not feele me, *Rome*? not yet? Is night
So heauy on thee, and my weight so light?
Can SYLLA's Ghost arise within thy walls,
Lesse threatning, then an earth-quake, the quick falls
Of thee, and thine? shake not the frighted heads
Of thy steepe towers? or shrinke to their first beds?
Or, as their ruine the large *Tyber* fills,
Make that swell vp, and drowne thy seuen proud hills?
What sleepe is this doth seize thee, so like death,
And is not it? Wake, feele her, in my breath:
Behold, I come, sent from the *Stygian* sound,
As a dire vapor, that had cleft the ground,
T'ingender with the night, and blast the day;
Or like a pestilence, that should display
Infection through the world: which, thus, I doe.
PLVTO be at thy councells; and into

Thy darker bosome enter SYLLA's spirit:
All, that was mine, and bad, thy brest inherit.
Alas, how weake is that, for CATILINE!
Did I but say (vaine voice!) all that was mine?
All, that the GRACCHI, CINNA, MARIVS would;
What now, had I a body againe, I could,
Comming from hell; what Fiends would wish should be;
And HANNIBAL could not haue wish'd to see:
Thinke thou, and practice. Let the long-hid seeds
Of treason, in thee, now shoot forth in deeds,
Ranker then horror; and thy former facts
Not fall in mention, but to vrge new acts:
Conscience of them prouoke thee on to more.
Be still thy incests, murders, rapes before
Thy sense; thy forcing first a *Vestall* nunne;
Thy parricide, late, on thine owne onely sonne,
After his mother; to make emptie way
For thy last wicked nuptialls; worse, then they,
That blaze that act of thy incestuous life,
Which got thee, at once, a daughter, and a wife.
I leaue the slaughters, that thou didst for me,
Of *Senators*; for which, I hid for thee
Thy murder of thy brother, (being so brib'd)
And writ him in the list of my proscrib'd
After thy fact, to saue thy little shame:
Thy incest, with thy sister, I not name.
These are too light. *Fate* will haue thee pursue
Deedes, after which, no mischiefe can be new;
The ruine of thy countrey: thou wert built
For such a worke, and borne for no lesse guilt.
What though defeated once th'hast beene, and knowne,
Tempt it againe: That is thy act, or none.
What all the seuerall ills, that visite earth,
(Brought forth by night, with a sinister birth)
Plagues, famine, fire could not reach vnto,
The sword, nor surfets; let thy furie doe:

Make all past, present, future ill thine owne;
And conquer all example, in thy one.
Nor let thy thought find any vacant time
To hate an old, but still a fresher crime
Drowne the remembrance: let not mischiefe cease,
But, while it is in punishing, encrease.
Conscience, and care die in thee; and be free
Not heau'n it selfe from thy impietie:
Let night grow blacker with thy plots; and day,
At shewing but thy head forth, start away
From this halfe-spheare: and leaue *Romes* blinded walls
T'embrace lusts, hatreds, slaughters, funeralls,
And not recouer sight, till their owne flames
Doe light them to their ruines. All the names
Of thy confederates, too, be no lesse great
In hell, then here: that, when we would repeat
Our strengths in muster, we may name you all,
And *Furies*, vpon you, for *Furies*, call.
Whilst, what you doe, may strike them into feares,
Or make them grieue, and wish your mischiefe theirs.

*

Is there a heauen? and gods? and can it be
They should so slowly heare, so slowly see!
Hath IOVE no thunder? or is IOVE become
Stupide as thou art? ô neere-wretched *Rome*,
When both thy *Senate*, and thy gods doe sleepe,
And neither thine, nor their owne states doe keepe!

The Forrest

XI

EPODE

Not to know vice at all, and keepe true state,
    Is vertue, and not *Fate*:
Next, to that vertue, is to know vice well,
    And her blacke spight expell.
Which to effect (since no brest is so sure,
    Or safe, but shee'll procure
Some way of entrance) we must plant a guard
    Of thoughts to watch, and ward
At th'eye and eare (the ports vnto the minde)
    That no strange, or vnkinde
Obiect arriue there, but the heart (our spie)
    Giue knowledge instantly,
To wakefull reason, our affections king:
    Who (in th'examining)
Will quickly taste the treason, and commit
    Close, the close cause of it.
'Tis the securest policie we haue,
    To make our sense our slaue.
But this true course is not embrac'd by many:
    By many? scarse by any.
For either our affections doe rebell,
    Or else the sentinell
(That should ring larum to the heart) doth sleepe,
    Or some great thought doth keepe
Backe the intelligence, and falsely sweares,
    Th'are base, and idle feares
Whereof the loyall conscience so complaines.
    Thus, by these subtle traines,
Doe seuerall passions inuade the minde,
    And strike our reason blinde.

Of which vsurping rancke, some haue thought loue
    The first; as prone to moue
Most frequent tumults, horrors, and vnrests,
    In our enflamed brests:
But this doth from the cloud of error grow,
    Which thus we ouer-blow.
The thing, they here call Loue, is blinde Desire,
    Arm'd with bow, shafts, and fire;
Inconstant, like the sea, of whence 'tis borne,
    Rough, swelling, like a storme:
With whom who sailes, rides on the surge of feare,
    And boyles, as if he were
In a continuall tempest. Now, true Loue
    No such effects doth proue;
That is an essence, farre more gentle, fine,
    Pure, perfect, nay diuine;
It is a golden chaine let downe from heauen,
    Whose linkes are bright, and euen,
That falls like sleepe on louers, and combines
    The soft, and sweetest mindes
In equall knots: This beares no brands, nor darts,
    To murther different hearts,
But, in a calme, and god-like vnitie,
    Preserues communitie.
O, who is he, that (in this peace) enioyes
    The'*Elixir* of all ioyes?
A forme more fresh, then are the *Eden* bowers,
    And lasting, as her flowers:
Richer then *Time*, and as *Time*'s vertue, rare.
    Sober, as saddest care:
A fixed thought, an eye vn-taught to glance;
    Who (blest with such high chance)
Would, at suggestion of a steepe desire,
    Cast himselfe from the spire
Of all his happinesse? But soft: I heare
    Some vicious foole draw neare,

That cryes, we dreame, and sweares, there's no such thing,
    As this chaste loue we sing.
Peace, Luxurie, thou art like one of those
    Who, being at sea, suppose,
Because they moue, the continent doth so:
    No, vice, we let thee know,
Though thy wild thoughts with sparrowes wings doe flye,
    Turtles can chastly dye;
And yet (in this t'expresse our selues more cleare)
    We doe not number, here,
Such spirits as are onely continent,
    Because lust's meanes are spent:
Or those, who doubt the common mouth of fame,
    And for their place, and name,
Cannot so safely sinne. Their chastitie
    Is meere necessitie.
Nor meane we those, whom vowes and conscience
    Haue fill'd with abstinence:
Though we acknowledge, who can so abstayne,
    Makes a most blessed gayne.
He that for loue of goodnesse hateth ill,
    Is more crowne-worthy still,
Then he, which for sinnes penaltie forbeares.
    His heart sinnes, though he feares.
But we propose a person like our Doue,
    Grac'd with a Phœnix loue;
A beautie of that cleere, and sparkling light,
    Would make a day of night,
And turne the blackest sorrowes to bright ioyes:
    Whose od'rous breath destroyes
All taste of bitternesse, and makes the ayre
    As sweet, as shee is fayre.
A body so harmoniously compos'd,
    As if *Nature* disclos'd
All her best symmetrie in that one feature!
    O, so diuine a creature

Who could be false to? chiefly, when he knowes
      How onely shee bestowes
The wealthy treasure of her loue on him;
      Making his fortunes swim
In the full floud of her admir'd perfection?
      What sauage, brute affection,
Would not be fearefull to offend a dame
      Of this excelling frame?
Much more a noble, and right generous mind
      (To vertuous moods inclin'd)
That knowes the waight of guilt: He will refraine
      From thoughts of such a straine.
And to his sense obiect this sentence euer,
      Man may securely sinne, but safely neuer.

The Staple of News

            Who can endure to see
The fury of mens gullets, and their groines?
What fires, what cookes, what kitchins might be spar'd?
What Stewes, Ponds, Parks, Coopes, Garners, Magazines?
What veluets, tissues, scarfes, embroyderies,
And laces they might lacke? They couet things
Superfluous still: when it were much more honour
They could want necessary: what need hath Nature
Of siluer dishes, or gold chamber pots?
Of perfum'd napkins, or a numerous family
To see her eate? poore, and wise, she requires
Meate only: hunger is not ambitious.
Say that you were the *Emperour* of pleasures,
The great *Dictator* of fashions for all *Europe*,
And had the pompe of all the Courts and Kingdomes
Laid forth unto the shew to make your self

Gaz'd and admir'd at: you must goe to bed
And take your naturall rest: then all this vanisheth.
Your brauery was but showen: 'twas not possest:
While it did boast it selfe it was then perishing.

JOHN WEBSTER (?1580–?1634)

Webster incorporated *Hippolytus/Phaedra* 615 (*'curae leues loquuntur ingentes stupent'*) in *The White Devil*, published and probably produced in 1612. This was a popular passage of Seneca among the Elizabethans – compare Shakespeare's *Macbeth* IV. iii. 209–10, Tourneur's *Revenger's Tragedy* I. iv, Chapman's *Widow's Tears* IV. i. 104–5, and Ford's *Broken Heart* V. iii.

The second excerpt, from *The Duchess of Malfi*, indicates a Stoical and Senecan philosophy; Ian Jack, in 'The Case of John Webster' (1949, reprinted in G.K. Hunter and S.K. Hunter, *John Webster*, Harmondsworth, Penguin, 1969, p. 149), writes of this and similar passages that Webster's 'attempt to shore up chaos with a sententious philosophy is a flagrant artistic insincerity', while M.C. Bradbrook, in 'Fate and Chance in *The Duchess of Malfi*' (1947, reprinted in Hunter and Hunter, op. cit., p.159) argues that Webster 'had a delicate balance to maintain between the theatrical and doctrinal', and that Seneca's work included 'physical atrocities' of a kind which are not paralleled in Webster.

Unkindnesse do thy office, poore heart breake,
Those are the killing greifes which dare not speake.

*

BOSOLA: We are meerely the Starres tennys-balls (strooke, and
banded
Which way please them) oh good *Antonio*,
I'll whisper one thing in thy dying eare,
Shall make thy heart breake quickly: Thy faire Dutchesse
And two sweet Children.

ANTONIO: Their very names
    Kindle a litle life in me.
BOSOLA: Are murderd!
ANTONIO: Some men haue wish'd to die.
    At the hearing of sad tydings: I am glad
    That I shall do't in sadnes: I would not now
    Wish my wounds balm'de, nor heal'd: for I haue no vse
    To put my life to: In all our Quest of Greatnes;
    (Like wanton Boyes, whose pastime is their care)
    We follow after bubbles, blowne in th'ayre.
    Pleasure of life, what is't? onely the good houres
    Of an Ague: meerely a preparatiue to rest,
    To endure vexation: I doe not aske
    The processe of my death: onely commend me
    To *Delio*.

SIR JOHN HARINGTON

(1561–1612)

A courtier and translator, educated at Cambridge; Queen Elizabeth was his godmother, and suggested that he translate Ariosto. He invented the first water closet, and his bawdy satires resulted in his briefly being banished from the queen's presence. His epigrams, published in several editions between 1618 and 1625, were popular; the one given below is taken from *Hercules Furens*, 250.

Treason doth never prosper: what's the reason?
Why, if it prosper, none dare call it treason.

Epigrams, Book iv. Ep. 5

JOHN FORD (c.1586–c.1640)

Ford, Cunliffe writes, 'abounds in his own kind of tragic horrors' yet he was a Senecan fatalist whose characters meet death calmly. These small excerpts from *The Broken Heart* (1629) echo many a Senecan speech.

> Put out thy Torches *Hymen*, or their light
> Shall meet a darkenesse of eternall night.
> Inspire me *Mercury* with swift deceits;
> Ingenious Fate has lept into mine armes,
> Beyond the compasse of my braine. – Mortality
> Creeps on the dung of earth, and cannot reach
> The riddles, which are purpos'd by the gods.
>   Great Arts best write themselues in their owne stories,
>   They dye too basely, who out-liue their glories.

*

> The Counsels of the gods are neuer knowne,
> Till men can call th' effects of them their owne.

HENRY CHETTLE (c.1560–c.1607)

Became a playwright after failing as a printer. While he helped write several dozen plays, few survive, although *The Tragedy of Hoffman* (c.1603, published 1631) is believed to be entirely his. A typically Senecan revenge play, it begins with thunder and lightning, and ends with a Stoic acceptance of Hell.

> HOFFMAN: Hence Clouds of melancholy
>   Ile be no longer subiect to your schismes,
>   But thou deare soule, whose nerues and arteris
>   In dead resoundings summon vp reuenge,

And thou shalt hate, be but appeas'd sweete hearse,
The dead remembrance of my liuing
          father,   *strikes ope a curtaine where*
And with a hart as aire, swift as thought   *appears a body.*
I'le execute iustly in such a cause.
Where truth leadeth, what coward would not fight?
Ill acts moue some, but myne's a cause that's
          right   *thunder and lightning.*
See the powers of heauen in apparitions,
And fright full aspects as insenced,
That I thus tardy am to doe an act
Which iustice and a fathers death excites,
Like threatening meteors antedates destruction.   *thunder*
Againe I come, I come, I come,
Bee silent thou effigies of faire virtue
That like a goodly syen wer't pluckt vp
By murderous, winds, infectious blasts and gusts
I will not leaue thee, vntill like thy selfe,
I'ue made thy enemies, then hand in hand
Wee'le walke to paradise – againe more blest
Ile to yon promonts top, and their suruey,
What shipwrackt passengers the belgique sea
Casts from her fomy entrailes by mischance.
Roare sea and winds, and with celestiall fires,
Quicken high proiects, with your highest desires.

*

HOFFMAN: A man resolu'd in blood, bound by a vow
     For noe lesse vengeance, then his fathers death,
     Yet become amorous of his foes wife!
     Oh sin against all conceit! worthy this shame
     And all the tortures that the world can name.
MARTHA: Call vpon heauen, base wretch, thinke on thy soule.
HOFFMAN: In charity and prayer
     To no purpose without charity.

DUKE OF SAXONY: We pardon thee, and pray for thy soules
    health.
HOFFMAN: Soe doe not I for yours, nor pardon you;
    You kild my father, my most warlike father,
    Thus as you deale by me, you did by him;
    But I deserue it that haue slackt reuenge
    Through fickle beauty, and a womans fraud;
    But Hell the hope of all dispayring men,
    That wring the poore, and eate the people vp,
    As greedy beasts the haruest of their spring:
    That Hell, where cowards haue their seats prepar'd,
    And barbarous asses, such as haue rob'd souldiers of
    Reward, and punish true desert with scorned death.

SIR FULKE GREVILLE,
Ist BARON BROOKE (1554–1628)

Councillor of Elizabeth and James, he was also a poet and playwright,
though his work was not published in his lifetime. He is best known
for his sequence of songs and sonnets, *Caelica*, published in 1633, along
with two tragedies whose 'verbal capers', Lucas writes, 'out-Seneca
Seneca'. Lucas almost fondly called him 'a weird obfuscated genius'.
Thom Gunn, in his selection of Greville's poems (1968), regarded him,
with Ralegh, as 'a kind of epitome of Elizabethan poetry, moving
through the different styles and never relinquishing what he learned
from each'. The excerpt below is from *Mustapha*.

    I spake: they cried: For *Mustapha*, and *Achmat*.
    Some bid away; some kill; some saue; some hearken.
    Those that cried, *Saue*, were those that sought to kill me.
    Who cried, *Hearke*, were those that first brake silence,
    They held that bad me *Goe*. Humilitie was guiltie;
    Words were reproch; Silence in me was scornfull;

They answer'd ere they ask'd; assur'd, and doubted.
I fled; their Furie followed to destroy me;
Fury made haste; Haste multiplied their Furie;
Each would doe all; none would giue place to other.
The hindmost strake; and while the formost lifted
Their armes to strike, each Weapon hindred other.
Their running let their strokes, strokes let their running.
Desire, mortall enemy to desire,
Made them, that sought my life, giue life vnto me.

SIR FRANCIS BEAUMONT
(1584–1616) and JOHN FLETCHER
(1579–1625)

Beaumont, educated at Oxford, collaborated with Fletcher, educated at Cambridge, on some fifteen dramatic works. Beaumont is buried in Westminster Abbey; Fletcher died of plague. *The Bloody Brother* (1616) contains some distinctly Senecan gore, as when the heads of Gisbert and Hamond are brought on the stage after their execution. The scene excerpted below seems to be a direct imitation of *Thebäis*, roughly lines 450–565.

GISBERT: . . . that ever Brothers should
    Stand on more nice terms, than sworn Enemies
    After a War proclaim'd, would with a stranger
    Wrong the reporters credit; they saluted
    At distance; and so strong was the suspicion
    Each had of other, that before they durst
    Embrace, they were by sev'ral servants searcht,
    As doubting conceal'd weapons, Antidotes
    Ta'ne openly by both, fearing the room
    Appointed for the enter-view was poyson'd,

The Chairs, and Cushions, with like care survay'd;
And in a word in every circumstance
So jealous on both parts, that it is more
Than to be fear'd, concord can never joyn,
Minds so divided.

*

[*Enter* SOPHIA]

SOPHIA: Make way, or I will force it, who are those?
My Sons? my shames; turn all your swords on me,
And make this wretched body but one wound,
So this unnatural quarrel find a grave
In the unhappy womb that brought you forth:
Dare you remember that you had a Mother,
Or look on these gray hairs, made so with tears,
For both your goods, and not with age; and yet
Stand doubtful to obey her? from me you had
Life, Nerves, and faculties, to use these weapons;
And dare you raise them against her, to whom
You owe the means of being what you are?

OTTO: All peace is meant to you.

SOPHIA: Why is this War then?
As if your arms could be advanc'd, and I
Not set upon the rack? your bloud is mine,
Your dangers mine, your goodness I should share in;
I must be branded with those impious marks
You stamp on your own foreheads and on mine,
If you go on thus: for my good name therefore,
Though all respects of honour in your selves
Be in your fury choakt, throw down your swords;
Your duty should be swifter than my tongue;
And joyn your hands while they be innocent;
You have heat of bloud, and youth apt to Ambition,
To plead an easie pardon for what's past:
But all the ills beyond this hour committed,
From Gods or men must hope for no excuse.

GISBERT: Can you hear this unmov'd?
　　No Syllable of this so pious charm, but should have power
　　To frustrate all the juggling deceits,
　　With which the Devil blinds you.
OTTO: I begin to melt, I know not how.
ROLLO: Mother, I'le leave you;
　　And, Sir, be thankful for the time you live,
　　Till we meet next (which shall be soon and sudden)
　　To her perswasion for you.
SOPHIA: O yet, stay,
　　And rather than part thus, vouchsafe me hearing,
　　As enemies; how is my soul divided?
　　My love to both is equal, as my wishes;
　　But are return'd by neither; my griev'd heart,
　　Hold yet a little longer, and then break.
　　I kneel to both, and will speak so, but this
　　Takes from me th' authority of a mothers power;
　　And therefore, like my self, *Otto*, to thee,
　　(And yet observe, son, how thy mothers tears
　　Outstrip her forward words, to make way for'em)
　　Thou art the younger, *Otto*, yet be now
　　The first example of obedience to me,
　　And grow the elder in my love.
OTTO: The means to be so happy?
SOPHIA: This; yield up thy sword,
　　And let thy piety give thy mother strength
　　To take that from thee, which no enemies force
　　Could e're despoil thee of: why do'st thou tremble,
　　And with a fearful eye fixt on thy Brother,
　　Observ'st his ready sword, as bent against thee?
　　I am thy armour, and will be pierc'd through,
　　Ten thousand times, before I will give way
　　To any peril may arrive at thee;
　　And therefore fear not.
OTTO: 'Tis not for my self,
　　But for you, mother; you are now ingag'd

In more tha[n] lies in your unquestion'd vertue;
For, since you have disarm'd me of defence,
Should I fall now, though by his hand, the world
May say it was your practice.

SOPHIA: All words perish,
Before my piety turn treasons parent,
Take it again, and stand upon your guard,
And while your Brother is, continue arm'd;
And yet, this fear is needless, for I know,
My *Rollo*, though he dares as much as man,
So tender of his yet untainted valour,
So noble, that he dares do nothing basely.
You doubt him; he fears you; I doubt and fear
Both; for others safety, and not mine own.
Know yet, my sons, when of necessity
You must deceive, or be deceiv'd; 'tis better
To suffer Treason, than to act the Traytor;
And in a War like this, in which the glory
Is his that's overcome; consider then
What 'tis for which you strive: is it the Dukedom?
Or the command of these so ready subjects?
Desire of wealth? or whatsoever else
Fires your ambition? This still desp'rate madness,
To kill the people which you would be Lords of;
With fire, and sword to lay that Country waste
Whose rule you seek for: to consume the treasures,
Which are the sinews of your Government,
In cherishing the factions that destroy it:
Far, far be this from you: make it not question'd
Whether you have interest in that Dukedom,
Whose ruine both contend for.

OTTO: I desire but to enjoy my own, which I will keep.

ROLLO: And rather than posterity shall have cause
To say I ruin'd all, divide the Dukedom,
I will accept the moiety.

OTTO: I embrace it.

SOPHIA: Divide me first, or tear me limb by limb,
    And let them find as many several Graves
    As there are villages in *Normandy*:
    And 'tis less sin, than thus to weaken it.
    To hear it mention'd doth already make me
    Envy my dead Lord, and almost Blaspheme
    Those powers that heard my prayer for fruitfulness,
    And did not with my first birth close my womb:
    To me alone my second blessing proves
    My first of misery, for if that Heaven
    Which gave me *Rollo*, there had staid his bounty,
    And *Otto*, my dear *Otto*, ne're had been,
    Or being, had not been so worth my love,
    The stream of my affection had run constant
    In one fair current, all my hopes had been
    Laid up in one; and fruitful *Normandy*
    In this division had not lost her glories:
    For as 'tis now, 'tis a fair Diamond,
    Which being preserv'd intire, exceeds all value,
    But cut in pieces (though these pieces are
    Set in fine gold by the best work-mans cunning)
    Parts with all estimation: So this Dukedom,
    As 'tis yet whole, the neighbouring Kings may covet,
    But cannot compass; which divided, will
    Become the spoil of every barbarous foe
    That will invade it.
GISBERT: How this works in both!
BALDWIN: Prince *Rollo*'s eyes have lost their fire.
GISBERT: And anger, that but now wholly possessed
    Good *Otto*, hath given place to pity.
AUBREY: End not thus Madam, but perfect what's so well begun.
SOPHIA: I see in both, fair signs of reconcilement,
    Make them sure proofs they are so: the Fates offer
    To your free choice, either to live Examples
    Of Piety, or wickedness: if the later
    Blinds so your understanding, that you cannot

Pierce through her painted out-side, and discover
That she is all deformity within,
Boldly transcend all precedents of mischief,
And let the last, and the worst end of tyrannies,
The murther of a Mother, but begin
The stain of bloud you after are to heighten:
But if that vertue, and her sure rewards,
Can win you to accept her for your guide,
To lead you up to Heaven, and there fix you
The fairest Stars in the bright Sphere of honour;
Make me the parent of an hundred sons,
All brought into the world with joy, not sorrow,
And every one a Father to his Country,
In being now made Mother of your concord.

JOHN MILTON (1608–1674)

These lines from *Hercules Furens* (922–4) were translated in his pamphlet, *The Tenure of Kings and Magistrates*, which appeared in 1649 following the execution of King Charles, which Milton defended. These lines are spoken by Hercules after he has killed the tyrant, Lycus.

There can be slain
No sacrifice to God more acceptable
Than an unjust and wicked king.

EDMUND PRESTWICH

(dates unknown)

Prestwich's translation of *Hippolytus/Phaedra* dates from 1651.

> Thou Almighty King
> Of Gods canst thou so mildly see, so mildly hear
> Her wickedness? if not the Heavens be clear,
> When wilt thou thunder? let the troubled air
> Now run on heaps, and day a Vizard wear.
> May the reversed stars now backwards run.
> And what dost thou, thou the irradiate sun
> Behold thy Grandchilds lusts? for shame lay be
> Thy beams, and into utter darkness fly.
> And why are thou idle Spectator turn'd
> Great *Jove*, the world not yet with lightning burn'd,
> Thunder at me; let thy quick flame consume
> Me, I am wicked, and deserve the doom.

SAMUEL PORDAGE (1633–?1691)

A noted follower of the doctrines of the German mystic and theosophist Jacob Boehme (1575–1624), Pordage published his annotated version of *Troades* in 1660. He refrained from including any dedication, to avoid embarrassing anyone by name in the event that his translation be judged flawed, explaining, 'I assure you I am not *Pigmalion* to be in Love with the work of my own hands ... If thou ask'st why I have offer'd it in publique view, I will not answer thee with that trivial and palliating Come-off, that the intreaties of Friends have forc'd me contrary to my will to tumble into the presse, where after so desperate a Squeeze, I appeare so misshapen, and besmear'd with black blood: No, I freely jumped in, and have indured the wrack only to pleasure the mere *English* reader ...'

Companions Sweeten Grief; 'tis found
Less hard when Cries whole Swarmes resound.
Sorrow and Tears more gently bite
When Troops with like tears are in flight.
Great grief desires still to see,
Many fellows in Miserie:
And not alone the pain to bear.
None nills when all suffer a share.
No man wretched himself doth hold
If all are so: Men rich in Gold
Remove: Remove all such that use
To Cut rich land with a hunder'd ploughs;
And then the poors Cast minds will rise.
None's poor but when he rich espies.
In great mishaps 'tis Sweet to see
In Sadness every face agree.
He doth his fate moan and deplore
Who naked gains the sought-for-shore,
By swimming from Shipwrack alone.
He danger less and's Chance doth moan,
Who a Thousand ships did see
Together swallow'd by the Sea:
Whilst Shipwrack'd planks spread on the Shore
When that the North-west wind doth rore,
Holding back the Constrained waves.
Phrixus for *Helle*'s drowning raves,
When that the Golden-fleeced Ram
On's guilded back bore she and him,
And she fell thence into the Sea.
Deucalion and *Pyrrha* they
When they nothing beheld but waves
Where all but they had made their graves,
Griev'd less together. Alas! all we
Anon shall separated be;
And tossed Ships disjoyn our tears,
When that the Sayles the Mariners

At Trumpet sound shall hoist; and when
With winds, and hasty oars they from
The flying Shores hast to the Deep.
What State of mind shall wretches keep
When Seas increase, and Earth grows small?
When *Ida* high, lye hidden shall,
Then Children to their Mothers, they
To th' Children where *Troy* stood shall shew,
And poynting with the fingers Cry,
That's *Troy* where the Smoak on high,
Creeps to Heav'n. The *Trojans* so
By black Smoak shall their country know.

ABRAHAM COWLEY (1618–1667)

Educated at Cambridge, Cowley had written a verse romance at the
age of ten, and went on to write plays, poems, satires, and prose. He
seems to have been a Royalist spy, and was briefly imprisoned in 1655,
though there were subsequent doubts about his loyalty to the Royalist
cause. He is buried in Westminster Abbey. The following is his version
of the chorus in the second act of *Thyestes*; it appeared in an essay
published in 1668 about living well.

Upon the slippery tops of humane State,
    The guilded Pinnacles of Fate,
Let others proudly stand, and for a while
    The giddy danger to beguile,
With Joy, and with disdain look down on all,
    Till their Heads turn, and down they fall.
Me, O ye Gods, on Earth, or else so near
    That I no Fall to Earth may fear,
And, O ye gods, at a good distance seat
    From the long Ruines of the Great.

Here wrapt in th' Arms of Quiet let me ly;
Quiet, Companion of Obscurity.
Here let my Life, with as much silence slide,
    As Time that measures it does glide.
Nor let the Breath of Infamy or Fame,
From town to town Eccho about my Name.
Nor let my homely Death embroidered be
    With Scutcheon or with Elegie.
    An old *Plebean* let me Dy,
Alas, all then are such as well as I.
    To him, alas, to him, I fear,
The face of Death will terrible appear:
Who in his life flattering his senceless pride
By being known to all the world beside,
Does not himself, when he is Dying know
Nor what he is, nor Whither hee's to go.

JOHN WILMOT, 2nd EARL OF ROCHESTER (1647–1680)

Poet, satirist, and one of the court wits associated with Charles II, Rochester went to Oxford, and later, at the age of 18, abducted and married an heiress. His translations, imitations, and scurrilous lampoons, as well as his frank verse about sex, made him famous, though he died young. He is also famous for having, in Johnson's words, 'blazed out his youth and health in lavish voluptuousness'. The following is a version of the chorus in the second act of *Troas*, written 1674, published 1680.

After Death, Nothing is, and Nothing, Death,
The utmost Limit of a gasp of Breath:
Let the Ambitious Zealot lay aside
His Hopes of *Heav'n* (whose Faith is but his Pride)

Let *Slavish Souls* lay by their Fear,
Nor be concern'd which way, nor where,
After this Life they shall be hurl'd,
Dead, we become the *Lumber* of the *World*,
And to that *Mass* of *Matter* shall be swept,
Where things *destroy'd* with things *unborne* are kept.
Devouring Time swallows us whole,
Impartial *Death* confounds *Body* and *Soul*:
For *Hell*, and the foul *Fiend*, that rules
God's everlasting fiery *Gaols*,
Devis'd by *Rogues*, dreaded by *Fools*,
(With his grim griezly *Dog*, that keeps the *Door*,)
Are sensless *Stories*, *idle Tales*,
Dreams, *Whimsies*, and no more.

JOHN WRIGHT (d. 1658)

Wright was a playwright for the popular stage who adapted *Thyestes* published in 1674. In this excerpt, Thyestes experiences forebodings upon his return home, fulfilled in the next excerpt when he is fed the remains of his own children by his brother, Atreus.

My Country's long'd for Sight I now possess,
The greatest good that can sad Exiles bless.
My Native Soil, and Country-gods I see;
(If Gods they are who so neglected me;)
I see the towrs the *Cyclops* work that are,
No Mortal can raise structures half so fair.
Oft with applause have I at that fam'd place
In *Pelops* Royal Chariot won the Race.
Me the whole Town will meet returning home;
Nay, *Atreus* too, whose sight I hate, will come,
Then let me back again to woods obscure,
And with the Beasts a life like theirs endure.

A Crowns false splendor shall not me enflame:
Mind not the Gift, but him that gives the same.
Chearful I was when in a low Estate;
Now I from Exile am recall'd, and Fate
Doth smile, I'me sad. Something within doth cry,
Turn back again: I move unwillingly.

*

THYESTES: Hark ye, Brother, does your Room
    Here, learn to dance? So I presume:
    It turns upon the Toe so smoothly,
    And quick withall, I tell you soothly,
    It makes me giddy with its wheeling
    Motion, and sets me to a Reeling –
ATREUS: Reeling, that's my cue. Now I may
    Discover the intrigue o'th'play.
    Since in that door the wind is got,
    'Tis time to reconcile the Plot. –
    How do you like your cats, my Friend?
THYESTES: Well; but I dare not much commend
    For fear you steal 'em, nor is this same
    Fear vain and Pannique, for I miss 'em.
ATREUS: 'Las they've miscarri'd all to day,
    Some hang'd, some drown'd, as one may say
    And 'cause they should not basely fall,
    'Twas I, dear heart, that kill'd 'em all.
THYESTES: Was this done like a loving Brother?
    Or like a Friend? Sure neither nother.
    But let that pass. I'le spare my Curses –
    Their skins will make me three good purses.
    I'le goe and flea 'em.
ATREUS: But the jest is
    You 'ave dined upon 'em, dear Thyestes.
    And I both Butcher was, and Cook
    To serve you Sir.

THYESTES: Now I could puke –
    O Cuckold Cook to treat me thus!
    O Hated Hang-dog to hang Puss!
    O Son of an old rotten Whore!
    In fine – I'le sleep and tell you more.
    [*lies down*]
ATREUS: Io, Victoria! now at last
    By me, and Fortune thou art cast.
    Lye there. Such Victories as these are
    Will swell me up as big as Cesar.
    When the High Germans he bumbasted,
    Less Triumph and content he tasted.
    Even now, since thus my Brother fell,
    I seem as tall as a High Constable.

SIR MATTHEW HALE (1609–1676)

Educated at Oxford, Hale became Lord Chief Justice, and wrote a *History of the Common Law*. His *Contemplations Moral and Divine*, published in the year of his death, included a snippet of translation of the chorus from the second act of *Thyestes*.

    Let him that will, ascend the tottering Seat
    Of Courtly Grandeur, and become as great
    As are his mountain Wishes; as for me,
    Let sweet Repose, and Rest my portion be;
    Give me some mean obscure Recess, a Sphere
    Out of the road of Business, or the fear
    Of Falling lower, where I sweetly may
    My Self, and dear Retirement still enjoy.
    Let not my Life, or Name, be known unto
    The Grandees of the Times, tost to and fro
    By Censures, or Applause; but let my Age
    Slide gently by, not overthwart the Stage

Of Publick Interest; unheard, unseen,
And unconcern'd, as if I ne're had been,
And thus while I shall pass my silent days
In shady Privacy, free from the Noise
And busles of the World, then shall I
A good old Innocent Plebeian dy.
Death is a mere Surprize, a very Snare,
To him that makes it his lifes greatest care
To be a publick Pageant, known to All,
But unacquainted with Himself, doth fall.

JOHN DRYDEN (1631–1700) and
NATHANIEL LEE (?1649–1692)

This version of the Oedipus tragedy dates from 1679. Lee was an actor-turned-popular-playwright; he was confined to Bedlam for several years, and died after a drinking bout. In a preface to the play, Dryden writes of the poet's obligation in constructing Oedipus's story, and observes that Seneca, 'as if there were no such thing as Nature to be minded in a Play, is always running after pompous expression, pointed sentences, and Philosophical notions, more proper for the Study than the Stage'. Nevertheless, Dryden seems not to have hesitated to borrow from Seneca as he saw fit – especially in his inclusion of the ghost of Laius – while blending Seneca with other sources from his reading.

TIRESIAS: The Gods are just. –
   But how can Finite measure Infinite?
   Reason! alas, it does not know it self!
   Yet Man, vain Man, wou'd with this short-lin'd Plummet,
   Fathom the vast Abysse of Heav'nly justice.
   Whatever is, is in it's causes just;

Since all things are by Fate. But pur-blind Man
Sees but a part o'th' Chain; the nearest links;
His eyes not carrying to that equal Beam
That poizes all above.

EURYDICE: Then we must dye!

TIRESIAS: The danger's imminent this day.

ADRASTUS: Why then there's one day less for humane ills:
And who wou'd moan himself, for suffering that,
Which in a day must pass? something, or nothing –
I shall be what I was again, before
I was *Adrastus*; –
Penurious Heav'n, canst thou not add a night
To our one day? give me a night with her,
And I'll give all the rest.

TIRESIAS: She broke her vow
First made to *Creon*: but the time calls on:
And *Lajus* death must now be made more plain.
How loth I am to have recourse to Rites
So full of horrour, that I once rejoice
I want the use of Sight. –

1ST PRIEST: The Ceremonies stay.

TIRESIAS: Chuse the darkest part o'th' Grove;
Such as Ghosts at noon-day love.
Dig a Trench, and dig it nigh
Where the bones of *Lajus* lye.
Altars rais'd of Turf or Stone,
Will th' Infernal Pow'rs have none.
Answer me, if this be done?

ALL PRIESTS: 'Tis done.

TIRESIAS: Is the Sacrifice made fit?
Draw her backward to the pit:
Draw the barren Heyfer back;
Barren let her be and black.
Cut the curled hair that grows
Full betwixt her horns and brows:

And turn your faces from the Sun:
Answer me, if this be done?

ALL PRIESTS: 'Tis done.

TIRESIAS: Pour in blood, and blood like wine,
To Mother Earth and *Proserpine*:
Mingle Milk into the stream;
Feast the Ghosts that love the steam;
Snatch a brand from funeral pile;
Toss it in to make 'em boil;
And turn your faces from the Sun;
Answer me, if all be done?

ALL PRIESTS: All is done.

[*Peal of Thunder; and flashes of Lightning; then groaning below the Stage*]

MANTO: O, what Laments are those?

TIRESIAS: The groans of Ghosts, that cleave the Earth with pain,
And heave it up: they pant and stick half way.

[*The Stage wholly darken'd*]

MANTO: And now a sudden darkness covers all,
True genuine Night: Night added to the Groves;
The Fogs are blown full in the face of Heav'n.

TIRESIAS: Am I but half obey'd: Infernal Gods,
Must you have Musick too? then tune your voices,
And let 'em have such sounds as Hell ne're heard
Since *Orpheus* brib'd the Shades.

[*The Ghost of* LAJUS *rises arm'd in his Chariot, as he was slain. And behind his Chariot, sit the three who were Murder'd with him*]

GHOST OF LAJUS: Why hast thou drawn me from my pains below,
To suffer worse above? to see the day,
And *Thebes* more hated? Hell is Heav'n to *Thebes*.
For pity send me back, where I may hide,
In willing night, this Ignominious head:
In Hell I shun the publick scorn; and then

> They hunt me for their sport, and hoot me as I fly:
> Behold ev'n now they grin at my gor'd side,
> And chatter at my wounds.

TIRESIAS: I pity thee:
> Tell but why *Thebes* is for thy death accurst,
> And I'll unbind the Charm.

GHOST: O spare my shame.

TIRESIAS: Are these two innocent?

GHOST: Of my death they are.
> But he who holds my Crown, – Oh, must I speak! –
> Was doom'd to do what Nature most abhors.
> The Gods foresaw it; and forbad his being,
> Before he yet was born. I broke their laws,
> And cloath'd with flesh his pre-existing soul.
> Some kinder pow'r, too weak for destiny,
> Took pity, and indu'd his new-form'd Mass
> With Temperance, Justice, Prudence, Fortitude,
> And every Kingly vertue: but in vain.
> For Fate, that sent him hood-winckt to the world,
> Perform'd its work by his mistaking hands.
> Ask'st thou who murder'd me? 'twas *Oedipus*:
> Who stains my Bed with Incest? *Oedipus*:
> For whom then are you curst, but *Oedipus*!
> He comes; the Parricide: I cannot bear him:
> My wounds ake at him: Oh his murd'rous breath
> Venoms my aiery substance! hence with him,
> Banish him; sweep him out; the Plague he bears
> Will blast your fields, and mark his way with ruine.
> From *Thebes*, my Throne, my Bed, let him be driv'n;
> Do you forbid him Earth, and I'll forbid him Heav'n.
> [GHOST *descends.*
> *Enter* OEDIPUS, CREON, HÆMON, *&c.*]

OEDIPUS: What's this! methought some pestilential blast
> Strook me just entring; and some unseen hand
> Struggled to push me backward! tell me why
> My hair stands bristling up, why my flesh trembles!

You stare at me! then Hell has been among ye,
And some lag Fiend yet lingers in the Grove.

TIRESIAS: What Omen saw'st thou entring?

OEDIPUS: A young Stork,
That bore his aged Parent on his back;
Till weary with the weight, he shook him off,
And peck'd out both his eyes.

ADRASTUS: Oh, *Oedipus*!

EURYDICE: Oh, wretched *Oedipus*!

TIRESIAS: O! Fatal King!

OEDIPUS: What mean these Exclamations on my name?
I thank the Gods, no secret thoughts reproach me:
No: I dare challenge Heav'n to turn me outward,
And shake my Soul quite empty in your sight.
Then wonder not that I can bear unmov'd
These fix'd regards, and silent threats of eyes:
A generous fierceness dwells with innocence;
And conscious vertue is allow'd some pride.

TIRESIAS: Thou know'st not what thou say'st.

OEDIPUS: What mutters he! tell me, *Eurydice*:
Thou shak'st: thy souls a Woman. Speak, *Adrastus*;
And boldly as thou met'st my Arms in fight;
Dar'st thou not speak? why then 'tis bad indeed.
Tiresias, thee I summon by thy Priesthood,
Tell me what news from Hell: where *Lajus* points,
And who's the guilty head!

*

HÆMON: Thrice he struck,
With all his force, his hollow groaning breast,
And thus, with out-cries, to himself complain'd,
But thou canst weep then, and thou think'st 'tis well,
These bubbles of the shallowest emptiest sorrow,
Which Children vent for toys, and Women rain
For any Trifle their fond hearts are set on;
Yet these thou think'st are ample satisfaction

For bloudiest Murder, and for burning Lust:
No, Parricide; if thou must weep, weep bloud;
Weep Eyes, instead of Tears. O, by the Gods,
'Tis greatly thought, he cry'd, and fits my woes.
Which said, he smil'd revengefully, and leapt
Upon the floor; thence gazing at the Skies,
His Eye-balls fiery Red, and glowing vengeance,
Gods, I accuse you not, tho' I no more
Will view your Heav'n, till with more durable glasses,
The mighty Souls immortal Perspectives,
I find your dazling Beings. Take, he cry'd,
Take, Eyes, your last, your fatal farewel-view.
When with a groan, that seem'd the call of Death,
With horrid force lifting his impious hands,
He snatch'd, he tore, from forth their bloody Orbs
The Balls of sight, and dash'd 'em on the ground.
CREON: A Master-piece of horrour; new and dreadful!

JOHN CROWNE (?1640–?1703)

Crowne spent part of his youth in Nova Scotia, and went on to become a successful writer of tragedies. He collaborated with Dryden and Shadwell on the satire, *Notes and Observations*. He characterized his own work as 'successful, and yet clean'. His version of *Thyestes*, based directly on Seneca, dates from 1681.

Things are miscall'd, I ne're was blest till now –
When I was great, I had not one delight:
Who needs a Taster has small joy in taste:
Who needs a Guard for safety, ne're are safe:
And who needs watching, has but little rest.
What solitude so bad, as throngs of knaves
What dwelling so uneasie as is his,
Who in a thousand Rooms can take no rest;

Till his proud Palace has beat back a Sea,
And lifted up a Forrest on its brow?
Say Poyson come not in a Princes Cup,
Care will, and that's as bad; say Care shou'd not,
Intemperance may, which is as bad as both;
A ling'ry Poyson that consumes our time,
Our nights in drunkenness, our Days in sleep
Say he ne're see the bloody face of war,
A thousand Dishes are a dangerous Camp,
Where very often men have met with Death,
Among those fair pretended friends of life;
Nor is his rest the more for silent peace,
In Calms of peace, when all without is still,
Factions within will make a kingdom rowl.

ANDREW MARVELL (1621–1678)

This translation of the chorus of the second act of *Thyestes* was published in 1681.

Climb at court for me that will
Giddy favour's slippery hill;
All I seek is to lie still.
Settled in some secret nest,
In calm leisure let me rest,
And far off the public stage
Pass away my silent age.
Thus when without noise, unknown,
I have lived out all my span,
I shall die, without a groan,
An old honest countryman.
Who exposed to others' eyes,
Into his own heart ne'er pries,
Death to him's a strange surprise.

JOHN TALBOT (dates uncertain)

Talbot published his translation of *Troas* in 1686. In his preface, he claimed not to know of Rochester's translation of the second chorus till he had completed his own work, saying that 'my Lord's is a Paraphrase, and Mine only a Translation'. In this excerpt, the chorus maintains that everything perishes with the body, while the soul passes into the void. The purpose of these considerations is, as F.J. Miller explains, 'to discount the story that Achilles's shade could have appeared with its demand for the death of Polyxena' (*The Tragedies of Seneca*, Chicago, University of Chicago Press, 1907, p. 488).

> Is't true? Or does some Fear our minds deceive,
>   That Souls their Bodies do out live?
>   When any wretched Mortal dies,
>   And his sad Kindred close his Eyes,
>   Does not Death finish all his Pain,
>   But must he dye, to live again?
>   Or rather, when our Bodies dye,
>   And with our Breath, our Souls too flye,
> Is Death the End, and Cure of all our Misery?
>   Where're all-seeing Phaebus goes,
>   Where're the watry Ocean flows,
>   Nimbler than both, Time posts away;
>   Nor Gods, nor Men his Course can stay,
>   Swift, as the rapid Orbs are hurl'd;
>   Swift, as the Eye of this great World,
>   Our hasty Sand does downwards run,
>   Our Minutes fly, our Life is gone;
>   And when the slipp'ry Guest takes flight,
> The rest is long Oblivion, and eternal Night.
>   As Smoak dissolves into the Air,
>   And Winds drive Clouds we know not where:
>   So when poor Mortals breathe their last,
>   Their Souls exhale too in a blast;

And when the mighty Nothing disappears,
    Death crowns our hopes, and cures our fears.
What place must, after Death our Souls receive?
That, where we lay, e're we began to live.
    Our Souls, as well as Bodies, die;
And all is swallow'd up in vast Eternity.
    Pluto, Elysium, Cerberus are naught
But the loose Image of a shapeless Thought.
    The Poet's, not the Wiseman's Theam.
The wild Idea of an empty Dream.

SIR EDWARD SHERBURNE

(1618–1702)

Sherburne translated four of Seneca's tragedies 'in this ultimate Decline of my great Age (broken with undeserved Sufferings)' as a gift to an infant kinsman – they were published the year he died. Johnson, in his *Life of Dryden*, characterizes Sherburne as 'a man whose learning was greater than his powers of poetry; and who, being better qualified to give the meaning than the spirit of Seneca, has introduced his version of these tragedies by a defence of close translation'. In this introduction, Sherburne pithily characterizes Seneca's 'Political Lesson', which is 'That the hidden Malice of revengeful (though seemingly reconcil'd) Enemies, together with the flagitious, unbridled Lusts of dissolute Princes, have been the Ruin of most flourishing Kingdoms.' In this excerpt from *Medea*, Medea murders her children; Jason curses her as she escapes on a dragon-borne chariot.

Act V. Scene I

[*Enter* NUNCIUS *and* CHORUS]

NUNCIUS: All's lost! our Kingdom's Glory sunk in Fire;
 The Princely Daughter and her Royal Sire
 In blended Ashes lie.

CHORUS: Say how betray'd?

NUNCIUS: Ev'n by those usual Trains for Kings are laid.
 By Gifts.

CHORUS: In those what Treachery could be?

NUNCIUS: Nay, that's my wonder: Nor, tho' th' Fact I see,
 Can my Belief receive't for possible.

CHORUS: The manner of so strange a Ruine tell.

NUNCIUS: As 'twas commanded, the devouring Flame
 Assaults each part o'th' Palace: the whole Frame
 In pieces falls; and now we fear the Town.

CHORUS: The raging Flames with thrown-on Water drown.

NUNCIUS: Ev'n that Astonishment and Wonder breeds
 In this Disaster, Fire on Water feeds;
 The more supprest, the more it burns; and grows
 By that which to extinguish we impose.

Scene II

[*Enter* MEDEA, *and her* NURSE]

NURSE: Fly! fly, *Medea*! quickly hence be gone,
 And seek with speed some other Region.

MEDEA: How should we fly! – No; were we fled, to see
 This Day, we would return again; to be
 Spectatress of these Gallant Nuptials. – Heart!
 Dost stop? pursue thy happy Rage; this part

Of thy enjoy'd Revenge, what is't? – Distraught!
Dost thou yet love? is widowed *Jason* thought
Sufficient? work, *Medea*, work! invent
Some strange unusual kind of Punishment.
Hence with all Right, expulsed Shame be gone.
That's poor Revenge, which Hands yet pure have done.
Be all intent on Wrath; bravely excite
Thy drooping Thoughts, and with more eager Might
Rouze up th' old sparks of Rage hid in thy Breast.
What we have done already, to the rest
W'intend, may be call'd Piety: now ply't;
Let the World know how vulgar and how slight
Our former Ills were, but as Preludes to
Ensuing Rage. What could such rude Hands do,
Might be term'd great? or by a Girl be shown?
We're now *Medea*; our Invention grown,
As our Ills multiply'd. Now, now we're joy'd,
We lopt our Brother's Head, and did divide
His bleeding Limbs; that we our Father spoil'd
Of his Crowns sacred Treasure; and beguil'd
Daughters to take up parricidal Arms.
Seek matter for thy Fury, for all Harms
That brings a Hand prepar'd. – Wrath whither, oh!
Transported art thou? 'Gainst what treach'rous Foe
Intend'st these Weapons? – Something my fierce Mind,
But what I know not, hath within design'd,
Nor dares t'her self disclos't – Fool, I have been
Too fondly rash. Oh that I could have seen
Some Children of the Strumpet got! – What's thine
By *Jason* think *Creusa* bore. This kind
Of Vengeance likes; and likes deservedly.
The height of Ills, with a Resolve as high
Attempt: You, we did once our Children call,
For your Sire's Crimes a Satisfaction fall,
– Horror invades my Heart; an icy Cold
Stiffens my Limbs; my Breast pants; Wrath his hold

Hath left, and there (a Wive's stern Passions quit)
A Mother's soft restor'd Affections sit.
We in our Childrens Blood our hands imbrue?
Ah! better Thoughts distracted Griefs pursue!
Far be it from *Medea* yet, to act
So foul a Sin, or so abhor'd a Fact.
What Crime, poor Wretches! shall they suffer for?
– Their Father's Crime enough, and greater far
Their Mother. Let 'em die, they're none of mine.
Hold! they're thine own: then perish because thine.
Alas! they're innocent: without a touch
Of Guilt: 'tis true; my Brother too was such.
Why stagger'st thou my Soul? or why do Tears
Water my Cheeks? whilst Passion this way bears
My wav'ring Mind, now that way Love divides;
Toss'd in an Eddy of uncertain Tides.
As when the Winds wage war, the passive Waves
Are counter-rockt, the Sea a Neuter raves.
So floats my wreckt Heart; now Wrath wins the Field,
Now Piety; to Piety Wrath yield.
Oh! you, the only Joy and Comfort left
Of our sad State! now of all else bereft;
Come hither, my dear Children! and with mine
Your little Arms in close Embraces join.
May in your Lives your Father yet delight,
Whilst I your Mother may – Exile and Flight
Inforce me on: strait from my Arms with Cries
Will they be torn; then perish from all Joys
Of Father as of Mother. Grief again
Renews; my Hate boils high, my heated Brain
Its old Rage fires, and stirs m'abhorred Hand
Up to new Mischief. On then, thy Command
We follow. Would an Issue from my Womb
As numerous as *Niobe*'s had come.
And twice seven Children had from us deriv'd
Their Births: our Barrenness hath ev'n depriv'd

Our Vengeance; yet w'have two: enough t'expire
As Victims to our Brother and our Sire.
– Whither does this dire Troop of Furies bend?
Whom seek they? where their fiery Strokes intend?
'Gainst whom shake they their bloody Brands? Snakes
    wound
In lashing Whips with horrid Hisses sound.
Whom does *Megæra* with infestive post
Pursue? what yet unknown dismember'd Ghost,
Is this appears? 'ts my Brother's, come to crave
Vengeance of us; and Vengeance shalt thou have.
But first, fix all these Fire-brands in my Eyes;
Tear, burn; my Breast to Furies open lies.
Hence these dread Ministers of Vengeance send,
And bid these Spirits satisfi'd descend.
Leave me to my self, Brother; to imploy
This Arm in thy revenge, that did destroy
Thy Life; thus with this Victim we appease
Thy injur'd Ghost. – What suddain Sounds are these?
What means this Noise? – Arms 'gainst my Life are bent.
Up to the Houses top force thy Ascent:
Finish thy Murder there. Come you with me
My small Companion: whilst this Body we
Convey along. Now, Soul, thy task intend,
Nor thy brave Mischief unregarded end
In secret; shew't the People, let them stand,
Th' amaz'd Spectators of thy Tragick hand.

Scene III

[*Enter* JASON, *cum Armatis*]

JASON: You whom the Murder of your Prince doth move
    With sad Resentments of a loyal Love,
    The Author of that execrable Deed
    Help to surprize; hither with Weapons speed

You armed Cohorts, here this House surround,
And lay the Fabrick level with the Ground.

MEDEA: Ay, now our Sceptre, Brother, Sire, again
W'enjoy, and *Colchans* their rich Spoil retain.
Our Kingdom and our lost Virginity
Are now restor'd: O long cross Destiny
At length grown kind! O festive Nuptials! On,
Give thy Revenge, as Crime, Perfection.
Dispatch while thy hand's in. – Why thus delays
My Soul? what Doubts? – Our potent Wrath decays;
Now of the Fact a shameful Penitent.
What have I done? Wretch! such tho I repent,
I've don't; an ample Joy m'unwilling Heart
Seizes: it grows upon me. Yet this part
Of Vengeance wanted, he not being here,
Nor a Spectator; without whom whate'er
W've done, is lost.

JASON: See where she sits, upon
Yon Houses shelving top! hither some one
Bring burning Brands, and Fire impose on Fire;
That scorch'd in her own Flames she may expire.

MEDEA: Do, raise your Sons a Fun'ral Pile; your Bride
And Father-in-law, our Kindness did provide
With Rites of Sepulture. His Doom this Son
Hath felt; the like shall this, whilst thou look'st on.

JASON: By all the Gods! by our Community
Of Flight and Bed, which uninforced I
Ne'er violated: spare this Child; O spare
Me this: the Crime is mine, then let me share
The Punishment; and let deserved Death,
Seize on my guilty Head, and loathed Breath.

MEDEA: No; where thou would'st not ha't, where thou dost
feel
Most Sense of Sorrow, will we force our Steel.
Go now, thou proud Insulter, go and wed
Young Virgins now, and leave a Mother's Bed.

JASON: Let one suffice t'have suffer'd.

MEDEA: If our Rage
    One Death, or single Slaughter could asswage
    We none had sought; and tho both die, yet that
    T'our Wrongs is not Revenge commensurate;
    If in our Womb a Pledge there be, ev'n there
    This Steel shall search't, and thence the *Embrion* tear.

JASON: Dispatch thy Villany; no more we crave:
    An End at least now let our Suff'rings have.

MEDEA: Haste not my Grief; but leisurely imploy
    Thy slow Revenge. This Day's our own; w'enjoy
    Th'accepted time.

JASON: Death, cruel! we implore,
    Kill me.

MEDEA: Thou Pity crav'st. All's done; nor more
    Had we (O Sorrow!) as a Sacrifice
    To offer thee. Erect thy humid Eyes,
    Ingrateful *Jason*, here look up; dost know
    Thy Wife? thus use we to escape: Heav'ns show
    Our flight clear way; see both our Dragons here,
    Who freely stoop their scaly Necks to bear
    Their willing Yoke. Now take your Sons, whilst I
    On winged Wheels through Airy Regions fly.

JASON: Go, thro' the high Ætherial Stages post,
    And shew there are no Gods where'er thou go'st.

MATTHEW PRIOR (1664–1721)

Educated at Cambridge, he became a secret agent for the Tories and
was sent to Paris in 1711 while the Treaty of Utrecht was being
negotiated. When Queen Anne died, he was recalled and imprisoned.
He is remembered for his epigrams and occasional verse. The following
is his version of the chorus from the second act of *Troas* (1708). After
this is a poem by Prior about Seneca, based on a portrait of him.

Is it a truth, or but a well told lye,
That Souls have being, when their Bodyes dye.
When the Sad Wife, has closed her Husbands Eyes
And pierct the Ecchoing Vaults with Doleful Cryes,
Is not the Husbands life entirely fled,
His Soul extinguisht, as His Body dead;
Or does that other part of Him remain
Still chain'd to life, and Still condemn'd to pain?
No, No, before Our Friends officious Care,
Can light the Torch and Solemn rites prepare,
Our Breath is mixt, and lost, with common Air,
As far as East or West extended go,
As far as Sun beams Gild or Waters flow,
All beings have a Destin'd Space to run,
And All must Perish, as they all begun.
The Sun, the Moon, and every Sign above
Fixt by Strong Fate, in destind Courses move.
Like Us for certain Periods they endure,
Their life much longer, but their end as sure.
As Smoke which rises from the Kindling Fires
Is seen this moment, and the next Expires;
As Empty Clouds by rising Winds are tost,
Their fleeting forms Scarse sooner found, than lost,
So Vanishes Our State, so pas Our days,
So life but opens now and now decays
The Cradle and the Tomb alas! so nigh
To live is scarce distinguisht from to dye.
After Death nothing Is, and very Death,
It's self is nothing, 'tis but want of Breath;
The utmost Limit of a Narrow Span,
And End of motion which with life began.
Death Shows Us only what we know was near,
It cures the Misers Wish, and Checks the Cowards fear,
Where shalt thou be when thou art laid in Earth
Where wert thou Timorous thing, before thy Birth?

Disolv'd in Chaos, in the formless Mass,
Of what may be contending with what was,
Old Night and Death extend their Noxious Power,
O'er All the Man, the Body they Devour;
Nor spare the Soul, a Kingdom in the Dark
Furies that howl, three headed Dogs that bark,
Are empty Rumors formed in Childrens Schools
The Tales of Pedants, and the Dreams of Fools.

Picture of Seneca dying in a Bath.
By Jordain.
At the Right Honourable the Earl of Exeter's at Burleigh-House.

While cruel NERO only drains
The moral SPANIARD's ebbing Veins,
By Study worn, and slack with Age,
How dull, how thoughtless is his Rage!
Heighten'd Revenge He should have took;
He should have burnt his Tutor's Book;
And long have reign'd supream in Vice:
One nobler Wretch can only rise;
'Tis he whose Fury shall deface
The Stoic's Image in this Piece.
For while unhurt, divine JORDAIN,
Thy Work and SENECA's remain,
He still has Body, still has Soul,
And lives and speaks, restor'd and whole.

INTERIM SENECA

INTRODUCTION

The influence of Seneca's tragedies, so strongly felt during the Renaissance, all but vanished by the Restoration and the eighteenth century. Only Dryden had any serious interest in the plays as dramatic works, an interest illuminated by the epilogue to his and Nathaniel Lee's *Oedipus* (ll. 1–6).

> What Sophocles could undertake alone,
> Our Poets found a Work for more than one;
> And therefore two lay tugging at the piece,
> With all their force, to draw the ponderous mass from *Greece*,
> A weight that bent ev'n *Seneca*'s strong Muse,
> And which *Corneille*'s shoulders did refuse.

Rochester produced a chorus, yet Pope and Swift passed over the plays in silence. That Samuel Johnson used Seneca's plays the way others had the prose works, as a source for mottoes, is typical of a period during which Seneca's oratorial impressiveness was seen to reside more in his short phrases than in the whole dramas (indeed, Prior's 'Picture of Seneca' (1718) literally reduced Seneca to an 'Image'!). Charles Wheelwright's (1810) were the only full translations into English verse of any of Seneca's plays to appear between 1702 and 1904, and these, unlike their predecessors, were never performed and scarcely read. What accounts for this long interim during which Senecan influence had become so attenuated?

One consideration is the political climate in which English literature was being produced. The early translators, adapters, and imitators of Seneca had reasons, as Eliot pointed out, for adding 'political innuendo to Senecan moralizing on the vanity of place and power' (*Selected Essays*, San Diego, Harcourt Brace Jovanovich, 1951, p. 87). H. A. Mason contrasts the 'perilous situation' of Renaissance poets such as Wyatt with 'the comparative security of gentlemen in Restoration England' (*Humanism and Poetry in the Early Tudor Period*, London, Routledge and Kegan Paul, 1959, p. 185). That during the eighteenth and nineteenth centuries England had no authoritarianism or terror must be a factor. Moreover, as Gilbert Highet suggests, the Renaissance was followed by the beginning of a 'revolutionary age', in which 'systems of thought which had been in existence for centuries' had become less vital, and more conventional:

The Renaissance meant the assimilation of Latin, while the revolutionary era meant a closer approach to Greek. Men of the Renaissance, like Montaigne, would speak of 'the ancients', but in practice think of the Romans . . . This attitude was now reversed. What stimulated Keats was Homer, more than Vergil . . . When Shelley and Goethe decided to write great plays, they thought nothing of Seneca, but strove to emulate Aeschylus and Euripides.

(*The Classical Tradition: Greek and Roman Influences on Western Literature*,
New York and London, Oxford University Press, 1949, p. 360)

Though they were well aware of him – both Coleridge's and Words-worth's signature appear on a copy of *L. Annaei Senecae philosophi, et M. Senecae rhetoris quae extant opera* (Antwerp, 1609) – the English Romantics had very little use for Seneca. Coleridge sometimes jotted down aphorisms from Seneca's prose and plays, and in a letter of 27 October 1826 he listed Seneca among writers who had 'a sort of *memorandum* character' that was essentially Roman. But in 1830, he remarked that 'You may get a motto for every sect or line of thought or religion from Seneca – yet nothing is ever thought out in him' (*Table Talk*, II, *Collected Works*, vol. 12, London, Routledge and Kegan Paul, 1969, p. 171). In all his verse, meanwhile, Wordsworth only appended a snippet from one of Seneca's *Moral Epistles* to the 'Ode to Duty' years after composing it, and quoted Samuel Daniel's quotation of Seneca in a few lines of *The Excursion*.

Saintsbury, writing of Daniel in 1885, tried to explain why Daniel, 'almost alone, amidst a generation of learned persons', had any interest in Seneca *tragicus* (Samuel Daniel, *Complete Works*, New York, Russell and Russell, 1963, vol. III, p. xi):

The peculiarity of the Senecan tragedy is to be found, first, in its exact and careful form; secondly, in the prominence which it gives to moral over romantic interest; thirdly, in the simplicity of its plot and situations. The precepts which Horace drew from the Greek drama seem to have been worked out in it almost without reference to the original material, except in points of form. It is entirely a school drama, an exercise in literature. It knew no sort of condescension to the audience: the audience were expected to make all the advances. Hardly any more words are needed to show how utterly opposed it is to our own form of play . . .   (p. ix)

He reflected that when Seneca's tragedies

took the French stage by storm, in the middle of the sixteenth century, and held it in their simple form till the first quarter of the seventeenth, in a very slightly changed form till the first quarter of the nineteenth, they had to deal with a people at least as fond of dramatic shows as the English, and even more generally accustomed to a rough but lively variety of them. Why was one people taken and the other left? Why did Seneca take captive the whole drama of France, from Jodelle, through Garnier and Montchrestien and even Hardy, through Corneille and Racine and Voltaire, leaving his traces even on Victor Hugo?   (p. x)

He declined to answer, deciding that 'It is not my business to answer these questions, for which of course I or any one else could give not one but half a dozen elaborate and more or less unsatisfactory answers.'

If we turn to Hazlitt for further guidance, we find a detailed recapitulation of 'our learned critic' Schlegel's remarks on Seneca:

whatever period may have given birth to the tragedies of Seneca, they are beyond description bombastical and frigid, unnatural in character and action – revolting, from their violation of every propriety – and so destitute of every thing like theatrical effect – that I am inclined to believe they were never destined to leave the rhetorical schools for the stage. Every tragical common-place is spun out to the very last; all is phrase; and even the most common remark is delivered in stilted language. The most complete poverty of sentiment is dressed out with wit and acuteness. There is even a display of fancy in them, *or at least a phantom of it*; for they contain an example of the mis-application of every mental faculty. The author or authors have found out the secret of being diffuse, even to wearisomeness; and at the same time so epigrammatically laconic, as to be often obscure and unintelligible. Their characters are neither ideal nor actual beings, but gigantic puppets, who are at one time put in motion by the string of an unnatural heroism, and, at another, by that of passions equally unnatural, which no guilt nor enormity can appal. – 'Yet not merely learned men, without a feeling for art, have judged favourably of them, nay preferred them to the Greek tragedies, but even poets have accounted them deserving of their study and imitation.'

> (William Hazlitt, *Complete Works*, ed. P. P. Howe, New York,
> AMS Press, 1967, vol. 16, p. 78)

As Hazlitt himself admits, these remarks are 'exceedingly harsh, dogmatical, and intolerant' – as bad, and worse, than the sentence pronounced by Cowley on 'The dry chips of short-lung'd Seneca'.

By 1884, Seneca's influence in English could itself be described in a phrase: Symonds, writing about Shakespeare's predecessors, dispensed with them as 'Senecasters of the purest water' – a coinage which wormed its way into the *OED*. Meanwhile, Seneca had fallen from the school syllabus. In 1907, however, Frank Justus Miller translated all of Seneca's tragedies, explaining that, stimulated by Fredericus Leo's text edition and researches into the influence of Seneca upon the Elizabethans, popular interest in them had been growing. Calling them 'the only connecting link between ancient and modern tragedy', Miller wrote that he sought for his edition 'to bring Seneca back to the notice of classical scholars, and at the same time to present to the English reader all of the values accruing from a study' of them; he produced versions for the Loeb Classical Library in 1917.

It would be left to T. S. Eliot to examine such 'values'. In *The Egoist* for July 1919 ('Reflections on Contemporary Poetry'), Eliot complained that 'contemporary poetry' was 'deficient in tradition', and discussed ways in which 'dead voices speak through the living voice'; Seneca figured directly in the discussion. Describing 'the *saturation* which sometimes combusts spontaneously into originality' he says that

> fly where men feel
> The cunning axletree: and those that suffer
> Beneath the chariot of the snowy Bear

is beautiful; and the beauty only appears more substantial if we conjecture that Chapman may have absorbed the recurring phrase of Seneca in

> signum celsi glaciale poli
> septem stellis Arcados ursae
> lucem verso termone vocat . . .
> > sub cardine
> glacialis ursae . . .

a union, at a point at least, of the Tudor and the Greek through the Senecan phrase.

By 1927, Eliot had written two full essays in which he explored Senecan influence. In 'Seneca', he noted that 'in modern times, few Latin authors have been more consistently damned' than Seneca; the prose Seneca 'still enjoys a measure of tepid praise, though he has no influence' (*Selected Essays*, p. 52). Observing that 'Latin literature provides poets for several tastes, but there is no taste for Seneca', Eliot explored the 'damaging' view that Senecan influence resulted in a predominance of declamatory rhetoric – which F. L. Lucas (*Seneca and Elizabethan Tragedy*, Cambridge, Cambridge University Press, 1922, p.55) described as 'exasperatingly false . . . with its far-fetched and frigid epigrams' – that would characterize Western drama from the Renaissance until the latter half of the nineteenth century. Eliot argued that such criticism could be attenuated by considering that Senecan drama was not intended for stage performance, but for private decla-mation: 'In the plays of Seneca, the drama is all in the word, and the word has no further reality behind it' other than the 'Latin sensibility which is expressed by the Latin language' (pp. 53–4): 'We should think of the long ranting speeches of Seneca, the beautiful but irrelevant descriptions, the smart stichomythia, rather as peculiarities of Latin than as the bad taste of the dramatist' (p. 57). As for deciding whether Seneca's English successors 'profited by the study' of his works, 'or whether they admired him and pillaged him to their own detriment, we must remember that we cannot justly estimate his influence unless we form our own opinion of Seneca first, without being influenced by his influence' (p. 61).

In this formulation, 'the English playwright was under the influence of Seneca by being under the influence of his own predecessors' (p. 63). Translations of Seneca consequently 'possess a particular value: whether they greatly affected the conception of Seneca, or greatly expanded his influence, they give a reflection of the appearance of Seneca to the Englishman of the time'. Eliot therefore found Senecan influence to be of more than documentary interest, since it represented the transformation of an older form of versification into a new, 'consequently the transformation of language and sensibility as well' (p. 84).

In 'Shakespeare and the Stoicism of Seneca', Eliot, distinguishing again between Seneca's work and its influence, writes of the 'continuity' as well as the 'violent contrast' (p. 114) which characterized the relationship between Seneca and the Elizabethans: 'The influence of Seneca on Elizabethan drama has been exhaustively studied in its formal aspect, and in the borrowing and adaptation of phrases and situations; the penetration of Senecan sensibility would be much more difficult to trace' (p. 120).

Ezra Pound, responding to Eliot's interest in and use of Seneca, commented drily that 'The time to be interested in Seneca may possibly have been before Mr. Shakespeare had written his plays.' He remarks that Eliot, 'applying what he has learned by being bored with as much of the rest of Seneca as he has bothered to read, is a vastly more vital Eliot, and a much more intensively critical Eliot than when complying with the exigencies of the present and verminous system for the excernment of book-reviews' (*Selected Prose, 1909–1965*, New York, New Directions, 1973, p. 399). (Elsewhere, Pound had written that 'the criticism of Seneca in Mr. Eliot's *Agon* is infinitely more alive, more vigorous than in his essay on Seneca' [*Literary Essays*, New York, New Directions, 1954, p. 75]; see Eliot's pieces in this book.) Pound distinguished between the critic and the poet: he had compiled *How to Read* for the 'specialist and practising writer' (*Selected Prose*, p. 396), and disapproved of the 'bureaucracy' of professors and students who might prefer more 'yatter' than 'exhibit' in an anthology. Pound was therefore troubled when Eliot inclined, for example, to a 'Christian interpretation' of a Senecan passage: 'I can't personally see that the old half-bore goes further than asserting that the gods are not in that particular district of the aether' (ibid.): it is evidence of Eliot's 'condescensions to the demands of British serial publication' (ibid. p. 394). William Empson, however, writing about Eliot establishing his position in the *Times Literary Supplement* – 'which was then wholly anonymous and chillingly learned' (*Argufying: Essays on Literature and Culture*, ed. John Haffenden, Iowa City, University of Iowa Press, 1987, p. 365) – gives an anecdote showing how Eliot could feel that the scholars 'deserved to have their legs pulled'. Having been asked to identify the Latin quotation which introduces 'Marina' (1930), Empson consulted a fellow poet, Ronald Bottrall.

He said, 'If it's poetry it's very unclassical poetry. It might be Seneca, for instance. In fact, it actually is from *Hercules Furens*,' and he raised his eyes from the paper, 'My God what a thing.'

Eliot's response:

I didn't know Bottrall was a scholar. Seneca isn't in the school syllabus, so all the classical men were caught out.

Yet in a letter to E. McKnight Kauffer, who provided drawings which accompanied the poem in a pamphlet, Eliot made it plain that his use of the Senecan epigraph constituted more than leg-pulling:

I dont [*sic*] know whether it is any good at all. The theme is paternity; with a criss-cross between the text and the quotation. The theme is a comment on the Recognition Motive in Shakespeare's later plays, and particularly of course the recognition of Pericles. The quotation is from 'Hercules Furens', where Hercules, having killed his children in a fit of madness induced by an angry god, comes to without remembering what he has done. (I didn't give the reference for fear it might be more distracting than helpful to the reader who did not grasp the exact point): the contrast of death and life in Hercules and Pericles . . .

(quoted in B. C. Southam, *A Student's Guide to the Selected Poems of T. S. Eliot*, 6th edn, Faber, 1990, p. 247)

The Stoic doctrine of *sumpatheia* held that different parts of the universe interact harmoniously; it was a view which Seneca's first English translators, under the influence of the Christian Church, modified (see

John Kerrigan, *Revenge Tragedy: Aeschylus to Armageddon*, London, Oxford University Press, 1996, pp. 112–13). Eliot, inaugurating a modern era in which interest in Seneca has greatly revived, established a kind of literary doctrine of *sumpatheia*: writers of various times and cultures intersect – 'criss-cross', to use his term – within the universe of the written word. It is a belief, outlined in 'Tradition and the Individual Talent' (1919), which saturates his own influential work, and helps explain how English-language writers in modern times could reach back, through a period in which Senecan drama was scarcely recognized, into the history of their own literature, in which Seneca had played such an important part.

SIR RICHARD BLACKMORE
(1654–1729)

Blackmore was a physician to Queen Anne and author of much lengthy verse mocked by Pope in his *Dunciad*. Dr Johnson, however, insisted that he be included in an edition of the works of the English poets; Johnson, in a preface to Blackmore's work published separately in the *Lives of the English Poets*, said of Blackmore that he, 'by the unremitted enmity of the wits, whom he provoked more by his virtue than his dulness, has been exposed to worse treatment than he deserved'. 'The Safety of Low State' (1718) is adapted from *Agamemnon*.

The Safety of Low State

The treach'rous Fortune of a Royal Crown
    Places whatever's Rich and Great,
    On a steep and slipp'ry seat;
Whence with an easy Blast all tumbles down.
Proud Monarchs can't command soft Peace and rest,
    Nor chase uneasy Fears away,
    They know no safe and happy Day,
But painful cares their Greatness still molest.

The Lybian Sea ne'er with such Fury raves,
    When new collected Hills of Sand
    Heap'd up by Tempests tott'ring stand,
And interrupt the loud impetuous waves.
Euxinus, Neighbour to the Snowy Pole,
    Where the bright Carman by the Main
    Untouch'd drives round his shining wain,
Can't with such Force his troubled Waters roll;

As when Kings fall, turn'd round by rapid Fate,
        Kings, whose Desire is to appear
        Awful to move their subjects Fear,
Which Fear must be in themselves the like create.
The Night, to hide them safe, do's Darkness want,
        Soft Sleep, by which a troubled Breast
        Is sooth'd, and lies dissolv'd in Rest,
Can't charm the anxious Cares, that Princes haunt,

The Men, who born by too kind Fortune rise,
        Soon sink and fall down from their Height,
        Prest by their own unequal Weight,
Whom those, who envy'd them, as much despise.
Great Fortunes can't their own vast Burden bear,
        So the swift ship's expanded Sails,
        Swol'n out with too indulgent Gales,
The Winds, they wish'd before, begin to fear.

So a proud Tow'r thrusts his aspiring Head
        Among the flying Clouds, but finds
        Th' uneasy Neighbourhood of Winds,
And Thunder-Claps, that are around him bred.
So the rude Storms that shake the bending Wood,
        Design an envious, fatal Stroke
        At the ancient well-spread Oak,
The Grove's Defence and Glory, while it stood.

High Hills, the fairest Mark for Thunder stand,
        Great Bodies are but seldom found,
        Such have most room to take a Wound,
And the fat Deer invites the Huntsman's Hand.
What fickle Fortune do's this Day advance,
        It throws down with a greater Fall;
        Estates, that are but low and small,
Last a long quiet Age secure from Chance.

He's only happy, who of meaner Rank,
    Will ne'er his humble State resent,
    But always in his Fate content,
With a safe Wind sails by the Neighb'ring Bank;
Whose wary Boat, that dares not trust the Oar
    To the rough Usage of the Wind,
    And the wide Ocean seldom kind,
Keeps still in prospect of the safer Shore.

LEWIS THEOBALD (1688–1744)

A Shakespeare scholar as well as poet and playwright, Theobald famously exposed Pope's incompetence in editing Shakespeare, earning himself a place in the *Dunciad*. Many of his corrections to the texts of Shakespeare still stand. Oddly, he claimed to have revised and adapted for the stage a lost Shakespeare play called *Cardenio*. This Senecan epigram is from *The Double Falsehood*, his version of this play, and comes from *Hercules Furens*, 84. Pope, in *The Art of Sinking in Poetry* (1727), singled out this line for ridicule, calling it 'Profundity itself . . . unless it may seem borrow'd from the Thought of that Master of a Show in Smithfield, who writ in large Letters, over the Picture of his Elephant, *This is the greatest Elephant in the world, except* Himself.'

None but himself can be his parallel.

SAMUEL JOHNSON (1709–1784)

Johnson produced these translations of Seneca as epigrams in 1751 and 1753.

Rambler No. 106. Saturday, 23 March 1751

> Non unquam dedit
> Documenta fors majora, quam fragili loco
> Starent superbi. SENECA, *Troades*, l. 4

Insulting chance ne'er call'd with louder voice,
On swelling mortals to be proud no more.

Rambler No. 178. Saturday, 30 November 1751

Pars sanitatis velle sanari fuit.
SENECA, *Hippolytus/Phaedra*, l. 248

To yield to remedies is half the cure.

Motto for Rambler No. 130. 15 June 1751

Johnson rewrote Elphinston's translation of Seneca's *Hippolytus/Phaedra*, 761–71, for the motto of *Rambler* 130, altering it so much that it is almost a new poem. Elphinston wrote:

No mist so blights the vernal meads,
When summer's sultry heat succeeds,
As one fell moment blasts the blow
That gave the tender cheek to glow.

Some beauty's snatch'd each day, each hour;
For beauty is a fleeting flow'r:
Then who that's wise, will e'er confide
In such a frail, so poor a pride?

Reprinted in *The Poems of Samuel Johnson*, ed. D. Nichol Smith and
E. L. McAdam. Jr. (Oxford, Clarendon Press, 1941, p. 382)

Not faster in the summer's ray
The spring's frail beauty fades away,
Than anguish and decay consume
The smiling virgin's rosy bloom.
Some beauty's snatch'd each day, each hour;
For beauty is a fleeting flow'r:
Then how can wisdom e'er confide
In beauty's momentary pride?

Rambler No. 40. Saturday, 24 March 1753

Solvite tantis animum monstris,
Solvite, Superi; rectam in melius
Vertite mentem.   SENECA, *Hercules Furens*, l. 1063

O! save ye Gods, omnipotent and kind,
From such abhor'd chimeras save the mind!
In truth's strait path no hideous monsters roar;
To truth's strait path the wand'ring mind restore.

Rambler No. 62. Saturday, 9 June 1753

O fortuna viris invida fortibus
Quam non aequa bonis praemia dividis.
                         SENECA, *Hercules Furens*, l. 524
Capricious fortune ever joys,
With partial hand to deal the prize,
To crush the brave and cheat the wise.

CHARLES APTHORP
WHEELWRIGHT (d. 1858)

Wheelwright translated several of Seneca's tragedies; they appeared in an edition of his work published in 1810. In this excerpt from *Octavia*, Seneca speaks as himself, concerned with the events of AD 62, when Nero became enamoured of Poppaea, who later invented a false accusation of adultery against Nero's wife, Octavia.

SENECA: Why, potent Fortune, have thy treach'rous smiles
    Allur'd my steps from low security,
    To where, upon the tow'ring eminence,
    Sits dark distrust, and thousand nameless fears,
    To antedate my ruin? Better still,
    Amid the rocks of Corsica, remote
    From rankling envy, to have pass'd the hours
    In happy, though inglorious, solitude –
    Reflecting on this universal world,
    The greatest work of the great Architect!
    The heav'nly vault, the sweet vicissitude
    Of light and dark, the lunar orb serene,
    Encircled with her starry diadem,
    And day's refulgent eye, doom'd to relapse
    In elemental chaos – Lo! thy hour
    Is fast approaching; shrink, devoted Earth,
    Shrink, impious Mortals, from th' impending crash
    Of orbs unnumber'd. Lo! the brighter day,
    Glad herald of a race more innocent,
    Dawns from the wreck of nature. As of old,
    When Saturn sway'd the Heav'ns, and sacred Faith
    With Justice, twin and virgin Deities,
    Left their celestial seats and rul'd the earth
    In mild conjunction – then no trumpet's blast
    To kindred slaughter rous'd the human race –

No jealous wall secur'd the peaceful town;
But ev'ry path to ev'ry step was free,
And all was common; then the joyful land
Pour'd the rich treasures from her teeming lap
Spontaneous – soon a hardier race succeeds,
Urg'd by a third, for piety renown'd,
And arts unknown before – the next, more skill'd
In restless turbulence, to chase the deer;
To drag, in treach'ous net, the scaly train
From out their native wave: with limed reed
To guile the airy choristers; to bend
Ferocious bulls beneath the iron yoke;
With unaccustom'd wounds to tear the earth;
And force the injur'd Mother to conceal,
Deep in her sacred breast, from murd'rous Man
The embryo treasures. Soon the bolder age
From her vex'd entrails dragg'd the iron forth,
And strife-promoting gold – then arm'd their hands
With slaught'rous weapons: rear'd the tow'ring wall;
Hemm'd in by narrow bounds the guarded realm,
And plied their weapons, unprovok'd by wrong,
Venal alike for rapine or defence.
Then first Astræa, Heav'n's bright ornament,
On earth neglected, sought her native sphere,
Scar'd at the blood-polluted race of Man –
Then rag'd the thirst of slaughter and of gold,
While luxury, a soft, but deadly pest,
By error nourish'd, and confirm'd by time,
Spread through the tainted land. From age to age
To us the congregated vices flow,
And find a welcome here. In our rank soil
Rage hideous vice and mad impiety;
Now av'rice grasps in her insatiate hands,
Devote to waste, the riches of the world.

LEIGH HUNT (1784–1859)

Poet, dramatist, essayist, and editor, Hunt was a friend and supporter to Keats and Tennyson. This translation of a chorus from *Thyestes* is from 1814.

'Tis not wealth that makes a king,
Nor the purple's colouring,
Nor a brow that's bound with gold,
Nor gates on mighty hinges rolled.

The king is he, who void of fear,
Looks abroad with bosom clear;
Who can tread ambition down,
Nor be sway'd by smile or frown;
Nor for all the treasure cares,
That mine conceals, or harvest wears,
Or that golden sands deliver,
Bosom'd in a glassy river.

What shall move his placid might?
Not the headlong thunderlight,
Nor the storm that rushes out
To snatch the shivering waves about,
Nor all the shapes of slaughter's trade
With forward lance or fiery blade.
Safe, with wisdom on his crown,
He looks on all things calmly down;
He welcomes fate, when fate is near,
Nor taints his dying breath with fear.

WILLIAM WORDSWORTH

(1770–1850)

Wordsworth quoted Samuel Daniel quoting Seneca in Book IV of *The Excursion*, 1814. Thirty-three years after writing 'Ode to Duty' (1805), Wordsworth added a motto from Seneca's description of a virtuous man in *Moral Epistles* CXX, 10, which illuminates the poem's Senecan tone.

> To see the moment, when the righteous cause
> Shall gain defenders zealous and devout
> As they who have opposed her; in which Virtue
> Will, to her efforts, tolerate no bounds
> That are not lofty as her rights; aspiring
> By impulse of her own ethereal zeal.
> That spirit only can redeem mankind;
> And when that sacred spirit shall appear,
> Then shall *our* triumph be complete as theirs.
> Yet, should this confidence prove vain, the wise
> Have still the keeping of their proper peace;
> Are guardians of their own tranquillity.
> They act, or they recede, observe, and feel;
> 'Knowing the heart of man is set to be
> The centre of this world, about the which
> Those revolutions of disturbances
> Still roll; where all the aspects of misery
> Predominate; whose strong effects are such
> As he must bear, being powerless to redress;
> *And that unless above himself he can*
> *Erect himself, how poor a thing is man!'*
>
> (*The Excursion*, Book IV, ll. 311–31)

Ode to Duty [*Composed 1805. – Published 1807.*]

'Jam non consilio bonus, sed more eò perductus, ut non tantum rectè
facere possim, sed nisi rectè facere non possim.'

Stern Daughter of the Voice of God!
O Duty! if that name thou love
Who art a light to guide, a rod
To check the erring, and reprove;
Thou, who art victory and law
When empty terrors overawe;
From vain temptations dost set free;
And calm'st the weary strife of frail humanity!

There are who ask not if thine eye
Be on them; who, in love and truth,
Where no misgiving is, rely
Upon the genial sense of youth:
Glad Hearts! without reproach or blot;
Who do thy work, and know it not:
Oh! if through confidence misplaced
They fail, thy saving arms, dread Power! around them cast.

Serene will be our days and bright,
And happy will our nature be,
When love is an unerring light,
And joy its own security.
And they a blissful course may hold
Even now, who, not unwisely bold,
Live in the spirit of this creed;
Yet seek thy firm support, according to their need.

I, loving freedom, and untried;
No sport of every random gust,
Yet being to myself a guide,
Too blindly have reposed my trust:
And oft, when in my heart was heard
Thy timely mandate, I deferred
The task, in smoother walks to stray;
But thee I now would serve more strictly, if I may.

Through no disturbance of my soul,
Or strong compunction in me wrought,
I supplicate for thy control;
But in the quietness of thought:
Me this unchartered freedom tires;
I feel the weight of chance-desires:
My hopes no more must change their name,
I long for a repose that ever is the same.

[Yet not the less would I throughout
Still act according to the voice
Of my own wish; and feel past doubt
That my submissiveness was choice:
Not seeking in the school of pride
For 'precepts over dignified,'
Denial and restraint I prize
No farther than they breed a second Will more wise.[1]]

Stern Lawgiver! yet thou dost wear
The Godhead's most benignant grace;
Nor know we anything so fair
As is the smile upon thy face:
Flowers laugh before thee on their beds

[1] In ed. 1807 only. – ED.

And fragrance in thy footing treads;
Thou dost preserve the stars from wrong;
And the most ancient heavens, through Thee, are fresh and
    strong.

To humbler functions, awful Power!
I call thee: I myself commend
Unto thy guidance from this hour;
Oh, let my weakness have an end!
Give unto me, made lowly wise,
The spirit of self-sacrifice;
The confidence of reason give;
And in the light of truth thy Bondman let me live!

ELLA ISABEL HARRIS (1859–1928)

Harris's translations of several of Seneca's tragedies gained wide currency
in Duckworth's *The Complete Roman Drama*. Her *Thyestes* was published
in 1904.

Act One. Scene I

[*Enter the* GHOST OF TANTALUS *and* MEGAERA]
GHOST: Who drags me from my place among the shades,
    Where with dry lips I seek the flying waves?
    What hostile god again shows Tantalus
    His hated palace? Has some worse thing come
    Than thirst amid the waters or the pangs
    Of ever-gnawing hunger? Must the stone,
    The slippery burden borne by Sisyphus,
    Weigh down my shoulders, or Ixion's wheel
    Carry my limbs around in its swift course,
    Or must I fear Tityus' punishment?

Stretched in a lofty cave he feeds dun birds
Upon his vitals which they tear away,
And night renews whatever day destroyed,
And thus he offers them full feast again.
Against what evil have I been reserved?
Stern judge of Hades, whosoe'er thou art
Who metest to the dead due penalties,
If something can be added more than pain,
Seek that at which the grim custodian
Of this dark prison must himself feel fear,
Something from which sad Acheron shall shrink,
Before whose horror I myself must fear;
For many sprung from me, who shall outsin
Their house, who, daring deeds undared by me,
Make me seem innocent, already come.
Whatever impious deed this realm may lack
My house will bring; while Pelops' line remains,
Minos shall never be unoccupied.

MEGAERA: Go, hated shade, and drive thy sin-stained home
To madness; let the sword try every crime,
And pass from hand to hand; nor let there be
Limit to rage and shame; let fury blind
Urge on their thoughts; let parents' hearts be hard
Through madness, long iniquity be heaped
Upon the children, let them never know
Leisure to hate old crimes, let new ones rise,
Many in one; let sin while punished grow;
From the proud brothers let the throne depart,
Then let it call the exiled home again.
Let the dark fortunes of a violent house
Among unstable kings be brought to naught.
Let evil fortune on the mighty fall,
The wretched come to power; let chance toss
The kingdom with an ever-changing tide
Where'er it will. Exiled because of crime,
When god would give them back their native land

Let them through crime reach home, and let them hate
Themselves as others hate them. Let them deem
No crime forbidden when their passions rage;
Let brother greatly fear his brother's hand,
Let parents fear their sons, and let the sons
Feel fear of parents, children wretched die,
More wretchedly be born. Let wife rebel
Against her husband, wars pass over seas,
And every land be wet with blood poured forth.
Let lust, victorious, o'er great kings exult
And basest deeds be easy in thy house;
Let right and truth and justice be no more
'Twixt brothers. Let not heaven be immune –
Why shine the stars within the firmament
To be a source of beauty to the world?
Let night be different, day no more exist.
O'erthrow thy household gods, bring hatred, death,
Wild slaughter, with thy spirit fill the house,
Deck the high portals, let the gates be green
With laurel, fires for thy arrival meet
Shall glow, crimes worse than Thracian shall be done.
Why idle lies the uncle's stern right hand?
Thyestes has not yet bewept his sons;
When will they be destroyed? Lo, even now
Upon the fire the brazen pot shall boil,
The members shall be broken into parts,
The father's hearth with children's blood be wet,
The feast shall be prepared. Thou wilt not come
Guest at a feast whose crime is new to thee:
Today we give thee freedom; satisfy
Thy hunger at those tables, end thy fast.
Blood mixed with wine shall in thy sight be drunk,
Food have I found that even thou wouldst shun.
Stay! Whither dost thou rush?

GHOST: To stagnant pools,
Rivers and waters ever slipping by,

To the fell trees that will not give me food.
Let me go hence to my dark prison-house,
Let me, if all too little seems my woe,
Seek other shores; within thy channels' midst
And by thy floods of fire hemmed about,
O Phlegethon, permit me to be left.
O ye who suffer by the fates' decree
Sharp penalties, O thou who, filled with fear,
Within the hallowed cave dost wait the fall
Of the impending mountain, thou who dreadst
The ravening lion's open jaws, the hand
Of cruel furies that encompass thee,
Thou who, half burned, dost feel their torch applied,
Hear ye the voice of Tantalus who knows:
Love ye your penalties! Ah, woe is me,
When shall I be allowed to flee to hell?

MEGAERA: First into dread confusion throw thy house,
  Bring with thee battle and the sword and love,
  Strike thou the king's wild heart with frantic rage.

GHOST: 'Tis right that I should suffer punishment,
  But not that I myself be punishment.
  Like a death-dealing vapour must I go
  Out of the riven earth, or like a plague
  Most grievous to the people, or a pest
  Widespread, I bring my children's children crime.
  Great father of the gods, our father too –
  However much our sonship cause thee shame –
  Although my too loquacious tongue should pay
  Due punishment for sin, yet will I speak:
  Stain not, my kinsmen, holy hands with blood.
  The altars with unholy sacrifice
  Pollute not. I will stay and ward off crime.
  [To MEGAERA]
  Why dost thou terrify me with thy torch,
  And fiercely threaten with thy writhing snakes?
  Why dost thou stir the hunger in my reins?

My heart is burning with the fire of thirst,
My parched veins feel the flame.

MEGAERA: Through all thy house
Scatter this fury; thus shall they, too, rage,
And, mad with anger, thirst by turns to drink
Each other's blood. Thy house thy coming feels
And trembles at thy execrable touch.
It is enough; depart to hell's dark caves
And to thy well-known river. Earth is sad
And burdened by thy presence. Backward forced,
Seest thou not the waters leave the streams,
How all the banks are dry, how fiery winds
Drive the few scattered clouds? The foliage pales,
And every branch is bare, the fruits are fled.
And where the Isthmus has been wont to sound
With the near waters, roaring on each side,
And cutting off the narrow strip of land,
Far from the shore is heard the sound remote.
Now Lerna's waters have been backward drawn,
Sacred Alpheus' stream is seen no more,
Cithaeron's summit stands untouched with snow,
And Argos fears again its former thirst.
Lo, Titan's self is doubtful – shall he drive
His horses upward, bring again the day?
It will but rise to die.

[*They vanish*]

FRANK JUSTUS MILLER (b. 1858)

A professor at the University of Chicago, Miller not only translated Seneca's tragedies, publishing them in 1907, but provided trots of the texts for the Loeb Classics. Dana Gioia comments, 'Having studied Miller's Loeb version so carefully . . . I cannot resist nominating it as the most regularly iambic prose translation in the language. Hardly a sentence doesn't scan' (*Seneca: The Tragedies*, Baltimore, Johns Hopkins University Press, 1995, p. 48). The excerpts are taken from *Hippolytus/Phaedra* and *Troades*.

> MESSENGER: When, fleeing forth, he left the city's walls,
>   With maddened speed he hurried on his way,
>   And quickly yoked his chargers to his car,
>   And curbed them to his will with close-drawn reins.
>   And then, with much wild speech, and cursing loud
>   His native land, oft calling on his sire,
>   He fiercely shook the reins above his steeds;
>   When suddenly, far out the vast sea roared,
>   And heaved itself to heaven. No wind was there
>   To stir the sea, no quarter of the sky
>   Broke in upon its peace; the rising waves
>   Were by their own peculiar tempest raised.
>   No blast so great had ever stirred the straits
>   Of Sicily, nor had the deep e'er swelled
>   With such wild rage before the north wind's breath,
>   When high cliffs trembled with the shock of waves,
>   And hoary foam smote high Leucate's top.
>   The sea then rose into a mighty heap,
>   And, big with monstrous birth, was landward borne.
>   For no ship's wrecking was this swelling pest
>   Intended; landward was its aim. The flood
>   Rolled shoreward heavily, something unknown
>   Within its laden bosom carrying.

What land, new born, will lift its head aloft?
Is some new island of the Cyclades
Arising? Now the rocky heights are hid,
Held sacred to the Epidaurian god,
And those high crags well known for Sciron's crime;
No longer can be seen that land whose shores
Are washed by double seas. While in amaze
We look in fear and wonder, suddenly
The whole sea bellows, and on every side
The towering cliffs re-echo with the roar;
While all their tops the leaping spray bedews.
The deep spouts forth and vomits up its waves
In alternating streams, like some huge whale
Which roves the ocean, spouting up the floods.
Then did that mound of waters strongly heave
And break itself, and threw upon the shore
A thing more terrible than all our fears.
The sea itself rushed landward, following
That monstrous thing. I shudder at the thought.
What form and bearing had the monster huge!
A bull it was in form, with dark-green neck
Uplifted high, its lofty front adorned
With verdant mane. Its ears with shaggy hair
Were rough; its horns with changing color flashed,
Such as the lord of some fierce herd would have,
Both earth and ocean-born. He vomits flames;
With flames his fierce eyes gleam. His glossy neck
Great couch-like muscles shows, and as he breathes,
His spreading nostrils quiver with the blast
Of his deep panting. Breast and dewlap hang
All green with clinging moss; and on his sides
Red lichens cling. His hinder parts appear
In monstrous shape, and like some scaly fish
His vast and shapeless members drag along;
As are those monsters of the distant seas
Which swallow ships, and spout them forth again.

The country-side was panic stricken; herds
In frenzied terror scattered through the fields;
Nor did the herdsmen think to follow them.
The wild beasts in the forest pastures fled
In all directions, and the hunters shook
With deadly fear. Hippolytus alone
Was not afraid, but curbed his frantic steeds
With close-drawn reins, and with his well-known voice
He cheered them on. The road to Argos runs
Precipitous along the broken hills,
On one side bordered by the roaring sea.
Here does that massive monster whet himself
And kindle hot his wrath; then, when he felt
His courage strong within his breast, and when
His power to attempt the strife he had rehearsed,
He charged Hippolytus with headlong course,
The ground scarce touching with his bounding feet;
And, fearful, stopped before the trembling steeds.
But this thy son, with savage countenance,
Stood steadfast, threatening, before the foe.
His features changed not, while he thundered loud:
'This empty terror cannot daunt my soul,
For 'twas my father's task to vanquish bulls.'
But straightway, disobedient to the reins,
The horses hurried off the car. And now,
The highway leaving, maddened by their fear,
They plunged along where'er their terror led,
And took their way among the rocky fields.
But he, their driver, as some captain strong
Holds straight his bark upon the boisterous sea,
Lest she oppose her side against the waves,
And by his art escapes the yawning floods;
Not otherwise he guides the whirling car.
For now with tight-drawn reins he curbs his steeds,
And now upon their backs he plies the lash.
But doggedly that monster kept along,

Now running by their side, now leaping straight
Upon them as they came, from every hand
Great fear inspiring. Soon all further flight
Was checked; for that dread, hornéd, ocean beast
With lowering front charged full against their course.
Then, truly, did the horses, wild with fear,
Break loose from all control; and from the yoke
They madly struggled to withdraw their necks,
Their master hurling to their stamping feet.
Headlong among the lossened reins he fell,
His form all tangled in their clinging strands.
The more he struggled to release himself
The tighter those relentless fetters bound.
The steeds perceived what they had done, and now,
With empty car, and no one mastering them,
They ran where terror bade. Just so, of old,
Not recognizing their accustomed load,
And hot with anger that the car of day
Had been entrusted to a spurious sun,
The steeds of Phoebus hurled young Phaëthon
Far through the airs of heaven in wandering course.
Now far and wide he stains the fields with blood,
His head rebounding from the smitten rocks.
The bramble thickets pluck away his hair,
And that fair face is bruised upon the stones.
His fatal beauty which had been his bane,
Is ruined now by many a wound. His limbs
Are dragged along upon the flying wheels.
At last, his bleeding trunk upon a charred
And pointed stake is caught, pierced through the groin;
And for a little, by its master held,
The car stood still. The horses by that wound
Were held awhile, but soon they break delay –
And break their master too. While on they rush,
The whipping branches cut his dying form,
The rough and thorny brambles tear his flesh,

And every bush retains its part of him.
Now bands of servants scour those woeful fields,
Those places where Hippolytus was dragged,
And where his bloody trail directs the way;
And sorrowing dogs trace out their master's limbs.
But not as yet has all this careful toil
Of grieving friends sufficed to gather all.
And has it come to this, that glorious form?
But now the partner of his father's realm,
And his acknowledged heir, illustrious youth,
Who shone refulgent like the stars – behold
His scattered fragments for the funeral pile
They gather up and heap them on the bier!

*

CHORUS: When in the tomb the dead is laid,
When the last rites of love are paid;
When eyes no more behold the light,
Closed in the sleep of endless night;
Survives there aught, can we believe?
Or does an idle tale deceive?
What boots it, then, to yield the breath
A willing sacrifice to death,
If still we gain no dreamless peace,
And find from living no release?
Say, do we, dying, end all pain?
Does no least part of us remain?
When from this perishable clay
The flitting breath has sped away;
Does then the soul that dissolution share
And vanish into elemental air?
Whate'er the morning sunbeam knows,
Whate'er his setting rays disclose;
Whate'er is bathed by Ocean wide,
In ebbing or in flowing tide:
Time all shall snatch with hungry greed,

With mythic Pegasean speed.
Swift is the course of stars in flight,
Swiftly the moon repairs her light;
Swiftly the changing seasons go,
While time speeds on with endless flow:
But than all these, with speed more swift,
Toward fated nothingness we drift.
For when within the tomb we're laid,
No soul remains, no hov'ring shade.
Like curling smoke, like clouds before the blast,
This animating spirit soon has passed.
Since naught remains, and death is naught
But life's last goal, so swiftly sought;
Let those who cling to life abate
Their fond desires, and yield to fate;
And those who fear death's fabled gloom,
Bury their cares within the tomb.
Soon shall grim time and yawning night
In their vast depths engulf us quite;
Impartial death demands the whole –
The body slays nor spares the soul.
Dark Taenara and Pluto fell,
And Cerberus, grim guard of hell –
All these but empty rumors seem,
The pictures of a troubled dream.
Where then will the departed spirit dwell?
Let those who never came to being tell.

MODERN SENECA

T. S. ELIOT (1888–1965)

'Marina' begins with an unattributed epigraph from *Hercules Furens*. The lines are spoken by Hercules when he comes to his senses after killing his wife and children in the fit of madness induced by Juno. Eliot's poem contains an echo of the lines, which can be translated as 'What place is this? what region? or of the world what coast?' Denis Donoghue notes that the poem is not for the illiterate reader: 'It is for initiates' ('Eliot's "Marina" and Closure', in *The Hudson Review*, Autumn 1996, vol. XLIX, no. 3, p. 368).

Marina

Quis hic locus, quae regio, quae mundi plaga?

What seas what shores what grey rocks and what islands
What water lapping the bow
And scent of pine and the woodthrush singing through the fog
What images return
O my daughter.

   Those who sharpen the tooth of the dog, meaning
Death
Those who glitter with the glory of the humming-bird, meaning
Death
Those who sit in the stye of contentment, meaning
Death
Those who suffer the ecstasy of the animals, meaning
Death

   Are become unsubstantial, reduced by a wind,
A breath of pine, and the woodsong fog
By this grace dissolved in place

What is this face, less clear and clearer
The pulse in the arm, less strong and stronger –
Given or lent? more distant than stars and nearer than the eye

Whispers and small laughter between leaves and hurrying
     feet
Under sleep, where all the waters meet.

Bowsprit cracked with ice and paint cracked with heat.
I made this, I have forgotten
And remember.
The rigging weak and the canvas rotten
Between one June and another September.
Made this unknowing, half conscious, unknown, my own.
The garboard strake leaks, the seams need caulking.
This form, this face, this life
Living to live in a world of time beyond me; let me
Resign my life for this life, my speech for that unspoken,
The awakened, lips parted, the hope, the new ships.

What seas what shores what granite islands towards my timbers
And woodthrush calling through the fog
My daughter.

Ezra Pound ('Date line', 1934) commented that 'the criticism of Seneca in Mr. Eliot's *Agon* is infinitely more alive, more vigorous than in his essay on Seneca'. Note the use of stichomythia.

Sweeney Agonistes

FRAGMENTS OF AN ARISTOPHANIC MELODRAMA

ORESTES: You don't see them, you don't – but *I* see them:
     they are hunting me down, I must move on.

                                   Choephoroi.

> Hence the soul cannot be possessed of the divine union,
> until it has divested itself of the love of created beings.
> *St. John of the Cross.*

FRAGMENT OF A PROLOGUE

DUSTY. DORIS.

DUSTY: How about Pereira?
DORIS: What about Pereira?
  I don't care.
DUSTY: You don't care!
  Who pays the rent?
DORIS: Yes he pays the rent
DUSTY: Well some men don't and some men do
  Some men don't and you know who
DORIS: You can have Pereira
DUSTY: What about Pereira?
DORIS: He's no gentleman, Pereira:
  You can't trust him!
DUSTY: Well that's true.
  He's no gentleman if you can't trust him
  And *if* you can't trust him –
  Then you never know what he's going to do.
DORIS: No it wouldn't do to be too nice to Pereira.
DUSTY: Now Sam's a gentleman through and through.
DORIS: I like Sam
DUSTY: *I* like Sam
  Yes and Sam's a nice boy too.
  He's a funny fellow
DORIS: He *is* a funny fellow
  He's like a fellow once I knew.
  He could make you laugh.
DUSTY: Sam can make you laugh:
  Sam's all right

DORIS: But Pereira won't do.
We can't have Pereira
DUSTY: Well what you going to do?
TELEPHONE: Ting a ling ling
Ting a ling ling
DUSTY: That's Periera
DORIS: Yes that's Pereira
DUSTY: Well what you going to do?
TELEPHONE: Ting a ling ling
Ting a ling ling
DUSTY: That's Pereira
DORIS: Well can't you stop that horrible noise?
Pick up the receiver
DUSTY: What'll I say!
DORIS: Say what you like: say I'm ill,
Say I broke my leg on the stairs
Say we've had a fire
DUSTY: Hello Hello are you there?
Yes this is Miss Dorrance's *flat* –
Oh Mr. Pereira is that you? how do you do!
Oh I'm *so* sorry. I *am* so sorry
But Doris came home with a terrible chill
No, just a chill
Oh I *think* it's only a chill
Yes indeed I hope so too –
Well I *hope* we shan't have to call a doctor
Doris just hates having a doctor
She says will you ring up on Monday
She hopes to be all right on Monday
I say do you mind if I ring off now
She's got her feet in mustard and water
I said I'm giving her mustard and water
All right, Monday you'll phone through.
Yes I'll tell her. Good bye. Goooood bye.
I'm sure, that's very kind of *you*.
Ah-h-h

DORIS: Now I'm going to cut the cards for to-night.
   Oh guess what the first is

DUSTY: First is. What is?

DORIS: The King of Clubs

DUSTY: That's Pereira

DORIS: It might be Sweeney

DUSTY: It's Pereira

DORIS: It might *just* as well be Sweeney

DUSTY: Well anyway it's very queer.

DORIS: Here's the four of diamonds, what's that mean?

DUSTY [*reading*]: 'A small sum of money, or a present
                  Of wearing apparel, or a party.'
               That's queer too.

DORIS: Here's the three. What's that mean?

DUSTY: 'News of an absent friend.' – Pereira!

DORIS: The Queen of Hearts! – Mrs. Porter!

DUSTY: Or it might be you

DORIS: Or it might be you
  We're all hearts. You can't be sure.
  It just depends on what comes next.
  You've got to *think* when you read the cards,
  It's not a thing that anyone can do.

DUSTY: Yes I know you've a touch with the cards
  What comes next?

DORIS: What comes next. It's the six.

DUSTY: 'A quarrel. An estrangement. Separation of friends.'

DORIS: Here's the two of spades.

DUSTY: The *two* of *spades*!
  THAT'S THE COFFIN!!

DORIS: THAT'S THE COFFIN?
  Oh good heavens what'll I do?
  Just before a party too!

DUSTY: Well it needn't be yours, it may mean a friend.

DORIS: No it's mine. I'm sure it's mine.
  I dreamt of weddings all last night.
  Yes it's mine. I know it's mine.

> Oh good heavens what'll I do.
> Well I'm not going to draw any more,
> You cut for luck. You cut for luck.
> It might break the spell. You cut for luck.

DUSTY: The Knave of Spades.

DORIS: That'll be Snow

DUSTY: Or it might be Swarts

DORIS: Or it might be Snow

DUSTY: It's a funny thing how I draw court cards

DORIS: There's a lot in the way you pick them up

DUSTY: There's an awful lot in the way you feel

DORIS: Sometimes they'll tell you nothing at all

DUSTY: You've got to know what you want to ask them

DORIS: You've got to know what you want to know

DUSTY: It's no use asking them too much

DORIS: It's no use asking more than once

DUSTY: Sometimes they're no use at all.

DORIS: I'd like to know about that coffin.

DUSTY: Well I never! What did I tell you?
> Wasn't I saying I always draw court cards?
> The Knave of Hearts!
> [*Whistle outside of the window.*]

                           Well I *never*

What a coincidence! Cards are queer!
> [*Whistle again*]

DORIS: Is that Sam?

DUSTY: Of course it's Sam!

DORIS: Of course, the Knave of Hearts *is* Sam!

DUSTY [*leaning out of the window*]: Hello Sam!

WAUCHOPE: Hello dear
> How many's up there?

DUSTY: Nobody's up here
> How many's down there?

WAUCHOPE: Four of us here.
> Wait till I put the car round the corner
> We'll be right up

DUSTY: All right, come up.

DUSTY [*to* DORIS]: Cards are queer.
DORIS: I'd like to know about that coffin.

    KNOCK KNOCK KNOCK
    KNOCK KNOCK KNOCK
    KNOCK
    KNOCK
    KNOCK

    DORIS. DUSTY. WAUCHOPE. HORSFALL. KLIPSTEIN.
      KRUMPACKER.

WAUCHOPE: Hello Doris! Hello Dusty! How do you do!
    How come? how come? will you permit me –
    I think you girls both know Captain Horsfall –
    We want you to meet two friends of ours,
    American gentlemen here on business.
    Meet Mr. Klipstein. Meet Mr. Krumpacker.
KLIPSTEIN: How do you do
KRUMPACKER: How do you do
KLIPSTEIN: I'm very pleased to make your acquaintance
KRUMPACKER: Extremely pleased to become acquainted
KLIPSTEIN: Sam – I should say Loot Sam Wauchope
KRUMPACKER: Of the Canadian Expeditionary Force –
KLIPSTEIN: The Loot has told us a lot about you.
KRUMPACKER: We were all in the war together
    Klip and me and the Cap and Sam.
KLIPSTEIN: Yes we did our bit, as you folks say,
    I'll tell the world we got the Hun on the run
KRUMPACKER: What about that poker game? eh what Sam?
    What about that poker game in Bordeaux?
    Yes Miss Dorrance you get Sam
    To tell about that poker game in Bordeaux.
DUSTY: Do you know London well, Mr. Krumpacker?
KLIPSTEIN: No we never been here before
KRUMPACKER: We hit this town last night for the first time
KLIPSTEIN: And I certainly hope it won't be the last time.
DORIS: You like London, Mr. Klipstein?

KRUMPACKER: Do we like London? do we like London!
  Do we like London!! Eh what Klip?
KLIPSTEIN: Say, Miss – er – uh – London's swell.
  We like London fine.
KRUMPACKER: Perfectly slick.
DUSTY: Why don't you come and live here then?
KLIPSTEIN: Well, no, Miss – er – you haven't quite got it
  (I'm afraid I didn't quite catch your name –
  But I'm very pleased to meet you all the same) –
  London's a little too gay for us
  Yes I'll say a little too gay.
KRUMPACKER: Yes London's a little too gay for us
  Don't think I mean anything *coarse* –
  But I'm afraid we couldn't stand the pace.
  What about it Klip?
KLIPSTEIN: You said it, Krum.
  London's a slick place, London's a swell place,
  London's a fine place to come on a visit –
KRUMPACKER: Specially when you got a real live Britisher
  A guy like Sam to show you around.
  Sam of course is at *home* in London,
  And he's promised to show us around.

FRAGMENT OF AN AGON

SWEENEY. WAUCHOPE. HORSFALL. KLIPSTEIN.
KRUMPACKER. SWARTS. SNOW. DORIS. DUSTY.

SWEENEY: I'll carry you off
  To a cannibal isle.
DORIS: You'll be the cannibal!
SWEENEY: You'll be the missionary!
  You'll be my little seven stone missionary!
  I'll gobble you up. I'll be the cannibal.

DORIS: You'll carry me off? To a cannibal isle?
SWEENEY: I'll be the cannibal.
DORIS: I'll be the missionary.
   I'll convert you!
SWEENEY: I'll convert *you*!
   Into a stew.
   A nice little, white little, missionary stew.
DORIS: You wouldn't eat me!
SWEENEY: Yes I'd eat you!
   In a nice little, white little, soft little, tender little,
   Juicy little, right little, missionary stew.
   You see this egg
   You see this egg
   Well that's life on a crocodile isle.
   There's no telephones
   There's no gramophones
   There's no motor cars
   No two-seaters, no six-seaters,
   No Citroën, no Rolls-Royce.
   Nothing to eat but the fruit as it grows.
   Nothing to see but the palmtrees one way
   And the sea the other way,
   Nothing to hear but the sound of the surf.
   Nothing at all but three things.
DORIS: What things?
SWEENEY: Birth, and copulation, and death.
   That's all, that's all, that's all, that's all,
   Birth, and copulation, and death.
DORIS: I'd be bored.
SWEENEY: You'd be bored.
   Birth, and copulation, and death.
DORIS: I'd be bored.
SWEENEY: You'd be bored.
   Birth, and copulation, and death.
   That's all the facts when you come to brass tacks:

Birth, and copulation, and death.
I've been born, and once is enough.
You dont remember, but I remember,
Once is enough.

SONG BY WAUCHOPE AND HORSFALL
SWARTS AS TAMBO. SNOW AS BONES

Under the bamboo
Bamboo bamboo
Under the bamboo tree
Two live as one
One live as two
Two live as three
Under the bam
Under the boo
Under the bamboo tree.

Where the breadfruit fall
And the penguin call
And the sound is the sound of the sea
Under the bam
Under the boo
Under the bamboo tree.

Where the Gauguin maids
In the banyan shades
Wear palmleaf drapery
Under the bam
Under the boo
Under the bamboo tree.

Tell me in what part of the wood
Do you want to flirt with me?
Under the breadfruit, banyan, palmleaf
Or under the bamboo tree?
Any old tree will do for me

Any old wood is just as good
Any old isle is just my style
Any fresh egg
Any fresh egg
And the sound of the coral sea.

DORIS: I dont like eggs; I never liked eggs;
And I dont like life on your crocodile isle.

SONG BY KLIPSTEIN AND KRUMPACKER
SNOW AND SWARTS AS BEFORE

My little island girl
My little island girl
I'm going to stay with you
And we wont worry what to do
We wont have to catch any trains
And we wont go home when it rains
We'll gather hibiscus flowers
For it wont be minutes but hours
For it wont be hours but years

diminuendo { *And the morning*
And the evening
And noontime
And night
Morning
Evening
Noontime
Night

DORIS: That's not life, that's no life
Why I'd just as soon be dead.
SWEENEY: That's what life is. Just is
DORIS: What is?
What's that life is?
SWEENEY: Life is death.
I knew a man once did a girl in –

DORIS: Oh Mr. Sweeney, please dont talk,
  I cut the cards before you came
  And I drew the coffin
SWARTS: *You* drew the coffin?
DORIS: I drew the COFFIN very last card.
  I dont care for such conversation
  A woman runs a terrible risk.
SNOW: Let Mr. Sweeney continue his story.
  I assure you, Sir, we are very inter*e*sted.
SWEENEY: I knew a man once did a girl in
  Any man might do a girl in
  Any man has to, needs to, wants to
  Once in a lifetime, do a girl in.
  Well he kept her there in a bath
  With a gallon of lysol in a bath
SWARTS: These fellows always get pinched in the end.
SNOW: Excuse me, they dont all get pinched in the end.
  What about them bones on Epsom Heath?
  I seen that in the papers
  You seen it in the papers
  They *dont* all get pinched in the end.
DORIS: A woman runs a terrible risk.
SNOW: Let Mr. Sweeney continue his story.
SWEENEY: This one didn't get pinched in the end
  But that's another story too.
  This went on for a couple of months
  Nobody came
  And nobody went
  But he took in the milk and he paid the rent.
SWARTS: What did he do?
  All that time, what did he do?
SWEENEY: What did he do! what did he do?
  That dont apply.
  Talk to live men about what they do.
  He used to come and see me sometimes
  I'd give him a drink and cheer him up.

DORIS: Cheer him up?

DUSTY: Cheer him up?

SWEENEY: Well here again that dont apply
>   But I've gotta use words when I talk to you.
>   But here's what I was going to say.
>   He didn't know if he was alive
>   and the girl was dead
>   He didn't know if the girl was alive
>   and he was dead
>   He didn't know if they both were alive
>   or both were dead
>   If he was alive then the milkman wasn't
>   and the rent-collector wasn't
>   And if they were alive then he was dead.
>   There wasn't any joint
>   There wasn't any joint
>   For when you're alone
>   When you're alone like he was alone
>   You're either or neither
>   I tell you again it dont apply
>   Death or life or life or death
>   Death is life and life is death
>   I gotta use words when I talk to you
>   But if you understand or if you dont
>   That's nothing to me and nothing to you
>   We all gotta do what we gotta do
>   We're gona sit here and drink this booze
>   We're gona sit here and have a tune
>   We're gona stay and we're gona go
>   And somebody's gotta pay the rent

DORIS: I know who

SWEENEY: But that's nothing to me and nothing to you.

FULL CHORUS: WAUCHOPE, HORSFALL, KLIPSTEIN, KRUMPACKER

When you're alone in the middle of the night and you wake in
    a sweat and a hell of a fright
When you're alone in the middle of the bed and you wake like
    someone hit you on the head
You've had a cream of a nightmare dream and you've got the
    hoo-ha's coming to you.
Hoo hoo hoo
You dreamt you waked up at seven o'clock and it's foggy and
    it's damp and it's dawn and it's dark
And you wait for a knock and the turning of a lock for you
    know the hangman's waiting for you.
And perhaps you're alive
And perhaps you're dead
Hoo ha ha
Hoo ha ha
Hoo
Hoo
Hoo
KNOCK KNOCK KNOCK
KNOCK KNOCK KNOCK
KNOCK
KNOCK
KNOCK

F. L. LUCAS (1894–1967)

Lucas, Fellow of King's College, Cambridge, was a scholar of Elizabethan literature. The excerpts below appeared in his text *Seneca and
Elizabethan Tragedy*, published in 1922. This snippet of *Oedipus* is from
the messenger's account of the self-blinding of Oedipus; it is followed
by an account of the demise of Hippolytus from the play of that name.

A sudden storm of tears burst o'er his face,
Flooded his cheeks. 'Are tears enough?' he cried.
'Only so gently shall mine eyes rain down?
Torn from their sockets they shall follow forth
Their tears; does that suffice, ye gods of wedlock?
Out with my eyes!' He spoke, and raved in fury:
His threatening visage blazed with a savage fire,
His eyes scarce held themselves within their sockets,
Fearless and fell his face, – maddened with rage, –
One burst of frenzy. He groaned and with a cry
Laid hands upon his face. To meet his hands
His glaring eyes stood out and straining followed
Of their own will the grasp that tore them free,
Running to meet their ravisher. Greedily
He groped with his hooked fingers for their orbs
And from the inmost socket dragged and wrenched
Both eyeballs loose at once . . .

*

The scattered members of his mangled frame,
O Father, set in order, and restore
To their true place his errant limbs: see here
His right hand goes, and here his left, so skilled
To hold the reins: I recognize the mark
Of his left side. How large a part, alas,
Remains yet lost and absent from our tears.
. . .
O trembling hands endure your mournful office,
O cheeks be dry and stay your flood of tears,
While this poor father numbers his son's limbs,
And forms his body. What thing is this so shapeless,
And so befouled, – torn, mangled every side?
Which part of thee, I doubt: but some part, sure;
Well, lay it here, not where it should belong,
But where there's room.

ASA M. HUGHES

Hughes provided this translation of a chorus from *Thyestes* for an anthology, *Latin Poetry in Verse Translation*, ed. L. R. Lind, published in 1957. A note to the text explains that 'The glyconic meter with four beats to the line is imitated in the translation.'

Wealth can never produce a king,
Robes of purple will not avail,
Nor broad brows of a kingly cast,
Nor great gates with a gleam of gold;
Nothing dug from a western mine,
Nothing dredged from the yellow flood
Tagus holds in its lucent bed,
Nor whatever from harvest fields
Boiling Libya threshes out.
King is he who has lost all fear,
All ill thoughts of an angry heart;
Whom no lawless ambition moves
Nor that ever fickle applause
Of massed men with their headlong haste.
He who stands upon solid ground
Sees within his own soul all things,
Meets his fate with a cheerful mind
Nor complains when it's time to die . . .
Let him have power's proud hall who will
Fly so high on a slippery peak;
Let sweet peace be enough for me:
Let my life in the silence flow
Quite unheeded by fellowmen.
So when all of my days have passed
Undisturbed by the world's loud noise,
Let me die as a plain old man.
Death comes hard for the man who lives
Known too well to his fellowmen,
Still unknown to himself in death.

ROBERT LOWELL (1917–1977)

This excerpt is from *Phaedra*, Lowell's 1960 version of Racine's *Phèdre*. While not intended as a translation of Seneca, it is, as George Steiner observed, closer to Seneca than to Racine.

THESEUS: Here is Theramenes. Where is my boy,
    my first-born? He was yours to guard and keep.
    Where is he? Answer me. What's this? You weep?
THERAMENES: Oh, tardy, futile grief, his blood is shed.
    My lord, your son, Hippolytus, is dead.
THESEUS: Oh gods, have mercy!
THERAMENES: I saw him die. The most
    lovely and innocent of men is lost.
THESEUS: He's dead? The gods have hurried him away
    and killed him? . . . just as I began to pray . . .
    What sudden thunderbolt has struck him down?
THERAMENES: We'd started out, and hardly left the town.
    He held the reins; a few feet to his rear,
    a single, silent guard held up a spear.
    He followed the Mycenae highroad, deep
    in thought, reins dangling, as if half asleep;
    his famous horses, only he could hold,
    trudged on with lowered heads, and sometimes rolled
    their dull eyes slowly – they seemed to have caught
    their master's melancholy, and aped his thought.
    Then all at once winds struck us like a fist,
    we heard a sudden roaring through the mist;
    from underground a voice in agony
    answered the prolonged groaning of the sea.
    We shook, the horses' manes rose on their heads,
    and now against a sky of blacks and reds,
    we saw the flat waves hump into a mountain
    of green-white water rising like a fountain,
    as it reached land and crashed with a last roar
    to shatter like a galley on the shore.

Out of its fragments rose a monster, half
dragon, half bull; a mouth that seemed to laugh
drooled venom on its dirty yellow scales
and python belly, forking to three tails.
The shore was shaken like a tuning fork,
ships bounced on the stung sea like bits of cork,
the earth moved, and the sun spun round and round,
a sulphur-colored venom swept the ground.
We fled; each felt his useless courage falter,
and sought asylum at a nearby altar.
Only the Prince remained; he wheeled about,
and hurled a javelin through the monster's snout.
Each kept advancing. Flung from the Prince's arm,
dart after dart struck where the blood was warm.
The monster in its death-throes felt defeat,
and bounded howling to the horses' feet.
There its stretched gullet and its armor broke,
and drenched the chariot with blood and smoke,
and then the horses, terror-struck, stampeded.
Their master's whip and shouting went unheeded,
they dragged his breathless body to the spray.
Their red mouths bit the bloody surf, men say
Poseidon stood beside them, that the god
was stabbing at their bellies with a goad.
Their terror drove them crashing on a cliff,
the chariot crashed in two, they ran as if
the Furies screamed and crackled in their manes,
their fallen hero tangled in the reins,
jounced on the rocks behind them. The sweet light
of heaven never will expunge this sight:
the horses that Hippolytus had tamed,
now dragged him headlong, and their mad hooves maimed
his face past recognition. When he tried
to call them, calling only terrified;
faster and ever faster moved their feet,
his body was a piece of bloody meat.

The cliffs and ocean trembled to our shout,
at last their panic failed, they turned about,
and stopped not far from where those hallowed graves,
the Prince's fathers, overlook the waves.
I ran on breathless, guards were at my back,
my master's blood had left a generous track.
The stones were red, each thistle in the mud
was stuck with bits of hair and skin and blood.
I came upon him, called; he stretched his right
hand to me, blinked his eyes, then closed them tight.
'I die,' he whispered, 'it's the gods' desire.
Friend, stand between Aricia and my sire –
some day enlightened, softened, disabused,
he will lament his son, falsely accused;
then when at last he wishes to appease
my soul, he'll treat my lover well, release
and honor Aricia . . .' On this word, he died.
Only a broken body testified
he'd lived and loved once. On the sand now lies
something his father will not recognize.
THESEUS: My son, my son! Alas, I stand alone
before the gods. I never can atone.

TED HUGHES (b. 1930)

Hughes published his adaptation of Seneca's *Oedipus* in 1968. Peter
Brook was the director for its production at the National Theatre. In
this excerpt, consisting of Acts Four and Five, Oedipus grasps his fate.

Act Four

OEDIPUS: Before   it was fear   but now   is it certainty
              how have I been trapped

I killed Laius
the voice of the oracle accuses me
his own ghost points at me and accuses me
but my conscience   acquits me
I know myself
better than any ghost   better than the god at
   Delphi knows me
Laius is nowhere in my conscience

Laius murdered   if I could remember something
if I could go back
two men only   two strangers   both together
long ago
I see it   I see myself shoved to the roadside
shoved into the thorns
the horses driven straight at me   to trample me
to go over me with the wheels
the lathered horses   that arrogant screaming old man
and the driver shouting
trying to run me down with the chariot
it was one half self defence what I did
I put my spear into the driver   and he fell out backwards
as the chariot passed the old man slashed at me
with his sword
I drove the spear through him and he fell between the
   horses
they ran on and dragged him tangled in the reins under the
   chariot
it was all done in a moment   as they passed me
a long time ago   a long way away   at a crossroads
JOCASTA: Oedipus   leave the dead alone   stop these
   diggings into the past   bringing my dead husband
   back to show his wounds and show himself still in
   death agony   leave him alone   hell cannot be
   opened safely   what can come out of it   only
   more pain and more misfortune   more confusion
   and more death

OEDIPUS: Jocasta   tell me this   when Laius died
how old was he

JOCASTA: at the end of middle age

OEDIPUS: on that last ride how many rode with him

JOCASTA: many set out   but the roads to Delphi are broken
the country difficult   and Laius was a hard traveller

OEDIPUS: how many stayed with him

JOCASTA: he outstripped them all   he went ahead alone

OEDIPUS: the King was alone

JOCASTA: when he arrived at the crossroads he was alone
with the driver of his chariot

OEDIPUS: the driver was also killed

JOCASTA: the driver fell there at the crossroads   the horses
dragged the body of Laius on towards Delphi
nobody saw the fight   so they were found

OEDIPUS: there is no escaping this   I know who saw that
fight   when did it happen

JOCASTA: let it lie Oedipus   it happened   no man can
alter what has happened   I make no secret of it
to you   that death was waiting for Laius   fate
only adjusted the balance when he fell to the earth
he owed me a life   I bore him a boy and before
my milk had entered its mouth he snatched it away
things I have never spoken   a crime I shall not
dig up were tangled in those reins that dragged his
dead body away from the crossroads   a man of
stone broken by stones   forget him Oedipus
finish with riddles   forget the oracle
burrowing in that darkness cannot save us   only
strength can save us

OEDIPUS: when was Laius killed   how long ago

JOCASTA: this is the tenth summer

[*Enter* MESSENGER]

MESSENGER: the men of Corinth call you to your father's
throne
Polybus has gone to his last rest

OEDIPUS: how did my father die

MESSENGER: asleep   smiling   in peace

OEDIPUS: my father is dead   without hurt   from any
man   no murder   witness   my hands   I
can raise them to the light   innocent   my hands
cannot be accused   but something is left   the
worse half of my destiny   the half I fear most
that still remains

MESSENGER: in your father's kingdom you need fear nothing

OEDIPUS: only one thing keeps me from running towards it
with all my strength

MESSENGER: what is that Oedipus

OEDIPUS: my mother

MESSENGER: your mother   why fear her   she is longing for
you to come now   quickly

OEDIPUS: her love is what I fear

MESSENGER: can you leave her a widow

OEDIPUS: those words go too deep

MESSENGER: who is tormenting you   what is your secret
tell me   kings have trusted me before   even
with their greatest secrets

OEDIPUS: long ago the oracle told me this   I shall marry my
mother

MESSENGER: then you can forget the oracle   this fear is
unreal
your speculations are empty   Merope was never
your mother

OEDIPUS: why should the King of Corinth adopt a stranger

MESSENGER: an heir to the throne forestalls many troubles

OEDIPUS: who shared such a secret with you

MESSENGER: it was these hands   these very hands   when
you
were a whimpering baby   these   handed you
to Merope

OEDIPUS: you gave me to my mother   then where did I
begin   who gave me to you

MESSENGER: a shepherd   on Mount Cithaeron

OEDIPUS: how did you come to be on that mountain

MESSENGER: with my flock   I was also a shepherd

OEDIPUS: there's a strange mark on my body   what do you know about it

MESSENGER: sharp iron hooked through your heels   to cripple
and hobble you   you were meant to die
the wounds were infected and swollen   and so
you are called Oedipus   that scar must be still on
your feet

OEDIPUS: who gave me to you   tell me that

JOCASTA: listen to my warning Oedipus   the dead man will
never be satisfied   not until you are dead and
under the ground with him   the dead hate the
living   they only want to murder the living
turn your eyes towards the living   give your
strength to us   darkness is too deep you will
never see to the bottom of it   the dead will rob
you of everything

CHORUS: listen to the Queen Oedipus

OEDIPUS: who gave me to you

MESSENGER: the master of the King's flocks

OEDIPUS: what was the man's name

MESSENGER: I am old   that was long ago   it has been too
long buried

OEDIPUS: his face   could you recognize that

MESSENGER: perhaps

OEDIPUS: call in the shepherds   let them drive all their
beasts to the altars   bring the head shepherds
bring them to me here

JOCASTA: Oedipus   listen to your wife

CHORUS: listen to her Oedipus

JOCASTA: the truth is not human it has no mercy why rush
into the mouth of it   you have a kingdom to
protect

OEDIPUS: I am enmeshed in a mystery worse than any death

CHORUS: you want to satisfy yourself   but your people will
have to pay   your queen will have to pay   it is
not chance that hides these things and keeps them
hidden   leave things as they are   let fate unfold
at its leisure   do not force it

OEDIPUS: if it were endurable I would endure it   why do
you all warn me back   what is the truth

CHORUS: you were born to the throne   isn't that enough
don't look any deeper Oedipus

OEDIPUS: what blood am I   I shall find it out   whatever
it means   here is Phorbas   this ancient man
was once master of the king's flocks   do you
remember the name   Phorbas   do you
remember the face

MESSENGER: the man is familiar   I have seen that face before
in the days of King Laius did your flocks graze
Mount Cithaeron

PHORBAS: the rich grass of lovely Cithaeron   that was our
summer pasture   we were there every summer

MESSENGER: do you recognize me

OEDIPUS: do you remember a baby boy   that you handed
to this man   one day long ago on the slope of
Mount Cithaeron   iron was twisted through his
ankles   you were meant to expose him on the
mountain   for the wild beasts   I see your face
change   you are searching for words too carefully

PHORBAS: you are digging too deep

OEDIPUS: the truth is as it is   let it come out as it is

PHORBAS: it is all too long ago

OEDIPUS: speak or I shall torture you till you speak

PHORBAS: on a day long ago   yes   I handed this man a
crippled baby boy   it was hopeless we were too
late   it could never have lived

OEDIPUS: why could it never have lived

PHORBAS: the iron through its feet   those cruel wires
   that knot of filthy iron   the wound was putrid
   it stank   the whole body festering   burning
OEDIPUS: it's enough   my fate has found me at last   who
   was this child   who was it
PHORBAS: I swore never to speak
OEDIPUS: I shall burn that oath out of you
PHORBAS: will you destroy a man for one little fact
OEDIPUS: I am not a madman   you only need to speak
   who was that child   you are the only man who
   knows   who was its father   who was its mother
PHORBAS: its mother
OEDIPUS: who was its mother
PHORBAS: its mother was your wife
OEDIPUS: birth   birthbed   blood   take this   open
   the earth bury it   bottom of the darkness
   under everything   I am not fit for the light
   Thebans your stones   now put a mountain on
   me   hack me to pieces   pile the plague fires
   on me   make me ashes   finish me   put me
   where I know nothing   I am the plague   I am
   the monster Creon saw in hell   I am the cancer
   at the roots of this city   and in your blood and in
   the air   I should have died in the womb
   suffocated   inside there   drowned in my
   mother's blood   come out dead   that first day
   before anything   Oedipus wait   now I need
   that strength   something to fit this error   drag
   up the root of it   and out   something for me
   alone   first I shall go to the palace   quickly to
   seek out my mother   and present her with her son
   my mother

CHORUS

If only our fate were ours to choose   you would see me on
quiet waters   where the airs are gentle   a full sail but a
light wind   no more than a breath   easy voyage   that is

best   no blast no smashed rigging no flogging downwind into
cliffs   under surge   nothing recovered   no vanishing in
mid ocean

give me a quiet voyage   neither under cliffs nor too far out
on the black water where the depth opens   the middle course
is the safe one   the only life   easily on   to a calm end
surrounded by gains

foolish Icarus   he thought he could fly
it was a dream
tried to crawl across the stars
loaded with his crazy dream   his crazy paraphernalia
the wings the wax and the feathers
up and up and up
saw eagles beneath him   saw his enormous shadow on the
    clouds beneath him
met the sun face to face
fell

his father Daedalus was wiser   he flew lower
he kept under clouds   in the shadow of the clouds
the same crazy equipment   but the dream different
till Icarus dropped past him   out of the belly of a cloud
past him
down
through emptiness
a cry   dwindling
a splash

tiny in the middle of the vast sea

Act Five

CHORUS: who is that   it is one of the king's slaves
     beating
  his head with his fists   something has happened
  what has happened   tell us
SLAVE: When Oedipus grasped his fate   and saw the full
  depth of wrong where he had lost himself   he
  understood the oracle   now he's condemned himself

  he hurried straight back to the palace
  his stride was savage and heavy   like a beast
    purposeful
  never paused
  went in under that terrible roof

  face deathly   he was groaning   muttering
  he was a crazed beast   a wounded lion
  that's going to die killing
  his eyes bulged   demented   blazing with all that
    torment inside him
  mad grimaces kept wrenching his face
  sweat poured on his temples and neck
  froth stood round his mouth
  his hands kept griping at his stomach
  he was trying to tear himself open
  to gouge out the bowels and liver and heart the whole
    mass of agony
  he was toiling for something
  some action something unthinkable
  something to answer all that has happened
  he began to shout   why delay it
  I should be stabbed   smashed under a rock
  I should be burned alive   there should be animals

ripping me to pieces
tigers eagles ripping me with their hooks
Cithaeron   you mountain
you began it all   it's your slopes should have had
    my carcase
your wild dogs should have cracked my riddles for me
where are your wolves
and that woman who wrenched her husband's head off
    on your lovely grass
wrenched it off and ran with it   send her   Agave

why be afraid of death it's nothing am I afraid
death   it's only death
can keep a man innocent

then he pulled out his sword and he was going to kill
    himself
but he stopped he began to reason
one little jab of pain   a few seconds of death in my
    eyes and in my mouth
can that pay for a lifetime like mine
can one stroke cut all my debts off
one death   that's for your father   that's good
but what about your mother
and what about that doubled blood in your children
what about their shame
what about Thebes   all the dead   all those living
    with their deaths on them
they are doing your penance for you Oedipus
and you cannot pay you cannot possibly pay
not in this lifetime
you need to be born again   suffer for everything
    again
and die again   over and over   lifetime after
    lifetime
every lifetime a new sentence

and length of penalties
think   death can come only once
think   this death has to last   has to be slow
find a death
find a death that can still feel
and go on feeling   a life in death   a death among
    the living
why are you hesitating Oedipus

suddenly he began to weep   everything that had been
torment suddenly it was sobbing   it shook his whole
body and he shouted   is weeping all I can give
can't my eyes give any more   let them go with their
tears   let them go   eyeballs too   everything
out   is this enough for you you frozen gods of
marriage   is it sufficient   are my eyes enough

he was raging as he spoke   his face throbbed dark
red   his eyeballs seemed to be jumping in their
sockets   forced out from the skull   his face was
no longer the face of Oedipus   contorted   like a
rabid dog   he had begun to scream   a bellowing
animal   anger   agony tearing his throat

his fingers had stabbed deep into his eyesockets   he
hooked them gripping the eyeballs   and he tugged
twisting and dragging with all his strength   till they
gave way   and he flung them from him   his
fingers dug back into his sockets he could not stop
he was gibbering and moaning insane with his fury
against himself   gouging   scrabbling with his
nails
in those huge holes in his face
the terrors of the light are finished for Oedipus
he lifted his face   with its raw horrible gaps
he tested the darkness
there were rags of flesh strings and nerve ends

still trailing over his cheeks   he fumbled for them
snapping them off   every last shred
then he let out a roar   half-screamed
you gods
now will you stop torturing my country
I've found the murderer   and look   I've punished
      him
I've forced him to pay the debt
and his marriage   I've found the darkness for it
I've found it the night it deserves
as he was screaming his face seemed to blacken suddenly
the blood vessels had burst inside his torn eyepits
the blood came spewing out over his face and beard
in a moment he was drenched

CHORUS: Fate is the master of everything   it is vain to fight
            against fate
      from the beginning to the end the road is laid down
            human
      scheming is futile   worries are futile   prayers are futile
      sometimes a man wins   sometimes he loses
      who decides whether he loses or wins
      it has all been decided long ago elsewhere
      it is destiny
      not a single man can alter it
      all he can do is let it happen

      the good luck the bad luck everything that happens
      everything that seems to toss our days up and down
      it is all there from the first moment
      it is all there   tangled in the knotted mesh of causes
      helpless to change itself
      even the great god lies there entangled
      helpless in the mesh of causes
      and the last day lies there tangled with the first
      a man's life is a pattern on the floor   like a maze
      it is all fixed   he wanders in the pattern

no prayer can alter it
or help him to escape it   nothing

then fear can be the end of him
a man's fear of his fate is often his fate
leaping to avoid it   he meets it

OEDIPUS: all is well   I have corrected all the mistakes and
my father has been payed what he was owed   I like
this darkness   I wonder which god it is that I've
finally pleased   which of them has forgiven me for all
that I did   he's given me this dark veil for my head
pleasant
the light   that awful eye   that never let me rest
and followed me everywhere   peering through every
crack   at last you've escaped it   you haven't driven
it away   you haven't killed that as   you killed your
father   it's abandoned you   left you to yourself
simply   it's left you to your new face   the true face
of Oedipus

CHORUS: Look   Jocasta coming out of the palace
         demented
look at Jocasta   why has she stopped   look at her
she's staring at her son   she hardly knows what's
happening   darkness is nearly swamping her
there he stands   blasted   his blind mask turned to
the sky   she wants to speak   she's afraid of him
she comes closer her grief stronger than everything
she's stepping towards him

JOCASTA: what can I call you now   what shall I call you
you're my son shall I call you my son
are you ashamed
you are my son   I lost you
you're alive   I've found you
speak to me
show me your face
turn your head towards me show me your face

OEDIPUS: you are making all my pains useless   you are
        spoiling
    my comfortable darkness   forcing me to see again
    go away   we must not meet   the salt bottomless
    ocean should be washing between our bodies   not to
    cleanse them nothing can cleanse them ·   if another
    world hangs somewhere   under some other sun
    and lost away among other stars   one of us should be
    there

JOCASTA: you were my husband   you are my son   you
    killed my husband   I bore your sons   nothing
    can be blamed   everything that has happened is here
    there is no road away from it

OEDIPUS: no more words mother   I beg you by all that in
        our
    names is right and wrong   let there be no more words
    between us two

JOCASTA: nothing in me moves   can I not feel   I shared
        the
    wrong   how do I share the punishment   it's me
    I'm at the root of it   I am the root   my blood is
    the dark twisted root   this womb   darkness
    swallowing all order and distinction   so die   let
    out this hell that lives in you   nothing would be
    enough to punish it   if god smashed his whole
    universe on to me it wouldn't be enough   a mother
    a morass   all I want is death   find it   you
    killed your father   finish it   the same hand
    your mother   finish it   is this the sword that
    killed him   is this it that killed my husband and my
    husband's father with a single stab   where shall I
    have the second stab   this point under my breast
    or this long edge across my throat   don't you know
    the place   it's here   this   the place the gods
    hate   where everything began the son the husband
    up here

CHORUS: look   her hand slackens from the hilt   the
          whelm
   of blood squeezes the blade out
OEDIPUS: you god of the oracle   you deceived me lied to
          me it
   has not turned out as you said   only my father's
   death was required it was enough   it has been
   doubled and the blame has been doubled   my mother
   is dead and her death comes from me   both my
   father and my mother are dead under my fate   it is
   more than I was promised   now go   the dark
   road   quickly   quickly begin   do not stumble
   on the body of your mother   you people of Thebes
   crushed under this plague your spirits broken look   I
   am going away   I am taking my curse off you
   now you can hope again   lift your faces   now you
   will see the skies alter   and the sun and the grass
   everything will change now   all you stretched out
   hoping only for death your faces pressed to your graves
   look up   if you can move now   if you can breathe
   suck in this new air   it will cure all the sickness
   go and bury your dead now without fear   because
   the contagion is leaving your land I am taking it with
   me   I am taking it away   fate   remorseless
   my enemy   you are the friend I choose   come with
   me
   pestilence   ulcerous agony   blasting consumption
   plague terror   plague blackness   despair
   welcome   come with me   you are my guides
   lead me

   [*The* CHORUS *celebrate the departure of* OEDIPUS *with a dance*]

DOUGLASS PARKER (b. 1927)

Parker translated *Thyestes* for an anthology of classical drama in translation published in 1980.

>[*Exit the Messenger*]
>CHORUS:
>>Sir,
>>>Sun,
>>>>source
>
>of all material, all establishment,
>stern chucker-out of every spangled charm
>that trims the night's round corners,
>>>>a query:
>
>>Whither, we ask, and why?
>
>>>Too soon for the voice of Vesper,
>>>>harbinger of tardiness,
>>>>to beckon the beacons of dark,
>>>Too soon for the occident wheelspin
>>>>to order its car
>>>>unhitched from a job well done,
>>>Too soon for the scheduled trump
>>>>to blat the onset
>>>>of night-bent day's third third.
>>>The plowboy gawks in his tracks:
>>>>So sudden supper,
>>>>too soon for bulls to tire?
>
>>What grounds have engendered this sharp decline
>>>>from your lofty causeway?
>>What assignable cause has spilled your team
>>>>from its curb's enclosure?

To advance a few unthinkable wherefores:

From Hell's ruptured jail
 do the Giants, down and now out,
 try war once more?
In Tityos' shivered breast
 does the inchoate wound
 renew his outdated hatred?
Out from under his shucked-off Alp,
 does Typhoeus unfold his cramp?
Through monstrous, rimy troops
 does a high road rise,
 from Thessaly transfer Pelion
 to dump it on Ossa in Thrace?

The world's appointed periodicitis: Dead.
 Rise and set will cancel out.

Dawn's jaw hangs down:
Dainty, dewspent mother of first light,
trained to tender the god his reins
  in bon voyage –
and now her kingdom's doorway
muddled beyond all housekeeping:

  How wash down a weary wagon?
  How slosh in sea the manes that smoke with sweat?

A freakish welcome to stranger Sun,
the very same: Set for setting,
he stares at Aurora, makes to muster
the rising murk . . .
 too soon for Night to be dressed.

  No stars proceed to their places,
  no twinkle flicks over the pole,
  no moon detaches the shadows.

AWAY with all conjecture:
> mere night this is,
>> and night may it remain.

Here is the thud,
> the thud of dread
>> that hammers the heart:

> The coming totter and glide of the sum of things
>> in destiny's wreck,
> The returning crush and press of gods and men
>> by shapeless chaos,
>> Till Nature again clasps earth and sea together
>>> and paves the footloose stars
>>>> that stipple the sky.

> No more at thrust of deathless torch
>> will the astral conductor, ages' lord,
>>> inscribe his brand on winter and summer.
> No more intercepting the blaze of Sun
>> will Moon purge Night of panic, and rout
>>> her brother's horsemanship,
>>> whizzing quick her truncated track.
>>>> The mob of gods
>>>> will roll in a lump
>>>> and drop
>>>>> to one
>>>>> sole
>>>>> pit.

Watch them:

> The sanctified Throughway of sainted stars
> cuts slant its track across the zones.
> star-studded, bends trudging years to end . . .

        slip, Throughway,
        watch your stars slip ahead.

The Ram, before the gentle spring is come,
spreads sail to genial westwind . . .

        dive, Ram,
        down to the waves,
        Where once you bore up Helle's tremor.

The Bull shakes five damp sisters
at his shiny horntip . . .

        pull down the Twins, Bull,
        drag along the claws of crooked Crab.

The Lion, once the game of Hercules,
seething with fervid glow . . .

        fall, Lion,
            down from heaven again;
        fall, Virgin,
            back to the earth you left;
        fall, Scales,
            weighty with Justice,
            draw down Scorpion's sting.

Old gaffer Sagittarius,
        feathered shaft nocked to Thessalian string . . .

        snap string, Centaur,
        snuff your shaft.

Chilly Capricorn, usher of sluggish winter . . .

        fall, Goat, fall,
        and fracture whatshisname's jug,
        and Fish, last stars in heaven,
        go share his fall,
        and Wagon, never damped by the sea,
        sink down out of sight in the gulf,

and slippery Snake, you replica river,
who keeps the Bears apart.
and monster Dragon's minuscule yokemate,
Dogtail frozen hard and stiff,
and barely mobile wagon-watcher,
Boötes, Bearward,
now not half so steady,
            fall all,
                    fall all,
                            fall all . . .

So many candidates,
            and the honor falls on us,
                    to be crushed when the universe slips its hinge?

Has the final stage of creation
            fixed on us as its target?

            Oh, at our birth we got
                    a most sad lot
                    in a most hard draw.

        Did we let the sun fall down,
                or did we push?

Laments leave us, and dread depart:

    The universe is ending.
    Unseemly greed for life
    has one who refuses to die
    among such company.

JANE ELDER

Elder translated *Thyestes* for a volume published for the Mid North-umberland Arts Group in 1982.

Chorus

If any god feels love

        for our Achaean Argos
        for Peloponnesian Pisa home of racing
        famous for chariots

if any loves

    Corinth   the Isthmus
    the twin harbours   the parted seas
    the snows of Taygetus

           seen from far off

    which the North wind

           blowing from Scythia
           has massed on winter heights

    snows which summer

        melts with warm breezes

    Etesian winds filling voyaging sails

if any god is moved

        by Alpheus' river

           its clean its cool its lucent stream
      running along beside

           Olympia's famous course

let that god turn

     his kindly power upon us

          and keep away all harm

forbid alternate crime

      that child's children should follow

worse than their parents

     than their grandfather

forbid
>   that greater wickedness
>>   should not decrease in his descendants
weary at last
>   may the whole impious race
>>   of thirsting Tantalus
>   give up aggression
they have sinned enough
>>   right has no power
nor shared wrongdoing
betrayed Myrtilus
>   betrayer of his master
>>   plunged headlong
>>>   fell
into the sea
>   faith kept to him as he kept faith
he took a journey he sent others on
>>   made a sea famous
>>>   gave it his name
>>   no story better known
>>>   to sailors of Ionian ships
another story
>   a child
>>   welcomed by the sword
>>>   as he ran to his father's kiss
>>   fell a young victim
>>>   slaughtered at the family hearth
>>   split up by your right hand
>>>   Tantalus
>>   carved so you might set a meal
>>>   before the gods your guests
such food brings
>   eternal hunger
>   eternal thirst

no fitter penalty
    for that savage
       hospitality
Tantalus stands weary
     throat empty wanting
over his guilty head
    plenty
    a prey more elusive
        than the winged harpies
        torments of blind Phineus' feast
here there
    the tree hangs down
       fruitful with heavy branches
curving with apple offspring
     trembling
      swaying
it plays with mocks
     his wide-stretched jaws
        useless, gaping
but he
   though eager
     impatient at delay
deceived so long refrains
     neglects to touch
turns eyes aside
    closes his lips
      clamps hunger in shut teeth
then all the grove
    drops riches down
      nearer and nearer
from above
   overhead
    the fruit is lowered

insolent
> it insults him
>> kindly-ripe
>>> boughs bent with heavy leafage

his kindled hunger
> tells him to hold out
>> to use his deluded hands

he stretches them out
> takes a moment's pleasure
>> being deceived

the whole rich autumn
> the mobile forest
>> is snatched away
>>> lifts up high up

thirst follows
> worse than hunger

his blood burns
> hot with unseen
>> fiery torches

he stands tortured
> his mouth catching

at waves that come near
> up to his face
>> but
> the elusive water

turns away
> deserts him
> abandons
>> a barren channel
>>> useless
>>> empty

he tries to follow
> the gurgling water
>> it leaves him

from the swift stream
> he drinks deep
>> dust

FREDERICK AHL (b. 1941)

Ahl translated three of Seneca's tragedies for a volume published in 1986. The first excerpt is from *Trojan Women*, the second from *Hippolytus/Phaedra*.

CHORUS: They say the soul lives on when we are dead –
Can this be true, or is it just a myth,
an opiate to dull our fears?
When one who loves us shuts our eyes in death –
on that last day without daylight –
when ashes are sealed in the urn –
do we live on, poor creatures,
can we not wholly consign
our being to the grave? –
Or then again –
is death complete and absolute,
does not one fragment of our life live on,
does soul flee, like a puff of air,
up into sky, mingled forever with clouds
when we take final breath,
when the cremating flames lick naked thighs? –

Sun rises, travels the world before he sets –
Ocean's blue waters lap every shore
in ebb and flow –
And everything Sun and Sea behold
scurries to doom, dragged by time,
soaring swift as Pegasus –

Cosmic winds ceaselessly whirl the zodiac –
Mighty Sun, king of galaxies,
as he rotates, spins on centuries –

Each night bewitching moon
in arching orbit
skimming skies,
follows the plan of Destiny –

And so do we –

Then, when we reach Hell's swirling streams,
the Styx, the ultimate boundary of truth,
binding oaths of gods irrevocably,
we cease to be, exist no more –
Like smoke from a hot fire,
we briefly soil the air,
then vanish and disperse to nothingness –

The souls ruling our bodies,
like rainclouds drifting in sky,
suddenly scatter in cold north wind,
gone traceless in vastness –

Nothing exists after death,
and death is not a state –
only the end of the final lap
of fleeting life –

Greedy men, stop hoping for reward –
Anxious men, stop fearing punishment –
Time's rapacious jaws devour us whole –
Death cannot be divided:
it destroys the body,
does not spare the soul –

There is no Hell, no savage god who rules the dead,
no guardian dog to hinder your escape –
These are just idle folktales, empty words,
myth, woven into nightmare –

'Where will I lie when I am dead?' you ask –

You will lie among things never born.

                    *

CHORUS: Fame tends to favor   things of bygone ages,
     but when compared with   you all ancient glory
     fades. For your beauty   outshines other brightness
     as moon outshines stars   when, circle completed,
     when, as her horns join   in a fiery roundness,
     Phoebe runs nightlong   in her rapid orbit,
     shows just a trace of   blushing on her fair face,
     and stars lose grip on   their less brilliant torches.
     Like evening starlight   introducing darkness,
     angel of nighttime,   fresh washed in the ocean;
     like morning star,   when grasp of night is broken,
     angel of daylight.

     You, from pine-carrying   peoples of India,
     Bacchus, perpetually   long-haired and young-looking,
     terror of tigers with   vine-covered javelin.
     Your turban taming a   head crowned with oxen-horns
     can't even vie with the   hair of Hippolytus.
     Don't take too flattering a   view of your own good looks.
     Word is round everywhere   that Phaedra's sister once
     had, and preferred to have,   Theseus to you, Bacchus.

     Beauty for mortals is good and bad:
     a gift – but brief; its time but short.
     Her foot so fleet, so quick her fall.

     I won't compare meadows,   true green in springtime,
     ravaged by heat-haze   of searing summers
     when high sun stands still,   cruel at noonday,
     when rapid night hurtles   short-wheeled, tight-circling.

As lilies, pale-petaled,   languidly shrivel,
so gorgeous tresses thin   drily on our heads.
The striking radiance,   the sheen of young cheeks –
erased in an instant.   Each passing day's light
spoils, erodes partially,   beauty of body.
For beauty is matter,   fugitive nature.
What wise man banks upon   things that must wither?
Use them while they blossom.   Tacit time saps you.
Bad hours wearied you;   worse catch you unawares.

Why seek the wilderness?   Though there are no
    pathways,
beauty is no safer.   Hide in a wooded glade.
But when hot mid-day sun   stands huge and motionless
water nymphs sundrily,   lustfully circle in,
grip handsome men tightly,   shameless in their spring
    flow.
Glade goddesses will slip   astride you lecherously
in your unguarded dreams.   Tree nymphs hunt every Pan
exploring mountain peaks.
                        The moon was born after
your chaste and pristine days   of old Arcadians.
As she looks down from skies   wild and starry above,
her power to steer a pure   and shining course will fail.
Not long ago she glowed   blush red though not a cloud
bridled with dirtied veil   her bright and willful face.

It sundered all our hearts   to see her power so bruised.
We clashed cymbals, rang bells,   we thought she was
    bewitched
by spells of Thessaly,   being forced down to earth.
But it was you. While she,   goddess of night, watched
    you,

she stopped in her swift course.   You held her back, and
     you
caused her suffering.

Cold's bite, we hope, will spare   the beauty of your face;
your looks should have but rare   exposure to the sun
so their sheen may be fair   as Parian marble.
How fine to see a face   fierce with virility
grim with old dignity   fashioned upon its brow!
Your radiant hair compares   with Phoebus' untrimmed
     locks
which tumble shoulder-length,   artlessly beautiful.
Yours lies lawless, brow-short,   yet ruggedly handsome.
In fighting strength you'd dare   challenge the roughest
     gods,
surpass them in the breadth   of your great, spreading
     limbs.
Although you're young, you match   the embedded
     muscles
of powerful Hercules.   Your chest is broader than
that of the war god, Mars.
                              And if you wished to ride
upon a hard-hoofed mount,   you could rein Cyllarus,
Castor's great Spartan horse,   with a more agile hand.
With thumb and forefinger   torque the javelin strap,
target the weapon, then   hurl with your mighty strength.
Cretan hands, though well skilled   with arrows and with
     bows,
shoot out their slender reeds   a far shorter distance.
Or if fancy takes you   to shoot in Parthian style,
spraying arrows skyward   none will return to earth
without a bird transfixed,   point plunged deep in its guts,
tumbling from veiling clouds.

                              Review the centuries:
        rarely does beauty go   unpunished among men.
        May god treat you better!   May he leave you safer,
        and may he pass you by   till your shapely beauty
        crosses the threshold of   age and shapelessness.

A. J. BOYLE (b. 1942)

Boyle, a classicist, published a translation of *Hippolytus/Phaedra* in 1987.

HIPPOLYTUS: There is no life so free and virtuous
    And which so cultivates our ancient ways
    As far from city walls to love the woods.
    No rage of avarice inflames the man
    Self-vowed to innocence on mountain heights;
    No people's breath, no base, disloyal mob,
    No poisonous spite or fickle favour.
    He serves no kingdom nor threatens kingship
    Pursuing vain honours and fleeting wealth,
    Liberated from hope and fear; no black,
    Gnawing envy bites him with base-born tooth.
    He knows nothing of crime spawned in teeming
    Cities: no dreading every noise in guilt,
    No lies told. He seeks no rich man's palace
    Propped on a thousand pillars, nor rafters
    Proud-encrusted with gold. No streaming blood
    Soaks pious altars, no white bulls sprinkled
    With sacred meal submit a hundred necks.
    No, he's lord of empty fields and wanders
    Blameless in open air. He knows only
    To lay subtle traps for beasts and soothes toil-
    Exhausted limbs in snowy Ilissos.

Now he skirts swift-flowing Alpheus' bank,
Now passes through the deep grove's dense demesne
Where cool Lerna's lucid waters shine pure,
And changes his abode. Here plaintive birds
Prattle and wind-struck branches gently quiver
And ancient beeches. His the joy to lie
By a vagrant stream or to drink soft sleep
On bare turf where a bounteous spring drops
Swirling waters or through the fresh-sprung flowers
There sounds an escaping brook's sweet murmur.
Fruit shaken from trees arrest his hunger,
And berries torn from tiny shrubs give food
Without effort. His instinct is to flee
Royal luxury. The arrogant drink
From anxious gold; he rejoices to catch
A spring with bare hands. Surer sleep grips him
On his hard bed tossing his carefree limbs.
He seeks no wanton, stolen joy in secret
Or on darkened couch nor hides terrified
In maze-like house; he courts the air and light
And lives beneath heaven's eye.
                                            Such a life
I think lived those the primal age produced
To mingle with the gods. No blind desire
For gold obsessed them, no sacred judgment-
Stone parted on the plains the people's fields.
No credulous vessels yet cut the sea,
Each knew his own waters; no massive wall
Or tower block enclosed a city's side.
No weapons filled the soldier's savage hand;
No hurling catapult's heavy stone shattered
Close-barred gates. The earth bore no master's rule
And endured the slavery of no ox's yoke.
Rather, self-productive fields nourished man
Without demand; the woods gave natural
Riches, shaded grottoes natural homes.

Impious rage for gain broke this covenant,
Precipitate wrath and mind-inflaming
Lust; then came the bloody thirst for power,
The weaker became spoils for the stronger,
Might in place of justice. At first men fought
Bare-handed and turned rocks and rough branches
Into weapons. There was no light cornel
Armed with tapered iron or long-edged sword
Gripping the side or high-crested helmets
Nodding from afar: grievance furnished arms.
War-loving Mavors invented new arts
And a thousand forms of death. Then streaming
Blood dyed each land and made the ocean red.
Crime – its limits now removed – invaded
Every home, no sin lacked example:
Brother slain by brother, father by the hand
Of son, husband lay dead beneath wife's sword,
And impious mothers destroyed their offspring.
Stepmothers – I'm silent: beasts are more gentle.
But evil's prince is woman. Mistress of crime,
She besieges minds; for her sinful lusts
So many cities burn, so many states war,
So many peoples crushed by fallen kingdoms.
Others pass unnamed; alone, Aegeus' wife,
Medea, will prove woman a damned race.

NURSE: Why blame all women for the crimes of few?

HIPPOLYTUS: I loathe them all, I dread, I shun, I curse them.
Be it reason, nature or insensate rage,
I choose to hate them. Fire will sooner mix
With water and shifting Syrtis give friendly
Waves to ships, sooner from her distant lap
Hesperian Tethys will bring bright day
And wolves look tenderly on does, before I
Defeated show gentleness to woman.

NURSE: Often love puts bridles on stubborn hearts
And transforms hate. Look at your mother's realm:

Even those savage women feel Venus' yoke.
You are proof of this, the tribe's only son.
HIPPOLYTUS: I've one consolation for my mother's loss:
That I may now detest all womankind.
CHORUS: O nature, great mother of gods,
And you, fiery Olympus' lord,
Who through whirling sky pull scattered
Stars and wandering planet's course,
Turn the world on speeding axis,
Why such care to spin eternal
The pathways of the soaring sky,
That now grey winter's frosts denude
The woods, now the plantation's shade
Returns, now the summer lion's
    Neck with fervent
Heap ripens Ceres' grain
And the year tempers its strength?
Why do you who have such power,
Beneath whom the vast world's balanced
Mass drives its wheeling courses,
Stand so far from man indifferent,
Not anxious to reward the good,

    To harm the wicked?
Human life without order
Fortune rules and with blind hand
Scatters gifts, fostering the worst.
Vile lust defeats purity,
Crime reigns in towering courts,
Mobs love to hand authority
To villains, they serve whom they hate.
Grim virtue gains perverse rewards
For honesty; the chaste are dogged
By evil want and, strong in vice,
Adulterers rule. O worthless shame
    And honour false.

J. P. SULLIVAN (1930–1993)

Sullivan translated this excerpt of *Hercules Oetaeus* for *Roman Poets of the Early Empire*, ed. and trans. with A. J. Boyle, Harmondsworth, Penguin, 1991.

> O barbarous Corsica, locked in by crags,
> Rugged and vast where endless deserts stretch,
> Fall brings no fruit, and summertime no crops,
> No Attic olives bend the winter's branch;
> From rainy spring no new births lure a smile,
> And no grass grows on this ill-omened earth;
> No bread, no taste of water, no fire in hearth:
> Only two things – the exiled and exile.

STEPHEN SANDY (b. 1934)

From 'A Cloak for Hercules (*Hercules Oetaeus*)' in Slavitt's collection, *Seneca: The Tragedies*, published in 1995.

> HERCULES: (*To himself*) What scorpion out of the Sahara or
> what crab
>   from a jungle pool burns in the marrow of my bones?
>   My heart was strong and steady, now it bursts my lungs;
>   my liver is being scraped dry; persistent fever saps
>   my blood. First, this plague gnaws at the skin; from there
>   it enters the body, ravages arms and legs; and next
>   it gets into the joints and ribs, undoing as it goes
>   each organ. I am in appalling pain, and it
>   calmly eats and drinks away my body. It
>   holds a life-lease of even the marrow of my bones;

1 *Corsica* – where Seneca was exiled by Claudius, AD 41–9.

my bones, which lose their old rock-hard solidity
and, as they soften, bend; they fall together like
an imploded building. My muscular body shrivels
and turns to mush. Not even all my massive limbs
will satisfy this venom's relentless appetite.
How great must be the illness that Hercules calls great!
Shocking abomination! Look at me, cities, see
what's left of him, that Hercules who helped you so.
Can you tell this is your son, father, your Hercules?
Did these once powerful arms pin that marauding beast,
The Nemean lion, and wring its massive neck? Are these
the hands that drew the bow and from the stars brought
      down
the Stymphalian birds, the hands that managed all those
      strenuous
achievements? Are these the shoulders that bore up the
      world?
Is this my tremendous build? The neck thick as a bull's?
My manhood's dead and buried, yet I am still above
      ground.
Poor man, how can I ask Jove now for a place in heaven?
   Whatever this poison is that festers in my guts
I pray it will leech away, stop suppurating, stop
dosing me with its invisible injuries.
Where did it come from, out of the icy Black Sea waters
or the muddy Tethys? From Gibraltar, or Morocco
across the straits? O killing punishment, are you
some worm that lifts his filthy hooded head within me,
or some other evil thing unknown before, even
to me? Did you breed in the bloody mire of the Hydra
or did you drop like a bloated tick from the Stygian dog?
   You are all calamities yet none — I cannot meet you
face to face. Let me at least behold my killer:
whatever plague, whatever creature you may be,
openly meet me! How did you take up residence
in the chambers of my bones? Look, my right hand's torn

the skin away, laid bare these pustulating coils
of viscera; and yet the germ of this lies deeper still!
O strong catastrophe, the equal of Hercules!
But why this grief? Why tears staining my cheeks? I never
was one to weep; no hurt has ever smeared my face
with tears, yet – shame on me! – at last I've learned to cry.
No one anywhere has ever witnessed Hercules
in tears; I've borne my hardships dry-eyed! My strength,
    which has
put down so many terrors, surrenders only to you,
my pestilence. You first brought tears to my eyes; my
    visage,
once more steady than rock, harder than tempered steel,
is going soft and helpless. Commander of the skies,
everyone here on earth has seen me sobbing and bawling,
yet greater torture for me is knowing that Juno sees!
But O, the fire comes once more and roasts my guts.
Oh where is the lightning bolt to deal the final blow?

CARYL CHURCHILL (b. 1938)

Churchill published a version of *Thyestes* in 1995, commenting, 'I don't
think it's just because I've been translating *Thyestes* that the news seems
full of revenge stories. Seneca could have brought a god on at the end
of the play, but he's made a world where gods either don't exist or
have left. Or he could have had the chorus back at the end saying the
kind of generally uplifting and resigned things they do in Greek plays.
But he didn't. The play ends bleakly except for our memory of a chorus
who'd hoped for something better' (p. xiii).

CHORUS

Will anyone believe this?
Atreus, who can't control his mind,
   stood amazed at his brother.
     No force is stronger
than what you feel for your family.
     Strangers' quarrels last
but if you're joined by love you're joined forever.

When both sides have good cause
   to make them angry,
and Mars keeps the swords striking
   in his thirst for blood,
love forces you into peace.

What god's made this sudden quiet?
Civil war was wrecking the city.
   Pale mothers clung to their sons.
     We mended the walls
and mouldy towers, and barred the gates.
     Pale watchmen stared at
anxious night: worse than war is the fear of war.

Now it's swords that have fallen.
   the trumpets are still,
clashing clarions are silent.
   Deep peace has come back
to the delighted city.

When a north wind churns the waves
sailors are afraid to put to sea
   as Charybdis gulps it in
     and vomits it out,

and Cyclops is afraid Etna's fire
    that roars in his forge
may be put out by a great surge of water.

But when the wind drops the sea's
    gentle as a pool.
Ships were afraid but now
    small boats are playing.
There's time to count the fishes.

No luck lasts, pain and delight
take it in turn – delight's turn's shorter.
    Time flings you from low to high.
        If you wear a crown
and tribes lay down their arms when you nod,
        soon everything shifts
and you fear how things move and the tricks of time.

Power over life and death –
    don't be proud of it.
Whatever they fear from you,
    you'll be threatened with.
All power is under a greater power.

You can be great at sunrise,
    ruined by sunset.
Don't trust good times too much or
    despair in bad times.
The old women mix things up
    and spin every fate.
No one has gods so friendly
he can promise himself tomorrow.
    God turns our quick things over
        in a fast whirlwind.

Sun, where have you gone?
how could you get lost
half way through the sky?
The evening star's not here yet,
the chariot hasn't turned in the west
and freed the horses,
the ploughman whose oxen still aren't tired
can't believe it's suppertime.

The way things take turns
in the world has stopped.
There'll be no setting
any more and no rising.
Dawn usually gives the god the reins,
she doesn't know how
to sponge down the tired sweating horses
and plunge them into the sea.

Whatever this is
I hope it is night.
I'm struck with terror
in case it's all collapsing,
shapeless chaos crushing gods and men.
No winter, no spring,
no moon racing her brother, planets
piled together in a pit.

The zodiac's falling.
The ram's in the sea,
the bull's bright horns drag
twins and crab, burning lion
brings back the virgin, the scales pull down
the sharp scorpion,
the archer's bow's broken, the cold goat
breaks the urn, there go the fish.

Have we been chosen
out of everyone
somehow deserving
to have the world smash up and
fall on us? or have the last days come
in our lifetime? It's
a hard fate, whether we've lost the sun
or driven it away.

Let's stop lamenting.
Let's not be frightened.
You'd have to be really
greedy for life
if you didn't want to die when the whole world's
dying with you.

KELLY CHERRY (b. 1940)

From 'Octavia' in Slavitt's collection, *Seneca: The Tragedies*, published
in 1995.

OCTAVIA: And now the tyrant dispatches me
To the place of darkness, where I will be
A flicker of dark, let's say, an un-
Being, a darkness among darknesses,
Impossible to see and the sound of silence.
Why do I try to delay the inevitable?
Be done with it – and me! – you
To whom fortune has delivered me.
I pray to God – *but are you crazy,*
Octavia? Do not pray
To gods who have no use for you!
I call on Tartarus and on
The gods of that dark realm, the goddesses

Who chase the wicked down, and you,
The shade of my father, to bring down
The tyrant – bring him all the way down,
To the death and punishment he deserves.
[*To* PALACE GUARDS]
I am not afraid to die.
Put in the oars, unfurl the sails,
And let the pilot make for the shores
Of Pandataria, of death!
[OCTAVIA *exits with* PALACE GUARDS]

CHORUS OF ROMANS: May breezes gentle as the touch
Of her hand, like the breezes
That once ferried Iphigenia
On a light cloud from the altar
Of a vindictive Diana,
Hold this young woman in the palm
Of their going, softly blowing her ship
Far from the awful punishment
Meant for her, to the temple
At Trivia. More merciful
Than Rome is Aulis; more merciful
Than Rome, the foreign land of Turin.
In those places the gods are content
With the blood of strangers, while
Rome's delight is in the blood
Of her children, the innocent and good.
Thus Time itself is in exile.

RACHEL HADAS (b. 1948)

From 'Oedipus' in Slavitt's collection, *Seneca: The Tragedies*, published in 1995.

> By fate propelled, to fate we yield.
> No fussy gestures set us free.
> It is decreed, our human doom,
> all from above. Lachesis' laws
> (tightly she grasps them) point one way.
> Through narrow channels our lives move:
> our first day singles out our last.
> No god can cause events to swerve
> which, meshed in motives, roll along;
> each life proceeds untouched by prayer.
> To some men, fear's the greatest bane:
> afraid of what is fated, blind,
> they blunder right into their fate.

DANA GIOIA (b. 1950)

From 'The Madness of Hercules' (*Hercules Furens*) in Slavitt's collection, *Seneca: The Tragedies*, published in 1995. Just like Jasper Heywood, one of the very first to translate Seneca into English, Gioia adds to and varies the original. Heywood added scenes and characters, and created a prologue in which he meets Seneca; this excerpt is an interpolation in which Seneca appears again.

> ETEOCLES: To rule is to be hated. They go together.
> To rule and be loved is an idle fancy any
> sovereign soon discards. The people's love
> is a drug, pleasant enough at first but it saps
> the courage one needs in order to govern well.

Their hatred, meanwhile is rather a tonic, I find.

JOCASTA: A hated king never rules for long.

ETEOCLES: We'll see.

Exile can last a good while, but for kingship,
I'd say . . .

JOCASTA: You're willing to risk your home, your city?
Your honor?

ETEOCLES: Pay any price – with my face on the money.

[*They freeze into a tableau*]

CHORAGOS: That's it? But what happens? What kind of an ending is that? Is this your idea of a play?

SENECA: But you know perfectly well what happens. Eteocles and Polynices kill one another. Eteocles is buried with honor, and Polynices is left out there on the field until Antigone defies Creon's order and buries her brother. And is put to death for what she's done. But we know all that. It follows inevitably, from the moment the two sons turn away from their mother's perfectly reasonable and, I think, quite eloquent arguments. That's where the tragedy is – that language itself is useless. That the passions, though stupid, are powerful and real, and that logic and rhetoric and all those things we say we live for are all but irrelevant.

CHORAGOS: Is this your idea of a play?

SENECA: No, probably, not. But it's my idea of the truth. Of reality. Of how we live. As I suggested earlier, the making of perfect plays seems wrong, somehow, when we live in such a shambles. Stupidity and blood cannot be represented by shapely verse dramas with decorous choruses mouthing platitudes.

CHORAGOS: They never did show up, those Phoenician women, did they?

SENECA: No. I'm sorry. Not for my play so much as for the world we live in, which is, I agree, outrageous. The eloquence of the characters seems to me heartbreaking, considering how ineffective it turns out to be. Antigone is eloquent too, even though she has nothing to say in this second scene, but she is

there, for us to look at and weep for. We know it is her life
they are throwing away. And sometimes, I have the notion,
she knows it too.

CHORAGOS: You might have indicated that. It would have been
effective.

SENECA: What would there have been for her to say? Or for me
to put into her mouth? Screams of agony? Tears at the stupidity
of what was happening – tears that would be all the more
bitter because these people are her family, the people she loves.
The Greeks understood that. And the Romans. I think you
understand it, too. Thank you for coming. I apologize for the
play, and for the world, and wish you a good night.

GLOSSARY OF ANCIENT AND
MYTHOLOGICAL TERMS

ACASTUS Son of Pelias, and one of the Argonauts. He demanded Jason and Medea from Creon as vengeance for the murder of his father, which was brought about in part by the machinations of Medea.

ACHERON One of the rivers of Hades. To enter the underworld, the dead had to cross Acheron on Charon's ferryboat. Acheron was later personified as the son of Gaia. The name is sometimes used to refer to the lower world in general.

AGAVE Daughter of Cadmus and Harmonia, mother of Pentheus, king of Thebes. With her sisters, she slew Pentheus on Mount Cithaeron and bore his head back to Thebes.

AGEUS Father of Theseus; Aegean Sea named for him.

ALCMENE (Alcmena) Mother of Hercules and Iphicles. Though her sons were twins, as they grew older it became clear that Hercules was the son of Zeus and Iphicles was the son of Alcmene's husband, Amphitryon.

ALECTO One of the Furies.

ALPHEUS The river which flows past Olympia. Alpheus was the son of Oceanus and Tethys, a hunter who fell in love with the huntress Arethusa. Not wishing to marry, she went away to Ortygia and became a spring. Out of love for her, Alpheus became a river flowing from the sea to the spring.

AMASIS A king of Egypt who permitted the Greeks to visit and gave them settlements along his coasts.

AMPHION He and Zethus were the twin sons of Zeus and Antiope, abandoned by their mother and raised by a shepherd. Amphion practised music and was the first to raise an altar to Hermes; his music and song were so powerful he could command inanimate objects.

ARGIVE FLEET The navy of Argos or Argolis.

ARGOS The capital of Argolis, sacred to Juno, the home of heroes.

ASTREA The daughter of Zeus and Themis. She used to live among men on earth and is also called Dike, or Justice. She left the earth when men became evil, and took her place among the stars as the constellation Virgo.

ATREUS Son of Pelops and grandson of Tantalus, on whose descendants a curse had been laid because he betrayed the gods. The effects of the curse were apparent in the subsequent history of the family: Atreus had a deadly feud with his brother, Thyestes. Aerope, Atreus's wife, bore his sons Agamemnon and Menelaus, but she loved Thyestes. When Atreus discovered her adultery, he boiled the limbs of Thyestes' three sons and showed him their hands and feet when Thyestes finished eating. Atreus was eventually killed by Aegisthus, son of Thyestes by his daughter Pelopia.

ATTIS Son of Nana, the daughter of the river god Saugarios; Attis was a beautiful youth and was beloved of Cybele. When he fell in love with the wood nymph Sagaritis, Cybele killed her in a jealous rage. Attis went mad with grief, castrated himself, and died at the foot of a pine. Violets grew from his blood. His myth is often considered a counterpoint to that of Adonis.

AULIS Boeotian city on the Euripus. The Greeks were becalmed there before sailing for Troy, and Agamemnon was forced by his troops to sacrifice his daughter Iphigenia in order to appease Artemis.

AVERNUS A holy lake near Cumae, called '*aorno*' or birdless by the Greeks because it gave off a poisonous vapour which killed the birds.

BACCHUS One of the names given to Dionysus, bringer of wine and ecstasy, the son of Zeus and Semele. The women followers of Dionysus who worshipped the god in a state of ecstasy were called Bacchae or Bacchantes.

BALISTAS Weapon used by the Romans.

BEARES OF ARCADYE The hinds or stags of Arcadia, which Hercules had to capture for his third labour.

BOÖTES Constellation of the Wagoner or Ploughman in the northern hemisphere, situated behind Ursa Major, thought to represent a man with a crook driving a bear.

BOREAS Brother of Zephyrus and Notus, son of Eos, the dawn, and Astraeus, the starry sky. Boreas is the personification of the north wind, sometimes appearing in the form of a horse.

CADMUS Son of Agenor and Telephassa. When Zeus carried off his sister Europa, Agenor sent Cadmus and his brothers to search for her. Though Cadmus journeyed all over the known world, he did not find her. When he came to Delphi, the Pythia told him not to search any longer but to follow a cow with the sign of the moon on her flanks. Cadmus did, and became founder of Thebes when the cow lay down on that site. Zeus gave him Harmonia in marriage; after their reign ended they both became snakes and were transported to Elysium by Zeus.

CALLISTO Daughter of Lycaon, king of Arcadia, and one of the companions of Artemis. Zeus took her against her will and turned her into a bear to escape the notice of Hera, though Hera found out anyway and persuaded Artemis to shoot the bear. Zeus sent Hermes to save the child Callisto bore in her womb, Arcas, and turned Callisto herself into the constellation of the Great Bear.

CERBERUS Monstrous three-headed dog, the guardian of Hades.

CERES Daughter of Saturn, sister of Jupiter, mother of Proserpina and goddess of agriculture. Ceres was identified with the Greek Demeter from the fifth century BC.

CEYX King of Trachis who died in a shipwreck. His wife, Alcyone, mourned him incessantly until both he and she were changed into kingfishers.

CHARON Aged man who ferried souls across the river Styx into the underworld. His fare was a silver coin, placed under the tongue of the dead by the bereaved.

CHARYBDIS Whirlpool between Italy and Sicily, opposite to Scylla, alternately sucking in and spewing out the sea. A monster.

CITHAERON Mountain near Thebes where the infant Oedipus had been exposed. The mountain took its name from King Cithaeron, the first king of Plataea.

CORINTH Named after Corinthus, king of the city and said to be the son of Zeus.

CYBEL Cybele, the great mother of the gods and of all living beings. She was first revered in Phrygia, and her cult spread to the west, where she was sometimes identified with Demeter. Cybele was also a protector of cities.

CYCLOPS Arges (the bright one), Steropes (lightning), and Brontes (thunder) were the sons of Uranus and Gaia and forged thunderbolts for Zeus. Uranus hated them and threw them into Tartarus. According to later tradition, there were also Cyclopes under Mount Aetna in Sicily, as well as the one-eyed Cyclopes, descendants of Poseidon and the nymph Thooa, said to have built the walls of Mycenae.

DAEDALUS Architect who killed his pupil and was exiled to Crete, where he helped bring about the Minotaur and designed the labyrinth. He escaped from Crete by flying on wings of wax and feathers he made himself.

DEUCALION Son of Prometheus, he married Pyrrha. Because of their goodness and piety they were saved from the flood Zeus inflicted on the earth. Deucalion built an ark in which he and Pyrrha kept animals in pairs;

when the flood ended Deucalion landed on Mount Parnassus. After the flood Zeus sent Hermes to Deucalion and Pyrrha and allowed them to choose anything they wished. They chose to have a new race of men.

DIANA Ancient goddess who was revered in groves and forests in central and southern Italy. In very early days Diana was the goddess of the moon, and philosophers later regarded her as a goddess of light. Diana was identified with the Greek concept of Artemis.

DIANIRE Deianeira, the wife of Hercules.

DIRCE Wife of Lycus, who imprisoned and tortured Antiope when she was returned to Thebes. Dirce tried to have Antiope tied to the horns of a raging bull, to be dragged to her death, but Antiope's twin sons, Amphion and Zethus, rescued her and visited that punishment on Dirce instead. She was transformed into the stream or spring in Thebes that bears her name.

DIS Alternative name for Pluto, father of the underworld.

DITIS Another name for Dis.

DON River running through the southwestern area of Russia. Known to the ancients as Tanais, it has been a trading channel since Scythian times.

ECHO Nymph who aroused the anger of Hera for thwarting her efforts to catch Zeus with a nymph by prolonging her chatter and giving the nymphs time to get away. When Hera discovered the trick she decreed that Echo should be unable to speak unless spoken to, and that she should only repeat the last words said to her. When Echo fell in love with Narcissus this caused misunderstandings, and she faded away to a mere voice.

EOAS Eos, the dawn, who brought forth the strong winds Zephyrus, Boreas and Notus as well as Phosphorus, the dawn star, and all the other stars. Eos is tenderhearted and frequently falls in love with mortals.

EPIDAURIAN GOD Asclepius, who was born in the city of Epidaurus on the Saronic coast of Argolis, which later became the centre of worship of him.

ERINIS (Erinyes/Erinys) The Furies – fearful deities whose chief duty is to avenge wrong, particularly murder.

ETEOCLES Oedipus, king of Thebes, unwittingly killed his father and married Jocasta, his mother. The children of this marriage were Eteocles and Polyneices, Antigone and Ismere. Eteocles and Polyneices agreed to rule Thebes in alternate years, but Eteocles would not cede to Polyneices after his year was over; they eventually went to war and killed each other before the walls of Thebes. Creon declared that Eteocles was to have a public funeral with all honours, but that Polyneices would remain unburied. Antigone performed funeral rites over him, however, and dragged him on to the pyre of Eteocles.

ETESIAN WINDS Winds blowing every year at a stated period, over the Aegean Sea. The winds prevail forty days after the setting of the Dog Star.

EURYSTHEUS Born at seven months, Eurystheus was a weakling and a coward all his life. He was killed in a battle for Athens and his head and body were buried in separate places along the borders of Attica, because he promised his body would protect Athens from invaders.

EUXINE SEA Ancient name for the Black Sea.

GORDIAN KNOT From Gordius, father of Midas, who became king of Phrygia as prophesied by an oracle. The wagon they came to Phrygia on was dedicated to Zeus. Later, there was a belief that whoever cut the knot tying the wagon to its yoke was destined to become king of Asia. The Gordian knot was tied in such a way that it was impossible to see its beginning and end. When Alexander the Great came to Phrygia, he finally cut it with his sword, fulfilling the prophecy.

GRACCHI Two popular leaders of the Sempronian gens; examples of men brought to ruin by popular renown.

GRIPE Vulture.

HEBRUS River in Thrace, one of the largest in Europe.

HECATE Daughter of Perses and Asteria; often identified with Proserpina as the underworld manifestation of the deity seen in Diana on earth and Luna in heaven. She taught magic to Medea, her priestess.

HECTOR Eldest son of Priam and Hecuba; husband of Andromache. The bravest warrior and chief defender of Troy.

HELLE With her brother, Phrixus, Helle fled Thessaly on the back of a golden-fleeced ram in order to escape the persecution of their stepmother, Juno. The ram flew through the air. Helle fell into the sea during their escape, so the sea was named for her: Hellespont.

HYDASPES Fourth and last battle fought by Alexander in his campaign to conquer Asia.

ICARUS Son of Daedalus who, attempting to escape Crete on wings his father had made, flew too close to the sun and melted the wax holding his wings together. He fell into the sea, which took its name from him.

IDA Mount Ida was the name for two famous ranges, one in west-central Crete and the other southeast of Troy, where many events of the Trojan war took place. Ida was also the name of a mountain nymph who, with her sister Adrasteia, nursed the infant Zeus on the milk of the goat Amaltheia.

ILIAOA By Mars, the mother of Romulus and Remus.

ILLISSUS/ILLISSOS Stream near Athens. Boreas carried off Oreithya from the banks of this river.

IPHIGENIA Daughter of Clytemnestra and Agamemnon, she was offered as a sacrifice to Artemis to enable the Greek fleet to sail to Troy.

ISTER/ISTRUS Another name for the Danube River.

ITYS Son of Tereus and Procne.

IXION Although Ixion was mortal, Zeus admitted him to the table of the gods, where he drank ambrosia, which gave immortality. Ixion forgot he was a mortal and attempted to seduce Hera. Zeus fashioned the cloud Nephele into the shape of Hera to entrap Ixion; the offspring of that union were the centaurs. For his insult to Zeus, Ixion was eternally punished in Hades, tied to an ever-revolving wheel entwined with snakes.

LACHEDEMON (Lacedaemon) King and eponym of Lacedemon. The son of Zeus and Taygete, Lacedemon married Sparta, daughter of the Laconaian king, Eurotas, from whom he inherited the kingdom. He renamed the region for himself and founded what was to become its principal city, naming it for his wife.

LACHESIS One of the Fates, who measures each person's portion of the thread of existence.

LAIUS Son of Labdacus, king of Thebes; expelled from Thebes by Amphion and Zethus, he was cursed by Hera or Pelops. Returning to Thebes, he married Jocasta; he was warned by Apollo not to have children but ignored the warning and his son, Oedipus, was born. As a precaution, Oedipus was exposed, but was found by a shepherd and survived. Oedipus killed Laius in a quarrel, not knowing Laius was his father.

LEDA Wife of Tyndareus, king of Sparta. She became mother to Helen and Pollux when Zeus took the form of a swan and impregnated her.

LERNAS Marshes near Argos where the Hydra lived, who was slain by Hercules in his second labour.

LEUCATE Island in the Ionian Sea.

LYDIA Country in Asia Minor situated between the waters of Hermes and Meander to the north and south, and Phrygia to the east. The home of Croesus.

MAENAD TROOPS Female votaries of Dionysus.

MAEON Theban warrior, the son of Creon's son Haemon.

MARIUS Roman warrior who joined forces with Cinna to take Rome in 87 BC.

MAVORS One of the names for Mars.

MEANDER River in Turkey known for its wandering course; the river god Maeander.

MEDEA Daughter of Aeëtes, king of Colchis; granddaughter of Sol and Persis.

She helped Jason carry off the golden fleece upon which her father's kingdom depended; she slew her brother, tricked the daughters of Pelias into murdering their father; killed her two sons; vanished in the air in a chariot drawn by dragons.

MEGAERA Daughter of Creon, given in marriage to Hercules. When Juno rendered him insane, Hercules threw the children he fathered by Megaera into the fire and perhaps killed Megaera as well. For this he was condemned to perform his twelve labours.

MINOS Son of Europa and Zeus; king of Crete. Among his children were Phaedra and Ariadne. Minos imprisoned Daedalus in the labyrinth.

MOPSUS A seer, the son of Apollo, who was given the gift of prophesying by watching the flight of birds.

MORPHEUS One of the thousand sons of Somnus, the Roman god of sleep.

MULCIBER Surname of Vulcan, from the verb '*mulceo*', to soften, alluding to the softening effect of fire on metals.

MYRRHA Mother of Adonis. Daughter of Cinyras, she conceived an unnatural passion for her father. Pursued by him, she changed into a myrrh tree, the gum of which resembles tears.

MYRTILUS Son of Mercury, charioteer of Oenomaus. Bribed by Pelops, he secretly withdrew the linchpins of his master's chariot, wrecking his master's car in the race which was to decide the success of Pelops's suit.

NEMEAN LION Hercules's first labour was to deliver the skin of the Nemean lion. It was invulnerable to weapons, which could not pierce it, but Hercules choked it with his arm.

NESSUS Centaur who ferried people across the river Evenus, claiming the gods had given him the post because of his righteousness. Hercules killed him when the centaur attempted to violate Deianeira, Hercules's wife.

NIOBE Daughter of Tantalus and Dione, wife of Amphion, she had six daughters and six sons, who were killed because Niobe insulted the goddess Leto. Niobe was shattered with sorrow at the deaths of her children and was changed into marble, from which tears ran in the form of a spring.

OETHA (Oeta) Mount Thessaly, where Hercules died.

ORPHEUS Greatest of all the poets to honour the gods with their songs. Son of the muse, Calliope; Apollo taught him to play the lyre and the muses taught him letters. His music and singing were so sweet that the rocks and trees were drawn to him.

OSSA Mountain range in Thessaly. It was supposed that Ossa and Olympus were once united, but that an earthquake had rent them asunder.

PADUS The river Po. This name was said to be derived from the word used by Gauls to denote a pine tree.

PALLAS The goddess Minerva, the friend and helper of Hercules in his various labours and the patron goddess of the Athenians.

PELION Mountain range in Thessaly, along a portion of the eastern coast. Homer alludes to it as the ancient abode of the centaurs.

PELOPONNESIAN PISA Olympia.

PELOPS Son of Tantalus, the king of Lydia. He was slain by his father and served as a meal to the gods, but the gods brought Pelops back to life and made him more beautiful than before – only his shoulder blade was missing.

PENTHEUS Son of Echion and Agave; king of Thebes. During his reign, Bacchus came from the east and sought to introduce his orgies. Women gave in enthusiastically to the new religion, though Pentheus tried to check it. He went to Mount Cithaeron and scaled a tree to watch the revels of the Bacchantes in secret; Bacchus caused the women to see Pentheus as a wild animal and they tore him to pieces.

PHAETON Son of Clymene and Phoebus. Desiring to prove himself to his father, he persuaded Phoebus to let him drive the four-horse chariot of the sun for one day. He could not control the horses so they ran too close to the earth, nearly burning it and creating the Libyan desert. Zeus hurled a thunderbolt at Phaeton to stop the earth and heavens being consumed and he fell dead in the river Eridanus (the Po).

PHASIS River flowing through Colchis to the Black Sea.

PHINEUS King of Salmydessus on the coast of Thrace, he was given the gift of prophecy by Apollo. Because he revealed too much of the counsels of the gods to men, Zeus blinded him and sent the Harpies to torment him.

PHLEGETHON Underworld river of flames which formed one of the boundaries of Hades.

PHOEBUS Apollo. Under this name, he is most frequently conceived of as the sun god, driving his chariot across the sky, seeing all things, withdrawing from the sky at the sight of monstrous sin.

PHORBAS An old man, head shepherd of the royal flocks, forced by Oedipus to tell the secret of the king's birth.

PHRIXUS Brother of Helle. They fled the persecution of Ino on a golden-fleeced ram obtained from Mercury. During their journey, Helle fell into the sea, called the Hellespont. Phrixus went on alone, sacrificed the ram at Colchis, and presented the golden fleece to Aeëtes. The golden fleece was the subject of the quest of the Argonauts. The Aegean Sea is also known as the Phrixian Sea.

PHRYGIAN Trojan.

PLUTO Hades, who ruled over the underworld with his queen, Persephone.

POLYNEICES Son of Oedipus and brother of Eteocles (see Eteocles).

PRIAM King of Troy. Among his children were Hector, Paris, and Cassandra. It was said that Priam had fifty sons and as many daughters. Priam rebuilt Troy, making it more powerful and splendid than before. Ruin came to Troy after Priam's son Paris abducted Helen, the wife of Menelaus. After the death of his son Hector, Priam foresaw the inevitable downfall of Troy; he fled to the altar of Zeus Herkeios where Neioptolemus, son of Achilles, killed him.

PROCNE Procne and Philomela were the daughters of Pandion of Athens. Pandion married Procne to his ally Tereus, king of Thrace; their son was Itys. Later Tereus fell in love with Philomela and married her, saying Procne had died; when she found this was not true he cut out her tongue to prevent her telling her story to her sister. Philomela wove a tapestry revealing her sorrows to her sister, and Procne took revenge by killing Itys and serving him for supper to the unsuspecting Tereus. Tereus pursued the two sisters to Parnassus, where they prayed to be changed into birds; Procne became a nightingale, and Philomela a swallow.

PSAMMETIQUE (Psammetichus) King of Egypt; he returned from exile to defeat his foes and become sole monarch.

PTOLEMIE (Ptolemaeus, Ptolemy) King of Egypt, friend and associate of Alexander; when the empire was divided after Alexander's death, Ptolemy obtained Egypt, Libya, and part of Arabia and was known for his benevolence and clemency and his cultivation of the arts.

RADAMANTH (Rhadamanthys) Son of Zeus and Europa, brother of Minos and Sarpedon, he ruled over Crete before Minos, who eventually expelled him. Rhadamanthys became one of the three judges in the underworld, judging whether the recently departed should be punished or rewarded for their conduct on earth.

RHOETEUM Promontory in Troy, on the shore of the Hellespont. The body of Ajax was buried on the sloping side of it.

SABEAN Yemenite; Yemen was one of the richest nations of the ancient world.

SCIRON Celebrated robber who trapped travellers on the narrow road between Megara and Athens and forced them to wash his feet; when they did, he kicked them over the cliffs and into the sea. Eventually Theseus came that way and slew him.

SCYROS Aegean island, now called Scyro. The island was named for Scyrius, said to be the true father of Aegeus. Theseus was said to have died there, either by falling or by being pushed down a precipice.

SCYTHIA Name given by the ancient Greeks and Romans to a large portion of northern Asia.

SIDON The oldest and most powerful city of Phoenicia, believed to have been founded by Sidon, the eldest son of Canaan.

SIPYLUS Mount Sipylus was celebrated in Greek mythology as the home of Tantalus and Niobe.

SISYPHUS King of Ephyra (Corinth), he was said to have received the throne from Medea. Sisyphus was known for his cunning, and fathered Odysseus. Various stories explain why Sisyphus was condemned to spend eternity in a futile attempt to push an enormous boulder to the top of a steep hill, and always fail.

SPARTA Capital of Laconia. It was noted for its militarism and reached the height of its power in the sixth century BC. A protracted rivalry with Athens led to the Peloponnesian Wars, and Sparta's hegemony over all of Greece.

STYMPHAL BYRDE (Stymphalian birds) For his sixth labour, Hercules had to drive away the Stymphalian birds, which used their feathers as arrows, ate humans, and destroyed crops with their droppings.

SYRTIS The two gulfs at either end of the Libyan Sea. The Argonauts were carried inland in this region by high seas and trapped for a time in the lake. Syrtis Major is now known as the Gulf of Sidra.

TAENARA Promontory at the southernmost point of the Peloponnesus, near which was a cave, said to be the entrance to the lower world.

TAGUS River in Spain, renowned for its golden sands.

TANTAL Tantalus – king of Lydia, son of Zeus and the nymph Pluto; father of Pelops and Niobe. Tantalus possessed untold riches. He was allowed to sit at the table of the gods because he was a son of Zeus; there, he drank nectar and ambrosia and became immortal. He became corrupted by his fortune, murdered his son Pelops, boiled him up, and served him to the gods to test their omniscience. But the gods knew, and punished him by making him suffer endless pangs of hunger and thirst in Hades, with fruit and water just out of reach.

TARTARUS The son of Aether and Gaia; the name was later used to designate the part of the lower world devoted to the punishment of the wicked, the abode of the Furies.

TAYGETUS Mountain range that divided Messenia from Laconia and took its name from its resident nymph, the Pleiad Taygete.

TETHYS Goddess of the sea, and consort of Oceanus.

THEBES Capital of Boeotia, founded by Cadmus.

THESSALEY (Thessaly) Region of east-central Greece between the Pindus mountains and the Aegean Sea. It reached the height of its power in the sixth century BC but soon declined because of internal conflicts.

THRACE Region and ancient country of the southeast Balkan peninsula north of the Aegean Sea. It was colonized by the Greeks in the seventh century BC and later passed under the control of Rome, Byzantium, and Ottoman Turkey.

TIBER River flowing through Rome to the Tyrrhenian Sea.

TITAN Family or race of giants whose power was destroyed by the gods.

TITYUS A giant, son of Gaia. He threatened violence against Leto, the mother of Apollo and Artemis. For this he was punished in Hades, where nine vultures kept feeding upon his liver.

TRIVIA An epithet of Hecate, also applied to Diana, because she presided over places where three roads meet.

TROIA Troy.

TYNDARIS (Tyndareus) King of Sparta, husband of Leda, who was loved by Zeus. It was commonly held that Castor and Clytemnestra were the children of Tyndareus and Leda. After his death, the Spartans worshipped Tyndareus as a hero.

TYPHOEUS Offspring of Gaia and Tartarus, Typhoeus brought forth all the whirlwinds which make the sea dangerous. Zeus attacked him, hurling Typhoeus into Mount Aetna where he was said to be the force under the volcano.

TYRE City on the eastern Mediterranean, the ancient capital of Phoenicia.

ZEPHIRUS (Zephyrus) The west wind, son of Eos and Astraeus. Flying through the air on perfumed wings, he scatters flowers and heralds the coming of spring. On the stream of Oceanus he met with the harpy Podarge and engendered Xanthus and Balius, the immortal horses of Achilles.

ZETHUS (Zethe/Zetus) Twin brother of Amphion, a hunter and herdsman.

Note: Many entries indebted to the *Concise Encyclopedia of Greek and Roman Mythology* by Sabine G. Oswalt (Glasgow, Collins, 1969) and *Harper's Dictionary of Classical Literature and Antiquities* (New York, Cooper Square Publishers, 1965).

EDITIONS OF SENECA IN ENGLISH: A SELECTION

Frederick Ahl, *Seneca: Three Tragedies*, Ithaca, Cornell University Press, 1986.

A.J. Boyle, *Seneca's Phaedra*, Leeds, Francis Cairns, 1987.

Caryl Churchill, *Thyestes*, London, Nick Hearn Books, 1995.

J. Crowne, *Thyestes*, London, 1681.

George E. Duckworth, ed., *The Complete Roman Drama*, New York, Random House, 1942.

Jane Elder, *Thyestes*, Manchester, Carcanet, 1982.

Moses Hadas, *The Plays of Seneca*, Indianapolis, Bobbs-Merrill, 1965.

Ted Hughes, *Seneca's Oedipus*, London, Faber and Faber, 1968.

Frank Justus Miller, *The Tragedies of Seneca*, Chicago, University of Chicago Press, 1907.

Frank Justus Miller, *Seneca in Nine Volumes: Tragedies*, Cambridge, Mass., Harvard University Press, 1917.

Thomas Newton, ed., *Seneca: His Tenne Tragedies*, London, 1581.

Douglass Parker, *Thyestes*, in *The Tenth Muse: Classical Drama in Translation*, ed. Charles Doria, Athens, Ohio University Press, 1980.

Samuel Pordage, *Troades*, London, 1660.

Edmund Prestwich, *Hippolitus*, London, 1651.

Edward Sherburne, *The Tragedies of L. Annaeus Seneca, the Philosopher*, London, 1702.

David R. Slavitt, ed., *Seneca: The Tragedies*, Baltimore, Johns Hopkins University Press, 1992–5.

J. Talbot, *Troas*, London, 1686.

E.F. Watling, *Seneca: Four Tragedies and Octavia*, London, Penguin Books, 1966.

Charles Apthorp Wheelwright, *Poems Original and Translated, Including Versions of the Medea and Octavia of Seneca*, London, 1810.

John Wright, *Thyestes*, London, 1674.

LIST OF TRANSLATORS

Ahl, Frederick
Blackmore, Sir Richard
Boyle, A. J.
Cherry, Kelly
Chettle, Henry
Churchill, Caryl
Cowley, Abraham
Crowne, John
Dyer, Sir Edward
Elder, Jane
Elizabeth I
Gioia, Dana
Hadas, Rachel
Hale, Sir Matthew
Harington, Sir John
Harris, Ella Isabel
Heywood, Jasper
Howard, Henry, Earl of Surrey
Hughes, Asa M.
Hughes, Ted
Hunt, Leigh
Johnson, Samuel

Lucas, F. L.
Marvell, Andrew
Miller, Frank Justus
Milton, John
Neville, Alexander
Newton, Thomas
Nuce, Thomas
Parker, Douglass
Pordage, Samuel
Prestwich, Edmund
Prior, Matthew
Sandy, Stephen
Sherburne, Sir Edward
Sidney, Sir Robert
Studley, John
Sullivan, J. P.
Talbot, John
Theobald, Lewis
Wheelwright, Charles Apthorp
Wilmot, John, Earl of Rochester
Wright, John
Wyatt, Sir Thomas

INDEX OF TRANSLATORS
AND ADAPTERS

READ MORE IN PENGUIN

In every corner of the world, on every subject under the sun, Penguin represents quality and variety – the very best in publishing today.

For complete information about books available from Penguin – including Puffins, Penguin Classics and Arkana – and how to order them, write to us at the appropriate address below. Please note that for copyright reasons the selection of books varies from country to country.

In the United Kingdom: Please write to *Dept. EP, Penguin Books Ltd, Bath Road, Harmondsworth, West Drayton, Middlesex UB7 ODA*

In the United States: Please write to *Consumer Sales, Penguin Putnam Inc., P.O. Box 999, Dept. 17109, Bergenfield, New Jersey 07621-0120.* VISA and MasterCard holders call 1-800-253-6476 to order Penguin titles

In Canada: Please write to *Penguin Books Canada Ltd, 10 Alcorn Avenue, Suite 300, Toronto, Ontario M4V 3B2*

In Australia: Please write to *Penguin Books Australia Ltd, P.O. Box 257, Ringwood, Victoria 3134*

In New Zealand: Please write to *Penguin Books (NZ) Ltd, Private Bag 102902, North Shore Mail Centre, Auckland 10*

In India: Please write to *Penguin Books India Pvt Ltd, 210 Chiranjiv Tower, 43 Nehru Place, New Delhi 110 019*

In the Netherlands: Please write to *Penguin Books Netherlands bv, Postbus 3507, NL-1001 AH Amsterdam*

In Germany: Please write to *Penguin Books Deutschland GmbH, Metzlerstrasse 26, 60594 Frankfurt am Main*

In Spain: Please write to *Penguin Books S. A., Bravo Murillo 19, 1° B, 28015 Madrid*

In Italy: Please write to *Penguin Italia s.r.l., Via Benedetto Croce 2, 20094 Corsico, Milano*

In France: Please write to *Penguin France, Le Carré Wilson, 62 rue Benjamin Baillaud, 31500 Toulouse*

In Japan: Please write to *Penguin Books Japan Ltd, Kaneko Building, 2-3-25 Koraku, Bunkyo-Ku, Tokyo 112*

In South Africa: Please write to *Penguin Books South Africa (Pty) Ltd, Private Bag X14, Parkview, 2122 Johannesburg*

READ MORE IN PENGUIN

A CHOICE OF CLASSICS

Aeschylus	**The Oresteian Trilogy**
	Prometheus Bound/The Suppliants/Seven against Thebes/The Persians
Aesop	**Fables**
Ammianus Marcellinus	**The Later Roman Empire (AD 354–378)**
Apollonius of Rhodes	**The Voyage of Argo**
Apuleius	**The Golden Ass**
Aristophanes	**The Knights/Peace/The Birds/The Assemblywomen/Wealth**
	Lysistrata/The Acharnians/The Clouds
	The Wasps/The Poet and the Women/ The Frogs
Aristotle	**The Art of Rhetoric**
	The Athenian Constitution
	De Anima
	Ethics
	Poetics
Arrian	**The Campaigns of Alexander**
Marcus Aurelius	**Meditations**
Boethius	**The Consolation of Philosophy**
Caesar	**The Civil War**
	The Conquest of Gaul
Catullus	**Poems**
Cicero	**Murder Trials**
	The Nature of the Gods
	On the Good Life
	Selected Letters
	Selected Political Speeches
	Selected Works
Euripides	**Alcestis/Iphigenia in Tauris/Hippolytus**
	The Bacchae/Ion/The Women of Troy/ Helen
	Medea/Hecabe/Electra/Heracles
	Orestes and Other Plays

READ MORE IN PENGUIN

A CHOICE OF CLASSICS

Hesiod/Theognis	**Theogony/Works and Days/Elegies**
Hippocrates	**Hippocratic Writings**
Homer	**The Iliad**
	The Odyssey
Horace	**Complete Odes and Epodes**
Horace/Persius	**Satires and Epistles**
Juvenal	**The Sixteen Satires**
Livy	**The Early History of Rome**
	Rome and Italy
	Rome and the Mediterranean
	The War with Hannibal
Lucretius	**On the Nature of the Universe**
Martial	**Epigrams**
Ovid	**The Erotic Poems**
	Heroides
	Metamorphoses
	The Poems of Exile
Pausanias	**Guide to Greece** (in two volumes)
Petronius/Seneca	**The Satyricon/The Apocolocyntosis**
Pindar	**The Odes**
Plato	**Early Socratic Dialogues**
	Gorgias
	The Last Days of Socrates (Euthyphro/ The Apology/Crito/Phaedo)
	The Laws
	Phaedrus and **Letters VII and VIII**
	Philebus
	Protagoras/Meno
	The Republic
	The Symposium
	Theaetetus
	Timaeus/Critias

READ MORE IN PENGUIN

A CHOICE OF CLASSICS

Plautus	**The Pot of Gold and Other Plays**
	The Rope and Other Plays
Pliny	**The Letters of the Younger Pliny**
Pliny the Elder	**Natural History**
Plotinus	**The Enneads**
Plutarch	**The Age of Alexander** (Nine Greek Lives)
	The Fall of the Roman Republic (Six Lives)
	The Makers of Rome (Nine Lives)
	Plutarch on Sparta
	The Rise and Fall of Athens (Nine Greek Lives)
Polybius	**The Rise of the Roman Empire**
Procopius	**The Secret History**
Propertius	**The Poems**
Quintus Curtius Rufus	**The History of Alexander**
Sallust	**The Jugurthine War/The Conspiracy of Cataline**
Seneca	**Four Tragedies/Octavia**
	Letters from a Stoic
Sophocles	**Electra/Women of Trachis/Philoctetes/Ajax**
	The Theban Plays
Suetonius	**The Twelve Caesars**
Tacitus	**The Agricola/The Germania**
	The Annals of Imperial Rome
	The Histories
Terence	**The Comedies (The Girl from Andros/The Self-Tormentor/The Eunuch/Phormio/The Mother-in-Law/The Brothers)**
Thucydides	**History of the Peloponnesian War**
Virgil	**The Aeneid**
	The Eclogues
	The Georgics
Xenophon	**Conversations of Socrates**
	A History of My Times
	The Persian Expedition